Calhoun County, Illinois

Births & Deaths

1878-1916

J. L. DICKSON

In association with

Personal Touch Genealogy
www.PersonalTouchGenealogy.com

and

ETC
ETCETERA
PUBLISHING

www.GenealogyBookPublisher.com

ISBN 978-0-9818351-4-3
Published by Etcetera Publishing LLC — Fort Worth, TX
Printed in the United States of America
First Edition

Please visit **www.PersonalTouchGenealogy.com**
to order this book or see Order Form on page 221.

— **JOE PAIGE BRIDGE**, Calhoun County, Illinois —

Explanation Of The Information In This Book

The listing contains the following information:

Surname	Indicate the family name
Given name	Name given at birth (if indicated)
Book	Book number where entry was documented
Page	Page number within the book where entry was documented
Year	A book may cover several years of documented entries hence may cover years 1878-1903 for said surname. Birth or death occurred during these years.

Please note ...

Books ONE and TWO look like they were merged together
at some point hence under book 1 & 2.

If left blank, no information was in source for that record.

The information in this book was collected from several entities.

All precautions were taken to transcribe all entries as
they were in the records.

Calhoun County Births

1878 - 1916

CALHOUN COUNTY BIRTHS

Surname	Given Name	Book	Page	Year
Abpel	Mary	1	31	1878-1887
Adams		4	186	1907-1916
Adams		3	18	1903-1915
Adams		1	52	1878-1887
Adams	Anna	4	333	1907-1916
Adcox	Leota	2	67	1887-1903
Aderton		1	50	1878-1887
Aderton	Clama Luciley	2	61	1887-1903
Aderton	Florence Eveline	2	68	1887-1903
Aderton	Gilbert Kring	2	20	1887-1903
Aderton	Grace Luzelle	2	84	1887-1903
Aderton	Imo	2	8	1887-1903
Aderton	Lenora	3	144	1903-1915
Aderton	Marcus Jerome	4	42	1907-1916
Aderton	Merle Edna	2	36	1887-1903
Aderton	Philip	2	20	1887-1903
Aderton	Susan Alma	1	66	1878-1887
Alexander		2	112	1887-1903
Alexander	Malinda M.	1	14	1878-1887
Aling	Elizabeth	4	496	1907-1916
Aling	John Henry	4	362	1907-1916
Alitizer		4	437	1907-1916
Allen	Susan	2	39	1887-1903
Alltizer	Ammel Henry	3	26	1887-1903
Alster		1	60	1878-1887
Altizer		2	118	1887-1903
Altizer	Nettie E.	3	162	1903-1915
Ames	Clarence	4	452	1907-1916
Anderson		2	128	1887-1903
Anderson		4	423	1907-1916
Anderson		2	86	1887-1903
Anderson	(Still Born)	3	282	1903-1915
Anderson	Alice Elizabeth	4	246	1907-1916
Anderson	Doloris V.	4	482	1907-1916
Anderson	Elvin R.	4	118	1907-1916

CALHOUN COUNTY BIRTHS

Surname	Given Name	Book	Page	Year
Anderson	Fred Olenta	2	105	1887-1903
Anderson	James E.	1	7	1878-1887
Anderson	Joseph Glen	4	524	1907-1916
Anderson	Julia Frances	2	70	1887-1903
Anderson	Lavina S.	1	76	1878-1887
Anderson	Leta Elaine	4	524	1907-1916
Anderson	Lillie Florence	2	86	1887-1903
Anderson	Lorraine Eleanor	4	249	1907-1916
Anderson	Mildred Bernice	3	182	1903-1915
Anderson	Myrtle E.	3	268	1903-1915
Anderson	Nebtern	3	112	1903-1915
Anderson	Robert WM	4	7	1907-1916
Anderson	Ruby Mildred	3	205	1903-1915
Anderson	Wayne Franklin	4	391	1907-1916
Anderson	Wilbur Shankland	4	259	1907-1916
Anderson	WM	4	443	1907-1916
Andreas	Frederick J.	1	34	1878-1887
Andrews		3	30	1903-1915
Andrews	Grace L.	1	23	1878-1887
Angel		2	123	1887-1903
Angel	Edith Viola	4	537	1907-1916
Angel	Nellie Marie	4	130	1907-1916
Angel	Oba Leonard	2	61	1887-1903
Angel	Roy	4	349	1907-1916
Angel	Homer Harvey	3	188	1903-1915
Ansell		1	11	1878-1887
Ansell		2	87	1887-1903
Ansell		2	61	1887-1903
Ansell	Opal Leota	4	44	1907-1916
Ansell		2	91	1887-1903
Ansell		2	80	1887-1903
Ansell		1	37	1878-1887
Ansell	Alice	3	270	1903-1915
Ansell	Anna Ora	2	95	1887-1903
Ansell	Bessie Estella	1	57	1878-1887

CALHOUN COUNTY BIRTHS

Surname	Given Name	Book	Page	Year
Ansell	Carl Washington	4	194	1907-1916
Ansell	Cuba Elsie	1	60	1878-1887
Ansell	Edith	1	24	1878-1887
Ansell	Ellsworth	3	125	1903-1915
Ansell	Eva	2	49	1887-1903
Ansell	Everett L.	1	70	1878-1887
Ansell	Harriett Mae	2	16	1887-1903
Ansell	Jacob L.	1	17	1878-1887
Ansell	Jake L.	2	119	1887-1903
Ansell	Jeanette J.	2	100	1887-1903
Ansell	Jos A.	1	10	1878-1887
Ansell	Ledda C.	1	37	1878-1887
Ansell	Lester A.	2	104	1887-1903
Ansell	Martha	2	69	1887-1903
Ansell	M. Willis	2	6	1887-1903
Ansell	Netta N.	2	40	1887-1903
Ansell	Nona	1	57	1878-1887
Ansell	Raymond V.	4	176	1907-1916
Ansell	Roy G.	3	5	1903-1915
Ansell	Winnie (Twin)	3	82	1903-1915
Ansell	Minnie (Twin)	3	83	1903-1915
Anson	Bessie Marie	4	214	1907-1916
Apple		1	13	1878-1887
Arentrout	Luther	1	34	1878-1887
Argust	Bertran C.	1	17	1878-1887
Argust	William Harold	1	38	1878-1887
Armstrong		2	94	1887-1903
Armstrong	Claude Eldon	2	102	1887-1903
Armstrong	Dora Irene	2	102	1887-1903
Armstrong	Dorothy	4	463	1907-1916
Armstrong	Flora Alice	3	126	1903-1915
Armstrong	Hugh Kenneth	4	41	1907-1916
Arnold		3	52	1903-1915
Arnold	Annie Catherine	2	104	1887-1903
Arnold	Eileen Marguerite	3	224	1903-1915

CALHOUN COUNTY BIRTHS

Surname	Given Name	Book	Page	Year
Arnold	Frederick W.	3	214	1903-1915
Arnold	Genevieve W.	4	472	1907-1916
Arnold	Irene Josephine	4	596	1907-1916
Arnold	Joseph Henry	2	29	1887-1903
Arnold	Lawrence Adolph	4	80	1907-1916
Arnold	Maggie	2	29	1887-1903
Arnold	Maria K.	1	15	1878-1887
Arnold	Mary Helena	2	56	1887-1903
Arnold	Norman J.	4	98	1907-1916
Arnold	Paul Edward	4	279	1907-1916
Arnold	Stanley George	4	234	1907-1916
Arter		2	97	1887-1903
Arter		3	116	1903-1915
Athy	Daniel	1	67	1878-1887
Athy	Ermina	1	45	1878-1887
Athy	Ruth	3	181	1903-1915
Attwell	Beatrice M.	3	185	1903-1915
Auer		1	77	1878-1887
Auer	Dora Hannah	1	50	1878-1887
Baalman	Alice Elizabeth	3	249	1903-1915
Baalman	Clara	2	112	1887-1903
Baalman	Emma E.	4	442	1907-1916
Baalman	Herman	2	59	1887-1903
Baalman	Raymond Carl	4	196	1907-1916
Baalman	Rosa Agnes	3	130	1903-1915
Bach		1	25	1878-1887
Bach		4	427	1907-1916
Bach	Carl S. (Twin)	2	1	1887-1903
Bach	Clarence A. (Twin)	2	1	1887-1903
Bach	Catherine Anna	4	303	1907-1916
Bach	C. John	4	488	1907-1916
Bach	Leola	4	479	1907-1916
Bach	Ruth Ardell	2	90	1887-1903
Bach	Fred	1	54	1878-1887
Backer	Louis	2	73	1887-1903

CALHOUN COUNTY BIRTHS

Surname	Given Name	Book	Page	Year
Backholdt	Louie	3	276	1903-1915
Bader		4	235	1907-1916
Bader	Mary	3	123	1903-1915
Bader	Tracy August	4	384	1907-1916
Bader	Tresa E.	4	172	1907-1916
Bader	Vincent Ethan	3	216	1903-1915
Baer		4	216	1907-1916
Bagger	Henry G.	2	36	1887-1903
Bailey		2	52	1887-1903
Bailey	Anna Eleanor	4	511	1907-1916
Bailey	Carl	2	13	1887-1903
Bailey	Clarence Evert	1	71	1878-1887
Bailey	Edward Frederick	4	586	1907-1916
Bailey	Elmer G.	4	174	1907-1916
Bailey	E. Leslie	2	39	1887-1903
Bailey	Gladys V.	2	81	1887-1903
Bailey	Harold Stephen	4	401	1907-1916
Bailey	Herbert WM.	4	292	1907-1916
Bailey	James	4	448	1907-1916
Bailey	Leroy Nelson	4	540	1907-1916
Bailey	Lillian Lucille	3	182	1903-1915
Bailey	Lorene H.	4	115	1907-1916
Bailey	Luther Raymond	2	113	1887-1903
Bailey	Mary	2	21	1887-1903
Bailey	Mary Melissa	3	204	1903-1915
Bailey	Milly	2	12	1887-1903
Bailey	Minnie N.	4	68	1907-1916
Bailey	Otto R.	2	39	1887-1903
Bailey	Waldo S.	1	20	1878-1887
Bailey	William	2	51	1887-1903
Bailey	Wilson R.	2	17	1887-1903
Bain		1	31	1878-1887
Bain		1	31	1878-1887
Bain	Aurie	1	8	1878-1887
Bain	Bertha	1	25	1878-1887

CALHOUN COUNTY BIRTHS

Surname	Given Name	Book	Page	Year
Bain	Carl William	4	361	1907-1916
Bain	Eva Rosa	1	73	1878-1887
Bain	Henry Floyd	1	77	1878-1887
Bain	James Orin	1	8	1878-1887
Bain	L. Allen	2	59	1887-1903
Bain	Mary Etta	1	63	1878-1887
Bain	Mary Luella	4	243	1907-1916
Bain	Rebecca	1	63	1878-1887
Bain	Rebecca	2	13	1887-1903
Bain	Walter	1	18	1878-1887
Baker	Elmor C.	3	19	1903-1915
Baker	Freda Louise	4	98	1907-1916
Baker	George	1	59	1878-1887
Baker	Herbert	4	359	1907-1916
Baker	John	1	3	1878-1887
Baker	Melvin Charles	4	271	1907-1916
Baker	Minnie Agnes	3	43	1903-1915
Baker	Oscar	1	26	1878-1887
Baker		2	85	1887-1903
Balke	Barney Herman	2	129	1887-1903
Balke	Katherine Helena	4	299	1907-1916
Balke	Theresa Caroline	4	34	1907-1916
Ball		1	78	1878-1887
Ball		1	48	1878-1887
Ball		1	13	1878-1887
Ball	Amos Ray	2	48	1887-1903
Ball	Arthur Alvin	3	198	1903-1915
Ball	Audrey P.	4	72	1907-1916
Ball	Carl Lesley	3	148	1903-1915
Ball	Frank A.	4	329	1907-1916
Ball	James O.	3	9	1903-1915
Ball	Ruby	4	389	1907-1916
Ball	Tully H.	2	40	1887-1903
Baltisberger		4	78	1907-1916
Baltisberger	Henry Abran	1	22	1878-1887

CALHOUN COUNTY BIRTHS

Surname	Given Name	Book	Page	Year
Bames	Osa Mayna	3	118	1903-1915
Banghardt	Esther	4	108	1907-1916
Banghardt	Frank W.	2	12	1887-1903
Banghardt	Lucille	4	278	1907-1916
Banghardt	Stella	4	444	1907-1916
Banghart		2	96	1887-1903
Banghart	Annie K.	2	28	1887-1903
Banghart	John Francis	2	42	1887-1903
Banker	Margaret Ellen	1	2	1878-1887
Barber		3	207	1903-1915
Barber		2	58	1887-1903
Barber		1	29	1878-1887
Barber	Cecil Claud	2	75	1887-1903
Barber	Thomas Richard	3	59	1903-1915
Barber	William R.	1	58	1878-1887
Bare	Mary Martha	2	81	1887-1903
Bare	Thomas Edward	3	59	1903-1915
Barker	Cecil Claud	2	75	1887-1903
Barlett	Florence Marguerite	4	49	1907-1916
Barlett	Freda A.	4	528	1907-1916
Barnard	Arthur Ray	3	140	1903-1915
Barnard	Charley H.	2	53	1887-1903
Barnard	Dennis Sylvester	4	45	1887-1903
Barnard	Grace	2	106	1887-1903
Barnard	Hazel Mytle	4	479	1907-1916
Barnard	Hester May Pearl	4	254	1907-1916
Barnes		4	210	1907-1916
Barnes		4	36	1887-1903
Barnes		2	25	1887-1903
Barnes		2	11	1887-1903
Barnes		1	11	1878-1887
Barnes		1	78	1887-1887
Barnes		1	3	1878-1887
Barnes		4	161	1907-1916
Barnes		1	78	1878-1887

CALHOUN COUNTY BIRTHS

Surname	Given Name	Book	Page	Year
Barnes	Clarence Dewey	2	81	1887-1903
Barnes	Dorris Odessa	4	397	1907-1916
Barnes	Elijah Moses	4	123	1907-1916
Barnes	Gladys Vernitia	4	276	1907-1916
Barnes	Herman Gilbert	3	187	1903-1915
Barnes	Herter	2	49	1887-1903
Barnes	Ida May	1	4	1878-1887
Barnes	Jessie Roscoe	4	434	1907-1916
Barnes	John Henry	4	429	1907-1916
Barnes	John M.	3	7	1903-1915
Barnes	Kyle	4	52	1907-1916
Barnes	Luda May	2	115	1887-1903
Barnes	Marvin Franklin	3	94	1903-1915
Barnes	Mary E.	3	8	1903-1915
Barnes	Maudie Jane	2	115	1887-1903
Barnes	Milo	4	577	1907-1916
Barnes	Minnie E.	4	320	1907-1916
Barnes	Morris Roland	4	397	1907-1916
Barnes	Norvel	2	128	1887-1903
Barnes	Orville	2	70	1887-1903
Barnes	Osa Marie	3	188	1903-1915
Barnes	Walter Elias	2	51	1887-1903
Barnes	William	2	119	1887-1903
Barnes	Winifred Felecia	4	122	1907-1916
Barnhard	Herman Henry	2	76	1887-1903
Barnhardt		1	43	1878-1887
Barry	Alloys	4	146	1907-1916
Barry	Dorothy	4	462	1907-1916
Barry	Edward E.	4	387	1907-1916
Barry	Edward S.	1	38	1878-1887
Barry	Leola Agnes	3	256	1903-1915
Barry	Morine Bernice	4	238	1907-1916
Barry	Robert E.	3	12	1903-1915
Barry	WM.	3	120	1903-1915
Barry	Zita Agnes	1	51	1878-1887

CALHOUN COUNTY BIRTHS

Surname	Given Name	Book	Page	Year
Bartholomew	Charles Dewey	2	77	1887-1903
Bartholomew	Ione	2	99	1887-1903
Bartholomew		2	77	1887-1903
Bartlett	Irene Inez	4	146	1907-1916
Batchhelder	Bertha J.	1	34	1878-1887
Batchhelder	Rosa Maude	1	73	1878-1887
Battershell		2	60	1887-1903
Battershell	Alden	1	36	1878-1887
Battershell	Meridice Virden	4	155	1907-1916
Battershell	Thomas Oren	2	58	1887-1903
Batz	John Hiram	4	600	1907-1916
Baugh		2	12	1887-1903
Baugh		2	56	1887-1903
Baugh		2	2	1887-1903
Baugh	Anna	2	117	1887-1903
Baugh	August	4	43	1907-1916
Baugh	Claybourn Winifred	4	552	1907-1916
Baugh	Frank	3	135	1903-1915
Baugh	Minnie	2	107	1887-1903
Baumann	Edward	4	463	1907-1916
Baumann	Francis Gertrude	4	233	1907-1916
Baumann	Grace	4	258	1907-1916
Baumann	Helena R.	4	136	1907-1916
Baumann	Hildegarde R.	4	74	1907-1916
Baumann	John M.	4	435	1907-1916
Baumann	Lilian	4	268	1907-1916
Baumann	Marie Regina	4	547	1907-1916
Baumgaertner		4	54	1907-1916
Baumgartner		3	268	1903-1915
Beach		1	2	1878-1887
Beach	Arnold L.	1	46	1878-1887
Beach	Meta Harriett	4	466	1907-1916
Beach	Minnie G.	1	58	1878-1887
Beaty	Ester	2	98	1887-1903
Beaty	Ione	2	3	1887-1903

CALHOUN COUNTY BIRTHS

Surname	Given Name	Book	Page	Year
Beaty	Lamont C.	2	21	1887-1903
Beaty	Theodore Longsworth	4	7	1907-1916
Becker		2	85	1887-1903
Becker		2	31	1887-1903
Becker		2	93	1887-1903
Becker		3	21	1903-1915
Becker		2	37	1887-1903
Becker	Anna Mary	2	64	1907-1916
Becker	Anna Matilda Edith	3	54	1903-1915
Becker	Carl	4	80	1907-1916
Becker	Chas. HY.	3	173	1903-1915
Becker	Ebert C.	4	195	1907-1916
Becker	Edith Francis	3	74	1903-1915
Becker	Ella Catherine	2	106	1887-1903
Becker	Ella Ruth	2	122	1887-1903
Becker	Emma Martha Minnie	2	10	1887-1903
Becker	Florence	2	33	1887-1903
Becker	Goldie	3	248	1903-1915
Becker	Grace	2	16	1887-1903
Becker	Harry	3	175	1903-1915
Becker	Helen Fredricka	4	485	1907-1916
Becker	Joseph I.	4	27	1907-1916
Becker	Margarette	2	76	1903-1915
Becker	Margarette Nancy	4	17	1907-1916
Becker	Mary Josephine	3	175	1903-1915
Becker	Velma Irene	4	521	1903-1915
Beckman		4	413	1878-1887
Beckman	Ethel Felicia	4	213	1907-1916
Beckman	Gleada Marie	4	38	1907-1916
Bedell		1	49	1878-1887
Beer		4	525	1907-1916
Beer	Henry	2	12	1887-1903
Beer	Lilly E.	2	38	1887-1903
Beer	Pauline Caroline	4	369	1907-1916
Behnen	Anna Claudine	4	322	1907-1916

CALHOUN COUNTY BIRTHS

Surname	Given Name	Book	Page	Year
Behnen	Lavada	4	322	1907-1916
Behrens	Alberta Louise	4	412	1907-1916
Behrens	Birdenia Henrietta	4	180	1907-1916
Behrens	Emma Regina	3	173	1903-1915
Behrens	Freda Helena	2	107	1887-1903
Behrens	Freda Helena	2	108	1887-1903
Behrens	Helen A.	4	440	1907-1916
Behrens	Irene Mary	4	179	1907-1916
Behrens	John W.	3	163	1903-1915
Behrens	Minnie F.	1	23	1878-1887
Behrens	Russell Otto	3	53	1903-1915
Behrens	Sophia Mary	4	3	1907-1916
Behrens	William Herman	4	17	1907-1916
Beisman		4	568	1907-1916
Beisman		2	79	1887-1903
Beisman	(Still Born)	3	286	1903-1915
Beisman	Paul Frances	2	123	1887-1903
Beisman	Charles J.	2	30	1887-1903
Beisman	Theresa C.	2	30	1887-1903
Bell		1	66	1878-1887
Bell		2	59	1887-1903
Bell	Chas. Doreen Taft	4	104	1907-1916
Bell	Elba C.	2	21	1887-1903
Bell	Evelyn Louise	4	280	1907-1916
Bell	Harriett Eliza	4	253	1907-1916
Bell	James Roosevelt	3	27	1903-1915
Bell	Jos. Somers	2	35	1887-1903
Bell	Martha May	2	15	1887-1903
Bell	Ordena U.	2	47	1903-1915
Bell	Richard Hanson	2	87	1887-1903
Bell	Ruth	3	109	1903-1915
Bell	Sarah	1	13	1878-1887
Bell	Thomas S.	1	47	1878-1887
Bell	WM. Nairn	3	170	1903-1915
Bellamy		1	62	1878-1887

CALHOUN COUNTY BIRTHS

Surname	Given Name	Book	Page	Year
Bellamy		1	75	1878-1887
Bellamy		1	32	1878-1887
Bellamy	Arthur	2	15	1887-1903
Belle	Vera Eileen	4	533	1907-1916
Bellm		2	102	1887-1903
Bellm	Frank	1	79	1887-1903
Bellm	Henry	2	20	1887-1903
Bellm	Mary C.	2	32	1887-1903
Bellm	Norbert Vincent	4	514	1907-1916
Bellmm	Clara	2	7	1887-1903
Belt	George Francis	1	31	1878-1887
Benedict	Colma	3	172	1903-1915
Benkert	Henry Anton	1	45	1878-1887
Bennet	Evelyn Elenor	3	171	1903-1915
Bennett	Alafair	2	3	1887-1903
Bennett	Burnice Eleanor	3	173	1903-1915
Bennett	Daisey	2	126	1887-1903
Bennett	Mary Josephine	3	79	1903-1915
Bennett	Tim E.	4	275	1907-1916
Benninger		2	90	1887-1903
Bens	John W.	4	402	1907-1916
Bensinger	Solomon Franklin	4	261	1907-1916
Bentrup	Katie	2	62	1887-1903
Benz		4	551	1907-1916
Benz	Aloys	3	93	1903-1915
Benz	Anna Frances	4	175	1907-1916
Benz	Catherine Anna	3	229	1903-1915
Benz	Ewin Alered	2	76	1887-1903
Benz	Evadna Irene	2	87	1887-1903
Benz	Frank John	4	78	1907-1916
Benz	Jospeph William	2	112	1887-1903
Benz	Martin Henry	2	127	1887-1903
Berge	James Henderson	2	11	1887-1903
Berke	Bessie E.	2	129	1887-1903
Bernt	Carl	3	66	1903-1915

CALHOUN COUNTY BIRTHS

Surname	Given Name	Book	Page	Year
Bernt	Henry	2	29	1887-1903
Berrey		1	33	1878-1887
Berrey		1	68	1878-1887
Berrey	James F.	2	129	1887-1903
Berrey	Joseph WM.	4	62	1878-1887
Berrey	Ralph C.	3	9	1903-1915
Berrey	Robert James	4	299	1907-1916
Berrey	Ruby Louisa	1	49	1907-1916
Berrey	Andrew K.	4	439	1907-1916
Berry	Beryl Virginia	1	108	1878-1887
Berry	Isaac Sidney	3	131	1903-1915
Berry	Mary Josephine	2	26	1887-1903
Berry	Mary Rosa Lee	4	168	1907-1916
Berry	Ruth A.	1	50	1907-1916
Besaw	Margaret D.	4	340	1907-1916
Besaw	Rita	3	208	1903-1915
Besaw	Viola Hill	3	119	1903-1915
Bess		1	5	1878-1887
Bess		2	64	1887-1903
Bess	Norris	2	99	1887-1903
Bess	Peter M.	4	411	1907-1916
Bess	William A.	4	410	1907-1916
Bethen		3	65	1907-1916
Bick		4	33	1907-1916
Bick	Alma Elizabeth	4	338	1907-1916
Bick	Clemen Hiram	4	262	1907-1916
Bick	Emme Catherine	4	581	1907-1916
Bick	Ghenry Frank	4	63	1907-1916
Bick	John Paul	4	384	1907-1916
Bick	Leo Herman	3	213	1903-1915
Bick	Loretta Mary	4	454	1907-1916
Bick	Mary Katharina	2	112	1887-1903
Bick	Robert Theodore	4	262	1907-1916
Bickman		2	128	1887-1903
Bimslager		2	116	1887-1903

CALHOUN COUNTY BIRTHS

Surname	Given Name	Book	Page	Year
Bimslager	Anna	1	14	1878-1887
Bimslager	Anna	4	334	1907-1916
Bimslager	Clara Elizabeth	2	99	1887-1903
Bimslager	Lena B.	4	169	1907-1916
Bimslager	Mary Agelina	4	46	1907-1916
Bimslager	Rosa M.	4	473	1907-1916
Bimslager	Wilford Herman	4	138	1907-1916
Bischoff	Edward Joseph	1	26	1878-1887
Bizaillion	Adaline	1	20	1878-1887
Bizaillion	Charley Holland	2	70	1887-1903
Bizaillion	Charlotte C.	3	13	1903-1915
Bizaillion	Forest	4	421	1907-1916
Bizaillion	Frances Z.	2	58	1887-1903
Bizaillion	Gerald	4	522	1907-1916
Bizaillion	Sarah Rose	2	40	1887-1903
Bizaillion	Thomas	3	172	1903-1915
Black		1	60	1878-1887
Black	Audrey Geraldine	4	196	1907-1916
Black	Regina Anne	4	320	1907-1916
Blackaby	Herman Hartcourt	2	25	1887-1903
Blackman	Allen Leroy	4	509	1907-1916
Blackorby		1	58	1878-1887
Blackorby		1	25	1878-1887
Blackorby		1	71	1878-1887
Blackorby		4	319	1907-1916
Blackorby		4	324	1907-1916
Blackorby	(Still Born)	3	277	1903-1915
Blackorby	Cecelia	4	488	1907-1916
Blackorby	Cecil	4	489	1907-1916
Blackorby	Delbert	1	35	1878-1887
Blackorby	Elby	3	190	1903-1915
Blackorby	Deo. Slocum	2	36	1887-1903
Blackorby	Harvey O.	4	438	1907-1916
Blackorby	Henry L.	4	426	1887-1903
Blackorby	Lemuel Lester	4	31	1887-1903

CALHOUN COUNTY BIRTHS

Surname	Given Name	Book	Page	Year
Blackorby	Lizzie Myrtle	2	61	1887-1903
Blackorby	Lucinda	1	13	1878-1887
Blackorby	Mary	4	71	1907-1916
Blackorby	Mary E.	4	467	1907-1916
Blackorby	Melvine	2	9	1887-1903
Blackorby	Minnie Irena	4	110	1907-1916
Blackorby	Ona M.	2	47	1887-1903
Blackorby	Orville F.	4	500	1907-1916
Blackorby	Zelmar Lee	2	67	1887-1903
Blackston		1	4	1878-1887
Blackston		1	70	1878-1887
Blackston		2	103	1887-1903
Blackston		2	40	1887-1903
Blackston	Hazel Eva	3	149	1903-1915
Blackston	Ida May	1	62	1878-1887
Blackston	Maudie Jane	1	74	1878-1887
Blackston	Hubert Edward	4	91	1907-1916
Blackstun		4	64	1907-1916
Blackstun		3	191	1903-1915
Blackstun		2	81	1887-1903
Blackstun		4	288	1907-1916
Blackstun	Alma Ruby	2	57	1887-1903
Blackstun	Arthur	3	135	1903-1915
Blackstun	Charlotte C.	14	163	1907-1916
Blackstun	Harry	2	108	1887-1903
Blackstun	Lesley Floyd	3	147	1903-1915
Blackstun	Mary Francis	4	506	1907-1916
Blackstun	Nona Myra	3	125	1903-1915
Blackwell		1	23	1878-1887
Blackwell		1	35	1878-1887
Blackwell		1	40	1878-1887
Blackwell		4	546	1907-1916
Blackwell	(Still Born)	3	270	1903-1915
Blackwell	Etna	2	74	1887-1903
Blackwell	Faye M.	2	61	1887-1903

CALHOUN COUNTY BIRTHS

Surname	Given Name	Book	Page	Year
Blackwell	Goldie Lee	2	61	1887-1903
Blackwell	Harry Stanley	2	22	1887-1903
Blackwell	Jewel	4	562	1907-1916
Blackwell	Lurena	1	68	1878-1887
Blackwell	Marshall Lamont	2	25	1887-1903
Blackwell	Melvina	1	68	1878-1887
Blackwell	Noah Albert	2	25	1887-1903
Blackwell	Ross	1	40	1878-1887
Blackwell	Stephen Roy	2	40	1887-1903
Blackwell	Thomas	4	460	1907-1916
Blackwell	Thomas A.	2	5	1887-1903
Blackwell	Wilson	1	69	1878-1887
Bland	Albert James	2	115	1887-1903
Bland	Austin Lee	2	60	1887-1903
Bland	Delbert	3	194	1907-1916
Bland	George	3	54	1907-1916
Bland	Howard Taft	4	308	1907-1916
Bland	Lester	4	566	1907-1916
Bland	Sylvester	1	48	1878-1887
Blondelon		1	19	1878-1887
Blondelon	Anton V.	1	39	1878-1887
Bloom	Fred Jospeh	4	75	1907-1916
Blooms		2	127	1887-1903
Blumenberg	Albert D.	4	115	1907-1916
Blumenberg	Lily Viva	2	109	1887-1903
Blumenberg	Vivian Ritta	2	96	1887-1903
Bockholder		4	140	1907-1916
Bockholt	Mary Ann	1	23	1878-1887
Boede		2	76	1887-1903
Boede	Andrew	2	105	1887-1903
Boede	Katy	1	43	1887-1903
Boede	Louise Mary	2	11	1887-1903
Boede	Minna	1	15	1878-1887
Boes	Joseph	2	28	1887-1903
Boes	Mary Gertrude	2	11	1887-1903

CALHOUN COUNTY BIRTHS

Surname	Given Name	Book	Page	Year
Boin		1	19	1878-1887
Bokamp	Eliza	1	39	1878-1887
Boland		4	220	1907-1916
Bolda	Frank Charles	1	9	1878-1887
Bollinger	Earl Judd	4	589	1907-1916
Bonard		2	80	1887-1903
Bonner	George F.	4	62	1907-1916
Bonner	Mary Catherine	2	123	1887-1903
Bonner	Michael Louis	3	130	1903-1915
Bonner	Ramond George	4	286	1907-1916
Bonner	Sylvester M.	4	164	1907-1916
Booth		1	76	1878-1887
Booth	Alma Jane	4	548	1907-1916
Booth	Arthur A.	3	231	1903-1915
Booth	Carrie Lee	2	2	1887-1903
Booth	Hattie L.	2	113	1887-1903
Booth	Iva Garnett	2	113	1887-1903
Booth	Marion Washington	2	126	1887-1903
Booth	Mary	3	91	1903-1915
Booth	Mary Jane	1	69	1878-1887
Booth	Rhoda M.	3	40	1903-1915
Booth	William Harrison	4	498	1907-1916
Booth	William Perry	2	13	1887-1903
Booth	WM. J.	3	7	1903-1915
Bopp		3	60	1903-1915
Bopp		2	114	1887-1903
Bopp	Anna Catherine	3	58	1903-1915
Bopp	May Frances	3	213	1903-1915
Borchers	Albert M.	2	56	1887-1903
Borchy	Myrtle Albertha	4	580	1907-1916
Borrowman		1	38	1878-1887
Borrowman	(Still Born)	3	280	1903-1915
Borrowman	Geo. Olin	2	89	1887-1903
Borrowman	Leno Clare	2	34	1887-1903
Borrowman	Plenna Loren	2	12	1887-1903

CALHOUN COUNTY BIRTHS

Surname	Given Name	Book	Page	Year
Borrowman	Roy Roscoe	1	55	1878-1887
Botts	Verna Bernie	2	125	1887-1903
Boucher	Susie E.	3	110	1903-1915
Boushey	Richard A.	2	82	1887-1903
Boushy	Woodroe W.	4	409	1907-1916
Bouyea	Dena	2	39	1887-1903
Bouyea	Esther M.	1	75	1878-1887
Bouyea	James Benj.	3	41	1903-1915
Bouyea	Moses	2	66	1887-1903
Bouyea	Ruby Viola	2	11	1887-1903
Bouyea	Willie Franklin	2	14	1887-1903
Bovee	Evaline B.	2	122	1887-1903
Bowers	Lemuel Everett	2	8	1887-1903
Bowser	Peral Victoria	4	157	1907-1916
Boyd	James Donald	4	558	1907-1916
Boyer		2	63	1887-1903
Boyer	Paul	4	404	1907-1916
Braden	James Andrew	4	73	1907-1916
Bradley	Oscar S.	1	39	1878-1887
Brainard		2	94	1887-1903
Brakeville		2	95	1887-1903
Brakeville	Nelson Oren Kenneth	3	85	1903-1915
Brakeville	Truemen Ludader	3	202	1903-1915
Brand	Charles Melbunn	3	235	1903-1915
Brandenberg	Carrie	3	208	1903-1915
Brandenberg	Clara	3	208	1903-1915
Brandenberg	Mabel Agnes	3	189	1903-1915
Brandenberg		2	100	1887-1903
Brands		3	37	1903-1915
Brands	Anna	4	417	1907-1916
Brands	Christopher	1	6	1878-1887
Brands	John	1	31	1878-1887
Brands	Otto Louis	4	102	1907-1916
Brands	Paul E.	4	94	1907-1916
Brands	Violet	4	257	1907-1916

CALHOUN COUNTY BIRTHS

Surname	Given Name	Book	Page	Year
Brandt		3	224	1903-1915
Brangenberg		4	359	1907-1916
Brangenberg		3	283	1903-1915
Brangenberg		4	96	1907-1916
Brangenberg		4	141	1907-1916
Brangenberg	Agnes Ann	3	164	1903-1915
Brangenberg		2	95	1887-1903
Brangenberg	(Still Born)	3	285	1903-1915
Brangenberg	Ester	4	315	1907-1916
Brangenberg	Goldie Loraine	3	227	1903-1915
Brangenberg	Hazel Elizabeth	4	215	1907-1916
Brangenberg	Henry	3	40	1903-1915
Brangenberg	Jospeph Jess	2	113	1887-1903
Brangenberg	Lela Ada	4	515	1907-1916
Brangenberg	Leona	3	48	1903-1915
Brangenberg	Paul	4	141	1907-1916
Brangenberg	Nellie	2	54	1887-1903
Branham	Arthur Lamont	2	54	1887-1903
Branham	Sarah Catherine	2	76	1887-1903
Brannon		2	68	1887-1903
Brannon	Basil R.	2	3	1887-1903
Brannon	Caroline Edna	1	29	1878-1887
Brannon	Eva Dora	1	12	1878-1887
Brannon	Rose Estella	1	2	1878-1887
Brant		1	65	1878-1887
Brant		2	94	1887-1903
Breden		2	82	1887-1903
Breden		2	97	1887-1903
Breden	Andrew Jackson	1	30	1878-1887
Breden	Edith	2	51	1887-1903
Breden	Edna Marie	4	239	1907-1916
Breden	Harold Glen	4	582	1907-1916
Breden	James Andrew	1	68	1878-1887
Breden	Leon	2	37	1887-1903
Breden	Leslie Edwin	2	114	1887-1903

CALHOUN COUNTY BIRTHS

Surname	Given Name	Book	Page	Year
Breden	Magie May	2	5	1887-1903
Breden	Maria J.	1	43	1878-1887
Breden	Mary L.	1	38	1878-1887
Breden	Mary S.	1	34	1878-1887
Breden	Rosita May	2	5	1887-1903
Breden	Sarah Louisa	1	54	1878-1887
Breden	Theodore	2	53	1887-1903
Breden	Theodore	4	114	1907-1916
Breden	WM. F.	2	25	1887-1903
Brenn	Hildegard Ida Bertha	2	248	1887-1903
Brewster		3	41	1903-1915
Brewster	Julia Silvinia	3	157	1903-1915
Brink	Frank	4	19	1907-1916
Brinkman	August Henry	4	105	1907-1916
Brinkman	Cecilia J.	2	101	1887-1903
Brinkman	Dorothy	4	270	1907-1916
Brinkman	Elmer W.	4	476	1907-1916
Brinkman	Emma Marguerite	4	14	1907-1916
Brinkman	Francisco	1	64	1878-1887
Brinkman	Frank A.	4	109	1907-1916
Brinkman	Herman Joseph	2	126	1887-1903
Brinkman	Hilda A.	4	433	1907-1916
Brinkman	Ida Josephine	3	136	1903-1915
Brinkman	Lora Musett	2	80	1887-1903
Brinkman	Marganna	2	22	1887-1903
Brinkman	Mary	2	80	1887-1903
Brinkman	Viloa Amelia Matilda	3	153	1903-1915
Brinkman	William Herman	4	15	1907-1916
Brissey	Lillian Alice	2	126	1887-1903
Briston	Lidda M.	1	33	1878-1887
Britton	Birdie Estella	2	116	1887-1903
Britton	Minnie May	2	47	1887-1903
Broaden	Jerry M.	1	34	1878-1887
Brock		4	137	1907-1916
Brock		4	140	1907-1916

CALHOUN COUNTY BIRTHS

Surname	Given Name	Book	Page	Year
Brock	Marie	4	311	1907-1916
Brodbeck	Ildra A. N.	4	434	1907-1916
Brodbeck	Minnie Matilda	3	140	1903-1915
Brodbeck	Thoms Herman	2	109	1887-1903
Brown		2	90	1887-1903
Brown	Perry W.	4	410	1907-1916
Browning	Biddy Rebecca	1	54	1878-1887
Brundies		3	68	1903-1915
Brundies	Agnes M.	4	169	1907-1916
Brundies	Alice E.	4	485	1907-1916
Brundies	Antone Henry	4	335	1907-1916
Brundies	Barney	3	120	1903-1915
Brundies	Emma Tickla	3	213	1903-1915
Brundies	Joseph Gerhard	4	181	1907-1916
Brundies	Joseph O.	4	20	1907-1916
Brundies	Leo	4	572	1907-1916
Brundies	Mary Ann	2	124	1887-1903
Brundies	Paul F.	4	350	1907-1916
Brunges		1	22	1878-1887
Brunges	Christian H.	1	41	1878-1887
Brunges	Mary Ann	1	45	1878-1887
Brunjes	Mayme	4	94	1907-1916
Brunjes	Orville Oran	3	214	1903-1915
Bruns	Harry M.	4	496	1907-1916
Bryan		3	235	1903-1915
Bryan	William Edward	4	180	1907-1916
Bryant		4	159	1907-1916
Bryant		4	160	1907-1916
Bryant		4	530	1907-1916
Bryant	Beulah William	4	311	1907-1916
Bryant	Charles Herman	4	50	1907-1916
Bryant	Erbie Alfred	3	9	1903-1915
Buchanan		1	65	1878-1887
Buchanan		3	215	1903-1915
Buchanan		4	162	1907-1916

CALHOUN COUNTY BIRTHS

Surname	Given Name	Book	Page	Year
Buchanan		3	215	1903-1915
Buchanan		4	355	1907-1916
Buchanan		4	132	1907-1916
Buchanan	Alphonse	4	369	1907-1916
Buchanan	Charles	4	229	1907-1916
Buchanan	Dorris Marlowe	4	257	1887-1903
Buchanan	Elmore C.	2	6	1887-1903
Buchanan	Harriet Amanda	4	295	1907-1916
Buchanan	John O.	1	17	1878-1887
Buchanan	Lillie Catherine	2	22	1887-1903
Buchanan	Otis C.	3	67	1903-1915
Buchanan	Roy	4	425	1907-1916
Buckholdt		1	79	1878-1887
Buckholdt	Louis	1	64	1878-1887
Buckingham	Irene Anna	4	398	1907-1916
Buckingham	Willard Douglas	4	570	1907-1916
Buhlman	John	1	2	1878-1887
Bull		2	79	1887-1903
Bull		1	56	1878-1887
Bull		1	11	1878-1887
Bull		1	19	1878-1887
Bull	(Still Born)	3	267	1903-1915
Bull	Alice B.	4	113	1907-1916
Bull	Alma	4	189	1907-1916
Bull	Cathrine Andrew	1	75	1878-1887
Bull	George W.	1	36	1878-1887
Bull	Grace Irene	1	36	1878-1887
Bull	Helen Lucile	2	117	1887-1903
Bull	Hettie Irene	2	117	1887-1903
Bull	Hubert Charles	2	116	1887-1903
Bull	James Lee	2	64	1887-1903
Bull	Leslie Jast	4	562	1907-1916
Bull	Maranda	1	74	1878-1887
Bull	Mary Agnes	4	405	1907-1916
Bullier	Margaret Mary	4	603	1907-1916

CALHOUN COUNTY BIRTHS

Surname	Given Name	Book	Page	Year
Bulon	Gabert Henry	4	447	1907-1916
Bunch		2	110	1887-1903
Bunch		1	17	1878-1887
Bunch		1	49	1878-1887
Bunch		2	61	1887-1903
Bunch	Lucy Alba	2	18	1887-1903
Bunch	Mary A.	2	11	1887-1903
Bunn		2	100	1887-1903
Bunn		2	83	1887-1903
Bunn	Dophine	2	126	1887-1903
Bunn	Eula Corine	3	171	1903-1915
Bunn	Mary Amanda	4	308	1907-1916
Bunn	Ross otto	2	95	1903-1915
Bunn	Roxey Rowene	3	148	1903-1915
Burbridge	Jesse U.	4	398	1907-1916
Burbridge	Raymond Kenneth	4	353	1907-1916
Burg		2	83	1887-1903
Burge		3	252	1903-1915
Burge		4	323	1907-1916
Burge	Bonna	4	457	1907-1916
Burge	Chas. Amos	2	63	1887-1903
Burge	Luther Henderson	4	227	1907-1916
Burge	Raymond	4	227	1907-1916
Burns		2	35	1887-1903
Burns		1	34	1878-1887
Burns		2	64	1887-1903
Burns	Byrta (Twin)	1	71	1878-1887
Burns	Bertha (Twin)	1	71	1878-1887
Burns	Carrie Leona	2	17	1887-1903
Burns	Charles Gerald	3	150	1903-1915
Burns	Dellia E.	1	14	1878-1887
Burns	Earl Waldsee	2	78	1887-1903
Burns	Eunice	4	209	1907-1916
Burns	James Irvin	2	107	1887-1903
Burns	Minnie Louisa	4	50	1907-1916

CALHOUN COUNTY BIRTHS

Surname	Given Name	Book	Page	Year
Burns	Minnie Rebecka	3	56	1903-1915
Burns	Robert	4	223	1907-1916
Burton	Mary Christina	1	26	1878-1887
Bush	Harry Osborn	1	54	1878-1887
Bush	Mary Elizabeth	2	23	1887-1903
Bushy		4	93	1907-1916
Bussen	John Henry	1	36	1878-1887
Bussen	Mildred	4	477	1907-1916
Buxton	Chas. Frederick	1	44	1878-1887
Byrd	Henry Earl	2	118	1887-1903
Byrd	John Everett	2	71	1887-1903
Byrd	Margaret Isabel	4	69	1907-1916
Cahill	Ellen	1	24	1878-1887
Cahill	Morris Michael	1	24	1878-1887
Calamme	Westley	2	117	1887-1903
Calloway		1	67	1878-1887
Calvey	Charles E.	1	30	1878-1887
Calvey	Donald Charles	4	5	1907-1916
Calvey	Emma Louisa	1	48	1878-1887
Calvey	Melvin E.	4	119	1907-1916
Calvin	Ada Lee B.	4	516	1907-1916
Camera		3	16	1903-1915
Camerea		2	86	1887-1903
Cameron		2	62	1887-1903
Campbell		2	105	1887-1903
Campbell		2	54	1887-1903
Campbell	Adie Lee	1	18	1878-1887
Campbell	Alma	1	79	1878-1887
Campbell	Andrew B.	1	22	1878-1887
Campbell	Bessie Ruth	3	40	1903-1915
Campbell	Chas. A.	3	59	1903-1915
Campbell	Clemory Cleo	4	90	1907-1916
Campbell	Cora Belle	1	61	1878-1887
Campbell	Cordelia Jane	2	65	1887-1903
Campbell	Earl Raymond	2	36	1887-1903

CALHOUN COUNTY BIRTHS

Surname	Given Name	Book	Page	Year
Campbell	Effe Lee	1	37	1878-1887
Campbell	Eva Elizabeth	2	28	1887-1903
Campbell	Eva Maxine	4	8	1907-1916
Campbell	Gerald Victor	4	164	1907-1916
Campbell	Helen V.	4	118	1907-1916
Campbell	James E.	3	211	1903-1915
Campbell	Jasper L.	3	211	1903-1915
Campbell	Jas. Carlton	4	14	1907-1916
Campbell	Jesse Hamilton	4	58	1907-1916
Campbell	John Obie Hirst	2	125	1887-1903
Campbell	Laura E.E.	4	229	1907-1916
Campbell	Lillian Evangeline	3	219	1903-1915
Campbell	Loyd Lionel	4	453	1907-1916
Campbell	Lucile M.	4	187	1907-1916
Campbell	Marie	4	207	1907-1916
Campbell	Martha Juanita	4	327	1907-1916
Campbell	Mary	2	44	1887-1903
Campbell	Mary Edna	2	7	1887-1903
Campbell	Merdes	2	98	1887-1903
Campbell	Mildred Fay	3	95	1903-1915
Campbell	Nellie Etta	3	34	1903-1915
Campbell	Norman L.	3	72	1903-1915
Campbell	Paul Willard	4	379	1907-1916
Campbell	Ruby Elizabeth	4	491	1907-1916
Campbell	Wiona	4	228	1907-1916
Canan	Catherine Ella	2	117	1887-1903
Canan	Gerard Lea	4	231	1907-1916
Canan	Laura Bernice	4	89	1907-1916
Canan	Timothy	3	122	1903-1915
Capel		2	123	1887-1903
Capher	Lucy D.	3	65	1903-1915
Cappel	Emil	4	190	1907-1916
Cappel	John	4	48	1907-1916
Capple		3	158	1903-1915
Capple		4	526	1907-1916

CALHOUN COUNTY BIRTHS

Surname	Given Name	Book	Page	Year
Capple	Charles	2	42	1887-1903
Carey	Mary (Twin)	2	56	1887-1903
Carey	Theresa (Twin)	2	56	1887-1903
Carlton		2	42	1887-1903
Carlton		4	561	1907-1916
Carlton		4	292	1907-1916
Carlton	Harry Everett	4	366	1907-1916
Carlton	Lillian Ester	4	211	1907-1916
Carlton	Orville Leo	4	350	1907-1916
Carlton	WM. L.	4	455	1907-1916
Carmidy	Mabel Edw.	2	57	1887-1903
Carnes		3	167	1903-1915
Carnes	Cyrus Chas.	2	118	1887-1903
Carnes	Martha Ellen	2	64	1887-1903
Carnes	Sadie	4	422	1907-1916
Carpenter		4	20	1907-1916
Carpenter	Bernice	4	590	1907-1916
Carpenter	Clarence Robert	4	455	1907-1916
Carpenter	Fred W.	4	283	1907-1916
Carpenter	Gertrude	4	590	1907-1916
Carpenter	Leona Agnes	4	420	1907-1916
Carpenter	WM. Arthur	2	62	1887-1903
Carpunky	Gerald Wallace	4	254	1907-1916
Carpunky	James	4	5	1907-1916
Carpunky	Mary Maria	1	30	1878-1887
Carpunky	Mildred Maria	4	380	1907-1916
Carpunky	Sarah	1	47	1878-1887
Carrel	Priney A.	2	47	1887-1903
Carroll		4	490	1907-1916
Carroll	John Walter	2	20	1887-1903
Carroll	Julia Josephine	2	70	1887-1903
Carrolton	Lottie J.	2	2	1887-1903
Carrolton	WM. Arthur	2	54	1887-1903
Carson		2	101	1887-1903
Carter	Chas.L. (Twin)	2	75	1887-1903

CALHOUN COUNTY BIRTHS

Surname	Given Name	Book	Page	Year
Carter	Grace (Twin)	2	75	1887-1903
Carter	Cuba M.	1	63	1878-1887
Carter	Frederick William	4	560	1907-1916
Carter	Nick Wesley	4	377	1907-1916
Carter	Nina S.	1	45	1878-1887
Carter	Sylia Lorain	4	245	1907-1916
Cary	Benjamin James	2	103	1887-1903
Cary	Lucina	1	12	1878-1887
Caselton	Evelyn Rosalie	4	221	1907-1916
Caselton	Helen Teresa	4	339	1907-1916
Caselton	John Antone	4	127	1907-1916
Caselton	Leona Margaret	3	152	1903-1915
Caselton	Mary Louisa	4	449	1907-1916
Casey	Elizabeth Ann	4	154	1907-1916
Casteel		4	345	1907-1916
Catlett	James Carl	1	44	1878-1887
Catlett	Zephania B.	1	27	1878-1887
Center	Mary Mollie	2	72	1887-1903
Centers		2	86	1887-1903
Chadowens		2	74	1887-1903
Champlin	Catherine V. E.	2	107	1887-1903
Champlin	Clinton J.	4	34	1907-1916
Champlin	Gladys B.	3	89	1903-1915
Champlin	Hattie	4	165	1907-1916
Charlton		4	144	1907-1916
Charlton		2	19	1887-1903
Charlton	(Still Born)	3	283	1903-1915
Charlton	Carmeline Daisy	4	342	1907-1916
Charlton	George Bernard	2	44	1887-1903
Charlton	Gibert C.	4	184	1907-1916
Charlton	Gladys Viola	4	344	1907-1916
Charlton	Homer	1	61	1878-1887
Charlton	Isa Oma	4	481	1907-1916
Charlton	Nettie Lorene	2	122	1887-1903
Child	Mary Richards	1	39	1878-1887

CALHOUN COUNTY BIRTHS

Surname	Given Name	Book	Page	Year
Christopher	Elda	1	32	1878-1887
Church		1	42	1878-1887
Church		1	40	1878-1887
Church		2	1	1887-1903
Church	Alice	2	41	1887-1903
Church	Elias T.	4	506	1907-1916
Church	Geo.	2	64	1887-1903
Church	Margaret Leona	2	27	1887-1903
Church	Thos. Edw.	2	12	1887-1903
Churchman	Charles Fremont	4	256	1907-1916
Churchman	James C.	4	23	1907-1916
Churchman	Joseph H.	4	272	1907-1916
Churchman	Mary Etta	4	129	1907-1916
Churchman	Meca Elizabeth	4	356	1907-1916
Clark		4	147	1907-1916
Clark	(Still Born Twin)	3	269	1903-1915
Clark	(Still Born Twin)	3	269	1903-1915
Clark	Robert	4	595	1907-1916
Clark	Zingora	1	3	1878-1887
Clemme	Quintin	3	196	1903-1915
Clendenny		1	41	1878-1887
Clendenny		1	58	1878-1887
Clendenny		2	56	1887-1903
Clendenny		4	521	1907-1915
Clendenny		2	41	1887-1903
Clendenny		1	17	1878-1887
Clendenny		2	6	1887-1903
Clendenny	Ethel	2	6	1887-1903
Clendenny	Faye	4	504	1907-1916
Clendenny	Harold	3	45	1903-1915
Clendenny	Harry William	2	71	1887-1903
Clendenny	James Freeman	3	180	1903-1915
Clendenny	James M.	3	233	1903-1915
Clendenny	James Otis	4	576	1907-1916
Clendenny	Leo N.	4	381	1907-1916

CALHOUN COUNTY BIRTHS

Surname	Given Name	Book	Page	Year
Clendenny	Lewis Kenneth	4	251	1907-1916
Clendenny	Logan L.	1	57	1878-1887
Clendenny	Lucy Janettie	4	553	1907-1916
Clendenny	Luly	1	18	1878-1887
Clendenny	Norma Gladlyn	4	99	1907-1916
Clendenny	Orland E.	4	83	1907-1916
Clendenny	Sylvia	4	376	1907-1916
Clendenny	William Alvin	1	76	1878-1887
Cleveland	Benjamin F.	1	7	1878-1887
Cleveland	Francis Marion	1	49	1878-1887
Cleveland	Hattie M.	1	36	1878-1887
Cloniger	Chester C.	3	156	1903-1915
Cloninger		2	10	1887-1903
Cloninger		2	24	1887-1903
Cloninger		4	108	1907-1916
Cloninger		2	42	1887-1903
Cloninger		1	12	1878-1887
Cloninger		1	8	1878-1887
Cloninger		4	27	1907-1916
Cloninger		1	18	1878-1887
Cloninger		4	82	1907-1916
Cloninger		1	45	1878-1887
Cloninger	Arthur	2	41	1887-1903
Cloninger	Arthur Glenn	2	41	1887-1903
Cloninger	Bessie Opal	3	84	1903-1915
Cloninger	Charles A.	1	21	1878-1887
Cloninger	Clarence Leroy	3	194	1903-1915
Cloninger	Esther A.	1	70	1878-1887
Cloninger	Luther	1	29	1878-1887
Cloninger	Luther Norman	2	125	1887-1903
Cloninger	Mable	1	51	1878-1887
Cloninger	Mary E.	4	370	1907-1916
Cloninger	Maxie Lee	3	250	1903-1915
Cloninger	Minnie Christina	2	56	1887-1903
Cloninger	Wilda Leota	4	567	1907-1916

CALHOUN COUNTY BIRTHS

Surname	Given Name	Book	Page	Year
Clowers		1	47	1878-1887
Clowers		2	82	1887-1903
Clowers	Bertha May	2	115	1887-1903
Clowers	Grace	1	72	1878-1887
Clowers	Milo Irvin	4	552	1907-1916
Clugsten		4	89	1907-1916
Clugsten	Esther	3	246	1903-1915
Clugsten	Hazel	4	387	1907-1916
Clugsten	Merlie	2	119	1887-1903
Cockrell		3	133	1903-1915
Cockrell		2	33	1907-1916
Cockrell	Forrest Leroy	4	10	1907-1916
Cockrell	Harold Elmore	4	16	1907-1916
Cockrell	Jesse Jerome	4	3	1907-1916
Cockrell	Martin Andrew	2	117	1887-1903
Cockrell	Ralph Abram	4	415	1907-1916
Cockrell	Robert Sidney	4	214	1907-1916
Cockrell	Sarah Juanita	2	88	1887-1903
Cockrell	Walter Marion	1	30	1878-1887
Cockshott	Winnie B.	2	17	1887-1903
Cole	Erma Mae	4	462	1907-1916
Collins		4	290	1907-1916
Collins		4	189	1907-1916
Collins		4	475	1907-1916
Collins	Eva	2	126	1887-1903
Collins		2	69	1887-1903
Collins	Frances Joseph	4	372	1907-1916
Collins	Sidney Leon	4	290	1907-1916
Colvin		2	91	1887-1903
Colvin	John	2	38	1887-1903
Conner	Edna Alma	4	218	1907-1915
Conner	Gladys	4	167	1907-1916
Conners	(Still Born)	3	266	1903-1915
Cook		1	15	1878-1887
Coombs	Chas. WM.	2	36	1887-1903

CALHOUN COUNTY BIRTHS

Surname	Given Name	Book	Page	Year
Cooshin	Minna Elizabeth	1	50	1887-1887
Copher	Isaac Christian	3	255	1903-1915
Copher	Maggie Ellen	3	177	1903-1915
Corbett		4	368	1907-1916
Corbett		4	65	1907-1916
Corbett	Adam B.	4	288	1907-1916
Corbett	Alvin E.	4	172	1907-1916
Corbett	Ella	4	501	1907-1916
Corbett	Helen M.	4	500	1907-1916
Corbett	Katie	3	154	1903-1915
Corbett	Lenora Helena	4	162	1907-1916
Corbett	Leo B.	4	544	1907-1916
Corbett	Nellie Catherine	4	492	1907-1916
Corbett	Frances Theresa	4	36	1907-1916
Corbett	William Bartholomew	4	26	1907-1916
Cornant	Chas. Joseph	2	54	1887-1903
Cornant	Mary	2	113	1887-1903
Cornelius	George	2	63	1887-1903
Cornelius	Gladys	2	81	1887-1903
Cornelius	Harry Fulton	3	110	1903-1915
Cornelius	Susan Rosena	2	94	1887-1903
Corven		2	95	1887-1903
Couch	Lula Arty	1	36	1878-1887
Coughlin	Martin	2	11	1887-1903
Cox		2	87	1887-1903
Cox	Aloys	2	2	1887-1903
Cox	Inez Elizabeth	2	112	1887-1903
Cox	James W.	1	9	1878-1887
Cox	William Elijah	1	26	1878-1887
Crader		1	65	1878-1887
Crader		4	206	1907-1916
Crader	Alta Mary	1	70	1878-1887
Crader	Beulah I.	2	57	1887-1903
Crader	Cassa	1	54	1878-1887
Crader	Dauty E.	1	68	1878-1887

CALHOUN COUNTY BIRTHS

Surname	Given Name	Book	Page	Year
Crader	Deforest	2	4	1887-1903
Crader	Earl	3	38	1903-1915
Crader	Edna	4	480	1907-1916
Crader	Elsie F.	3	124	1903-1915
Crader	Elsworth	3	124	1903-1915
Crader	Grover	2	8	1887-1903
Crader	Henry Selby	1	50	1878-1887
Crader	Inuz	1	31	1878-1887
Crader	Irene	2	15	1887-1903
Crader	Lamont	2	24	1887-1903
Crader	Leta Mae	3	225	1903-1915
Crader	Margaret Elizabeth	2	66	1887-1903
Crader	Myrtle Odessa	4	65	1907-1916
Crader	Olie Everett	3	230	1903-1915
Crader	Olie Jane	2	22	1887-1903
Crader	Oneita P.	4	289	1907-1916
Crader	Opal Loretta	4	378	1907-1916
Crader	Phydella L.	4	438	1907-1916
Crader	Roy W.	2	56	1887-1903
Crader	Slocum	2	41	1887-1903
Crader	Timothy Otto	3	50	1903-1915
Crader	Viola C.	4	550	1907-1916
Crader	Viola Maxine	4	133	1907-1916
Craig	Charley	2	102	1887-1903
Craig	Violet C.	2	94	1887-1903
Craigmile	William H.	1	8	1878-1887
Craigmiles		4	368	1907-1916
Craigmiles		2	104	1887-1903
Craigmiles	Albert R.	1	48	1878-1887
Craigmiles	Alonzo S.	3	22	1903-1915
Craigmiles	Dorris Elizabeth	2	109	1887-1903
Craigmiles	Stephen Eugene	3	168	1903-1915
Crater	Isaac	2	107	1887-1903
Crater	Rufus	1	47	1878-1887
Crater	Sarah Emily	2	6	1887-1903

CALHOUN COUNTY BIRTHS

Surname	Given Name	Book	Page	Year
Crater	Willie M.	2	73	1887-1903
Crawford		4	170	1907-1916
Crawford	Florence Augusta	3	232	1903-1915
Crawford	Leona B.	3	18	1903-1915
Crawford	Sopha Sadie	2	96	1887-1903
Creech		1	43	1878-1887
Creech		1	56	1878-1887
Creech	Ernest Everett	1	34	1878-1887
Creech	Ernest Hugh	4	565	1907-1916
Creech	Ionez Eliza	4	2	1907-1916
Creech	Myra E.	4	459	1907-1916
Creech	Robert Caral	3	131	1903-1915
Cress		1	53	1878-1887
Cress		1	74	1878-1887
Cress	(Still Born)	3	287	1903-1915
Cress	Effie Ethel	2	3	1887-1903
Cress	Mildred Eliza	4	97	1907-1916
Cress	Opal Elizabeth Vernetta	4	286	1907-1916
Cress	William Bryan	2	107	1887-1903
Cress	William Earl	2	104	1887-1903
Cresswell		1	72	1878-1887
Cresswell		3	33	1903-1915
Cresswell	John	1	77	1878-1887
Creswell		2	97	1887-1903
Creswell	Carroll	2	23	1887-1903
Criss		1	60	1878-1887
Croner	Charles	2	24	1887-1903
Crosby		1	3	1878-1887
Crosby		1	78	1878-1887
Crosby		2	9	1887-1903
Crosby	Cecil V.	2	90	1887-1903
Crosby	Darsey Anna A.	1	39	1878-1887
Crosby	Elby Ray	2	31	1887-1903
Crosby	Evalena	1	34	1878-1887
Crosby	Margaret Florence	2	107	1887-1903

CALHOUN COUNTY BIRTHS

Surname	Given Name	Book	Page	Year
Crouch		1	30	1878-1887
Crouch	Charles Harvey	1	7	1878-1887
Crull	George C.	1	20	1878-1887
Cunningham		4	147	1907-1916
Cunningham		1	8	1878-1887
Cunningham	Clifton J.	2	48	1887-1903
Cunningham	Emily	4	115	1907-1916
Cunningham	Grant Monroe Jr.	4	337	1907-1916
Cunningham	John A.	4	441	1907-1916
Cunningham	Lena V.M.	4	395	1907-1916
Cunningham	Lola H.	4	41	1907-1916
Cunningham	Margaret C.	1	26	1878-1887
Cunningham	Reba Florence	4	230	1907-1916
Cunningham	William Harry	4	556	1907-1916
Curtis		2	80	1887-1903
Curtis	Alpha Grace	4	48	1907-1916
Curtis	Arnold Owen	4	331	1907-1916
Curtis	Cecil R.	4	474	1907-1916
Curtis	Freda Irene	4	79	1907-1916
Curtis	Oca Florence	3	151	1903-1915
Cushen	Bridget R.	2	9	1887-1903
Cushing		2	32	1887-1903
Cushing	Morris (Twin)	1	65	1878-1887
Cushing	Maude (Twin)	1	65	1887-1887
Daack	Dorothy Elmina	4	318	1907-1916
Daack	WM. Oscar	4	321	1907-1916
Daak		4	446	1907-1916
Daak	Carrie Louise	4	216	1907-1916
daarh	Samuel J.	2	23	1887-1903
Dalton		2	83	1887-1903
Dalton	George O.	2	100	1887-1903
Damnitz	Frank H.	1	11	1878-1887
Daniels	Helen	4	411	1907-1916
Daprato	Louis F.	4	574	1907-1916
Darling	Rosa	1	30	1878-1887

CALHOUN COUNTY BIRTHS

Surname	Given Name	Book	Page	Year
Darr	Ernest Lee	1	25	1878-1887
Darr	Vesta	1	45	1878-1887
Daugherty	Leola Marie	3	93	1903-1915
Daugherty	James	1	22	1878-1887
Daugherty	William Adlai	2	57	1887-1903
Davidson		3	194	1903-1915
Davis		1	57	1878-1887
Davis		2	38	1887-1903
Davis		2	15	1887-1903
Davis		2	58	1887-1903
Davis		3	243	1903-1915
Davis	(Still Born)	3	280	1903-1915
Davis	(Still Born)	3	281	1903-1915
Davis	Alma	3	258	1903-1915
Davis	Elba	4	469	1907-1916
Davis	Harry Somers Berry	3	255	1903-1915
Davis	James William	1	13	1878-1887
Davis	Jessie May	3	147	1903-1915
Davis	Lawrence Evert	4	10	1907-1916
Davis	Lee Marion	2	78	1887-1903
Davis	Nettie M.	3	189	1903-1915
Davis	Ramonia Louisa	4	258	1907-1916
Davis	Robley Willard	2	88	1887-1903
Davis	Russell	4	106	1907-1916
Davis	WM. Mayo	2	130	1887-1903
Day		4	554	1907-1916
Day	Catherine F.	4	456	1907-1916
Day	Elsie	4	82	1907-1916
Day	Eula	4	203	1907-1916
Day	Howard Joseph	2	84	1887-1903
Day	John Bartholomew	4	369	1907-1916
Day	Loretta Margaret	4	328	1907-1916
Day	Mary Eleanor	4	117	1907-1916
Day	Murril Roy	3	230	1903-1915
Day	Murril Roy	3	230	1903-1915

CALHOUN COUNTY BIRTHS

Surname	Given Name	Book	Page	Year
Day	Theodore Winfield	3	151	1903-1915
Dayle	Ivy Orland	4	520	1907-1916
Deal	Grace Blanche	2	71	1887-1903
Dean	Mahalla	4	245	1907-1916
Deer		2	72	1887-1903
Degerlia		4	580	1907-1916
Degerlia	Albert	1	11	1878-1887
Degerlia	Amos A.	4	601	1907-1916
Degerlia	Amos Olney	3	182	1903-1915
Degerlia	Anna M.	1	32	1878-1887
Degerlia	Blanche Pauline	4	247	1907-1916
Degerlia	Charles Allen	4	290	1907-1916
Degerlia	Effa Viola	2	24	1887-1903
Degerlia	Margaret Ann	1	21	1878-1887
Degerlia	Mary M.	2	9	1887-1903
Degerlia	Robert F.	4	482	1907-1916
Degerlia	Rupert	2	43	1887-1903
Degerlia	William	4	249	1907-1916
Deickeiman	Levi Lewis	1	38	1878-1887
Delany		2	92	1887-1903
Delany	Alvora	3	146	1903-1915
Delany	Charles A.	2	19	1887-1903
Delany	Chas. William	1	48	1878-1887
Delany	Cora M.	1	12	1878-1887
Delany	Laura	1	79	1878-1887
Delear		2	114	1887-1903
Delona	WM. Samuel	2	110	1887-1903
Delonay	Joseph	4	430	1907-1916
Deloney	Alice Ottillia	4	512	1907-1916
Deloney	Ethel Pauline	4	337	1907-1916
Deloney	James Franklin	3	184	1903-1915
Deloney	Mary Alice Rector	4	24	1907-1916
Deloney	William Walter	4	168	1907-1916
Delong		4	223	1907-1916
Delong		1	65	1878-1887

CALHOUN COUNTY BIRTHS

Surname	Given Name	Book	Page	Year
Delong		1	40	1878-1887
Delong	(Still Born)	3	256	1903-1915
Delong	Canel Logan	1	59	1878-1887
Delong	Everet Gill	4	290	1907-1916
Delong	Lillian Jeanette	4	537	1907-1916
Delong	Louis Henry	4	370	1907-1916
Delong	Luther Ray	2	60	1887-1903
Delong	Mary D.	1	40	1878-1887
Delong	Mary Lucrela	4	534	1907-1916
Delong	William Allen	1	27	1878-1887
Delong	William Allen	4	483	1907-1916
Delong	Winnie E.	1	43	1878-1887
Delong	Winnie B.	3	1	1903-1915
Dennis		2	40	1887-1903
Dennis	Cora Alice	2	81	1887-1903
Dennis	David	2	31	1887-1903
Dennis	Estella Dolores	2	122	1887-1903
Depper		2	17	1887-1903
Depper		1	51	1878-1887
Depper	Anna	2	30	1887-1903
Depper	Edward Henry	3	116	1903-1915
Deshehr		2	99	1887-1903
Desherlia	Adam Henry	4	530	1907-1916
Desherlia	Everett Lyle	2	50	1887-1903
Desherlia	Harvey A.	2	86	1887-1903
Desherlia	Jaunita	4	367	1907-1916
Desherlia	William E.	4	489	1907-1916
Desherlia	William Jesson	1	54	1878-1887
Devault	John Lewis	1	6	1878-1887
Develin	Theodore E.	4	112	1907-1916
Deverger		1	14	1878-1887
Deverger	Mildred E.	4	486	1907-1916
Deverger	Pearl K.	4	142	1907-1916
Deverger	Rose Christina	4	321	1907-1916
Devine		2	94	1887-1903

CALHOUN COUNTY BIRTHS

Surname	Given Name	Book	Page	Year
Devine	A. M.	1	33	1878-1887
Devine	Eva Valara	3	96	1903-1915
Devine	Ezekiel H.	2	22	1887-1903
Devine	Gertie M.	2	76	1887-1903
Devine	Nellie Lee	2	68	1887-1903
Devine	Pansy	4	116	1907-1916
Devine	Teddy Bernard	3	206	1903-1915
Dewey	Rachael E.	1	32	1878-1887
Dewitt	Chas Bryan	2	75	1887-1903
Dewitt	William Harrison	2	54	1887-1903
Dickerman	John Wesley	1	73	1878-1887
Dickerman	Mildred Irene	4	314	1907-1916
Dickerman	Smythe Tone	2	31	1887-1903
Diekhoff	Anna Carolina Louisa	3	51	1903-1915
Dierking		4	4	1907-1916
Dierking		4	91	1907-1916
Dierking		4	294	1907-1916
Dierking	Bonnavier	4	435	1907-1916
Dierking	Emma	4	358	1907-1916
Dierking	Jewell Harlow	4	445	1907-1916
Dierking	Lela	2	100	1887-1903
Dierking	Lois	2	121	1887-1903
Dierking	Mavis Maxine	4	518	1907-1916
Dierksmeyer	Bertha Maria	4	379	1907-1916
Dietman	Cora Odella	2	74	1887-1903
Dietman	Mary Rosa Sylvia	2	52	1887-1903
Dillon		1	24	1878-1887
Dillon	Charles H.	2	13	1887-1903
Dillon	Harriet Ellen	1	2	1878-1887
Dillon	Lester Raymond	2	74	1887-1903
Dillon	Martin Edward	1	68	1878-1887
Dillon	Martin Edward	1	69	1878-1887
Dillon	Mary Etta	1	57	1878-1887
Dillree	Robert Franklin	2	118	1887-1903
Dinnis	Ople Leona	4	212	1907-1916

CALHOUN COUNTY BIRTHS

Surname	Given Name	Book	Page	Year
Dirking	Cornelius Fredrick	3	105	1903-1915
Dirking	Morrison	4	267	1907-1916
Dirking	Owen D.	4	267	1907-1916
Dirksmeyer		4	184	1907-1916
Dirksmeyer		2	91	1887-1903
Dirksmeyer	Lola Darlene	4	559	1907-1916
Dirksmeyer	Verlie Elizabeth	4	80	1907-1916
Dirksmeyer	Verna Luella	4	501	1907-1916
Dirksmeyer	Virginia Ilene	4	23	1907-1916
Dirksmeyer	William Otto	3	69	1903-1915
Dirksmeyer	WM.	4	326	1907-1916
Disernes	Cordelia C.	1	21	1878-1887
Diverger	Opal Eula	3	242	1903-1915
Dixon		1	56	1878-1887
Dixon		2	76	1887-1903
Dixon		1	53	1878-1887
Dixon	Albert Lewis	1	75	1878-1887
Dixon	Anna Myrtle	1	62	1878-1887
Dixon	Della	1	23	1887-1887
Dixon	Estella Margaret	3	101	1903-1915
Dixon	Harry	3	167	1903-1915
Dixon	Lee Alfred	2	90	1887-1903
Dixon	Lenard Milo	4	239	1907-1916
Dixon	Nancy Fern	2	113	1887-1903
Dixon	Nona Beatrice	1	42	1878-1887
Dixon	Ruby E.	3	1	1903-1915
Dixon	Violet	2	113	1887-1903
Dixon	William Jacob	3	145	1903-1915
Doak	Esther (Twin)	4	144	1907-1916
Doak	Hester (Twin)	4	144	1907-1916
Doak	Orvil Edgar	4	385	1907-1916
Dohme	Louis	2	50	1887-1903
Dorris	Lena Kathie	2	122	1887-1903
Dorworth	Lewis Berry	3	141	1903-1915
Dorworth	Alvin Nauss	1	10	1878-1887

CALHOUN COUNTY BIRTHS

Surname	Given Name	Book	Page	Year
Dorworth	Clark	2	15	1887-1903
Dorworth	Fern	2	35	1887-1903
Dorworth	Mable Clare	2	48	1887-1903
Dorworth	Mary Opal Jane	2	114	1887-1903
Dorworth	Ruby Isabella	4	244	1907-1916
Dorworth	WM. Earl	2	69	1887-1903
Dossett	Velma Lorene	4	219	1907-1916
Dota	James L.	1	70	1878-1887
Doty	Robert E.	1	52	1878-1887
Douglas	Benjamin Todd Jr.	3	98	1903-1915
Douglas	Gordon Carr	1	67	1878-1887
Douglas	Mary E.	4	404	1907-1916
Douley		3	175	1903-1915
Drake		2	25	1887-1903
Drake	Bernice	4	66	1907-1916
Draper		4	480	1907-1916
Draper	James	2	121	1887-1903
Draper	Lulu Minerva	3	100	1903-1915
Droege	Anna	2	79	1887-1903
Droege	Alma E.	2	39	1887-1903
Droege	Alvi	4	476	1907-1916
Droege	Celia Elizabeth	4	231	1907-1916
Droege	Clara Margaret	2	49	1887-1903
Droege	Clara Scharlote	4	293	1907-1916
Droege	Edward	4	85	1907-1916
Droege	Elizabeth	2	112	1887-1903
Droege	Gabriella Josepha	4	78	1907-1916
Droege	Helena	3	200	1903-1915
Droege	Henry	1	72	1878-1887
Droege	Herman Joseph	4	393	1907-1916
Droege	John	2	28	1887-1903
Droege	Leona Margaret	4	534	1907-1916
Droege	Margaret Tukla	2	102	1887-1903
Droege	Marie Ann	4	393	1907-1916
Droege	Mary Elizabeth	3	179	1903-1915

CALHOUN COUNTY BIRTHS

Surname	Given Name	Book	Page	Year
Droege	Peter	2	17	1887-1903
Droege	Raymond John	4	153	1907-1916
Droege	Stephen Garrett	4	165	1907-1916
Droege	Verdina Margaret	4	278	1907-1916
Droege	William Henry	3	42	1903-1915
Ducep	George Warren	2	20	1887-1903
Ducep	Joseph	1	22	1878-1887
Ducep	Julia Delina	1	3	1878-1887
Ducep	Julius	1	40	1878-1887
Ducep	Luther M.	3	81	1903-1915
Ducept		4	269	1907-1916
Duetman	Maggie Wilhelmina	2	79	1887-1903
Dunch	Charles	1	52	1878-1887
Dunse	Charlie Monroe	2	1	1887-1903
Dupy		4	157	1907-1916
Dupy	Jacob	3	254	1903-1915
Durking		4	574	1907-1916
Duteman	Barney	2	42	1887-1903
Dwyer	Eva	4	536	1907-1916
Dwyer	Leo Lawrence	4	107	1907-1916
Earley	James William	1	4	1878-1887
East	Harvey Leroy	4	145	1907-1916
East	Minnie Alma	1	70	1878-1887
Eaton	Cora Fern	4	330	1907-1916
Eberlin		4	160	1907-1916
Eberlin		4	61	1907-1916
Eberlin	Augusta	2	57	1887-1903
Eberlin	Clemens Elias	2	86	1887-1903
Eberlin	Edward Leonard	4	285	1907-1916
Eberlin	Golda Louisa	2	126	1887-1903
Eberlin	Henry	3	75	1903-1915
Eberlin	Raymond Henry	4	597	1907-1916
Eberlin	Gertrude C.	3	158	1903-1915
Echart	William R.	3	72	1903-1915
Eckart	(Still Born)	3	262	1903-1915

CALHOUN COUNTY BIRTHS

Surname	Given Name	Book	Page	Year
Eckart	Charles H.	1	54	1878-1887
Eckart		2	49	1887-1903
Eckart		3	251	1903-1915
Eckart	Artie Benjamin	4	206	1907-1916
Eckart	Lilian Lucile	3	1998	1903-1915
Eckart	Lula Leona	4	85	1907-1916
Eckart	Opal Runa	3	146	1903-1915
Eckart	William Elmer	2	66	1887-1903
Eckart	Mary Melvina	1	64	1878-1887
Eddington	David Joseph	4	375	1907-1916
Edson		2	13	1887-1903
Edwards		1	19	1878-1887
Edwards	Charles Saylor	2	103	1887-1903
Edwards	Early S.	1	54	1878-1887
Edwards	Edith Katherine	2	114	1887-1903
Edwards	Ernest Charles	4	309	1907-1916
Edwards	Lucy Lillian	4	318	1907-1916
Edwards	Mable V.	1	16	1878-1887
Edwards	Martha	4	10	1907-1916
Edwards	Ruth Virginia	3	56	1903-1915
Edwards	Viola	3	139	1903-1915
Eilerman	Catherina Mary	2	48	1887-1903
Eilerman	Clara Myrtle	4	200	1907-1916
Eilerman	Dora F.	2	116	1887-1903
Eilerman	Emma (Twin)	2	70	1887-1903
Eilerman	Minnie (Twin)	2	70	1887-1903
Eilerman	Louise Mary	3	73	1903-1915
Eilerman	Mary	4	447	1907-1916
Eilers	Mary	4	418	1907-1916
Eilers	Mathew	1	12	1878-1887
Eillerman	John August	2	91	1887-1903
Elder	Dorothy Marie	4	527	1907-1916
Elder	Helen Faye	4	141	1907-1916
Elder	Terry	4	197	1907-1916
Elledge		3	217	1903-1915

Surname	Given Name	Book	Page	Year
Elledge	Cleo Pearl	2	64	1887-1903
Elledge	Eluea D.	4	399	1907-1916
Elledge	Thomas Floyd	2	51	1887-1903
Emerick		2	74	1887-1903
Emerick	George William	1	77	1878-1887
Emerick	Lizzie	2	111	1887-1903
Emerick	Silas Richard	2	66	1887-1903
Emert	Floyd	2	46	1887-1903
Emery	Franklin E.	1	34	1878-1887
Emory		4	32	1907-1916
Engle	Laural	1	17	1878-1887
Engle	Minnie Alice	1	28	1878-1887
English	Mary Elizabeth	1	76	1878-1887
Enlow	Bertha	2	108	1887-1903
Ertil	Pauline	4	106	1907-1916
Eschbach	Edward Herman	4	565	1907-1916
Eschbach	Irene	4	361	1907-1916
Eschbach	Zelora Catherine	4	271	1907-1916
Etter		2	103	1887-1903
Etter	Charles Alfred	3	219	1903-1915
Etter	Clara	4	113	1907-1916
Etter	Earl	4	386	1907-1916
Etter	Emma	2	43	1887-1903
Etter	Florence	3	75	1903-1915
Etter	Mary L.	2	56	1887-1903
Etter	Mary M.	1	79	1878-1887
Etter	Raymond Willard	4	524	1907-1916
Etter	Tillie May	2	88	1887-1903
Etter	Wilhelmina Elizabeth	2	75	1887-1903
Etter	Willis Oliver	4	257	1907-1916
Evan		2	84	1887-1903
Evens		3	228	1903-1915
Evering	Loretta Ann	4	46	1907-1916
Evering	Mary Enda	3	157	1903-1915
Evering	Minerva	4	439	1907-1916

CALHOUN COUNTY BIRTHS

Surname	Given Name	Book	Page	Year
Ewen	Anna Marie	3	106	1903-1915
Ewen	Ed J.	4	403	1907-1916
Ewen	John Michael	4	107	1907-1916
Ewen	Karl M.	3	154	1903-1915
Ewen	Katherine C.	4	156	1907-1916
Ewen	Magdalena Francis	2	125	1887-1903
Ewen	Philip Frank	4	559	1907-1916
Ewen	William	4	28	1907-1916
Ewens	Joseph Herman	3	115	1903-1915
Ewens	Josephone Philomenia	3	115	1903-1915
Ewings	William Archie	2	64	1887-1903
Fabrum	Margaret	4	73	1907-1916
Fanning	Louisa M.	1	28	1878-1887
Fanning	Ruby Ann	1	5	1878-1887
Fanning	Samuel M.	1	25	1878-1887
Farley	Brau	1	15	1878-1887
Farnbach		4	505	1907-1916
Farnbach	Gerald	4	67	1907-1916
Farnbach	Joseph	1	44	1878-1887
Farnbach	William Harold	4	331	1907-1916
Farnbach	William	1	73	1878-1887
Farrow		4	153	1907-1916
Farrow		4	278	1907-1916
Farrow		4	131	1907-1916
Farrow	Cecil Fay	2	27	1887-1903
Farrow	Edwin Albert	4	265	1907-1916
Farrow	Florence Marie	2	89	1887-1903
Farrow	Loretta Mae	4	332	1907-1916
Farrow	Loyd N.	3	126	1903-1915
Farrow	Mary Jane	2	77	1887-1903
Farrow	Ruledge	4	462	1907-1916
Feilder	Henry Nicholas	3	67	1903-1915
Feilder	Homer Henry	3	23	1903-1915
Feilder	Raus N.	3	61	1903-1916
Ferguson		1	59	1878-1887

CALHOUN COUNTY BIRTHS

Surname	Given Name	Book	Page	Year
Ferguson		1	61	1878-1887
Ferguson		1	71	1878-1887
Ferguson	Carl Richard	2	14	1887-1903
Ferguson	Cuba May	2	53	1887-1903
Ferguson	George W. Norman	1	57	1878-1887
Ferguson	Grace E.	1	3	1878-1887
Ferguson	Sarah Agnes	1	66	1878-1887
Ferry	Jarvis Allen	4	228	1907-1916
Ferry	William	3	76	1903-1915
Fester		1	71	1878-1887
Feyler	Frederick Donald	2	121	1887-1903
Ficker	Anna Maggie	2	21	1887-1903
Ficker	Elizabeth B.	1	50	1878-1887
Ficker	Katie	2	56	1887-1903
Ficker	Lena	1	74	1878-1887
Field	Nancy Clementine	1	2	1878-1887
Fielder		2	97	1887-1903
Fielder		2	32	1887-1903
Fielder		3	269	1903-1915
Fielder	Albert C.	2	26	1887-1903
Fielder	Anna Maria	1	65	1887-1887
Fielder	Barbara	4	313	1907-1915
Fielder	Bertha V.	4	119	1907-1916
Fielder	Bessie Leona	2	102	1887-1903
Fielder	Chris	2	124	1887-1903
Fielder	Dorothy Virginia	4	55	1907-1916
Fielder	Etta	2	10	1887-1903
Fielder	Frederick William	1	77	1878-1887
Fielder	Izella Lavina	3	127	1903-1915
Fielder	John Henry	1	64	1878-1887
Fielder	Lilly Ann	2	103	1887-1903
Fielder	Mary M. E.	2	37	1887-1903
Fielder	Paul Henry	2	68	1887-1903
Fielder	Rosa Wilhelmina	2	32	1887-1903
Fielder	Sadia M.	3	144	1903-1915

CALHOUN COUNTY BIRTHS

Surname	Given Name	Book	Page	Year
Fields		2	69	1887-1903
Fields		3	49	1903-1915
Fields		4	376	1907-1916
Fields		4	60	1907-1916
Fields	Edna Lydia	2	127	1887-1903
Fields	Lulu Edith	2	49	1887-1903
Fields	Mary Ethel	2	26	1887-1903
Fields	Millie Myrtle	2	36	1887-1903
Fields	Virgil Jesse	3	217	1903-1915
Fields	Walter	3	122	1903-1915
Fischer		4	12	1907-1916
Fischer	Catherine Frances	2	11	1887-1903
Fischer	Freda	2	78	1887-1903
Fischer	Hildagard Tagkla	3	39	1903-1915
Fischer	John Dee	1	15	1878-1887
Fischer	Thresia E.	1	15	1878-1887
Fisher		2	50	1887-1903
Fisher		2	60	1887-1903
Fisher		2	70	1887-1903
Fisher		4	135	1907-1916
Fisher	Carl Rhuford	4	25	1907-1916
Fisher	Edna Corinne	4	421	1907-1916
Fisher	Emma Christina	2	113	1887-1903
Fisher	George Forest	1	29	1878-1887
Fisher	Henry C.	1	27	1878-1887
Fisher	Jacob G.	3	178	1903-1915
Fisher	John	4	328	1907-1916
Fisher	Lee Allen McDowell	1	54	1878-1887
Fisher	Myrtle Odessa	4	65	1907-1916
Fisher	Rosa Daisy	1	57	1878-1887
Fisher	Sarah Leone	3	36	1903-1915
Fisher	Sarah M.	1	42	1878-1887
Fisher	Sylvia Marie	1	71	1878-1887
Fisher	Walter C.	1	58	1878-1887
Fisher	William Morris	1	9	1878-1887

CALHOUN COUNTY BIRTHS

Surname	Given Name	Book	Page	Year
Fitzgearl	William I.	2	87	1887-1903
Flagge		1	38	1878-1887
Flagge		1	8	1878-1887
Flamm	Gertrude Annie	2	98	1887-1903
Flamm	Helen A. K.	3	205	1903-1915
Flamm	John Elston	2	73	1887-1903
Flamm	Myrtle Luella	2	129	1887-1903
Flamm	Thomas Joseph	2	60	1887-1903
Flanigan		2	80	1887-1903
Flanigan		3	52	1903-1915
Flanigan		4	42	1907-1916
Flanigan	Charles Leo	4	219	1907-1916
Flanigan	Charles E.	4	440	1907-1916
Flanigan	Elmer M.	4	401	1907-1916
Flanigan	George	2	16	1887-1903
Flanigan	Korene Helen	4	588	1907-1916
Flanigan	Laurence Frank	4	300	1907-1916
Flanigan	Thomas Joseph	2		1887-1903
Flaningan	Charles Leonard	2	10	1887-1903
Flaningan	Lucas Raymond	4	34	1907-1916
Flannigan	Ida Zeta	3	212	1903-1915
Flatt		4	282	1907-1916
Flatt		4	182	1907-1916
Flatt	Portia D.	3	145	1903-1915
Fleming		2	84	1887-1903
Fleming	Ruth	3	22	1903-1915
Fleming	Virginia Alice	4	351	1907-1916
Flemming	Columbus Bryan	2	71	1887-1903
Flemming	Ova Catherine	2	108	1887-1903
Flory	Eleeta Myrtle Marie	4	444	1907-1916
Flory	Thomas Leroy	1	72	1878-1887
Foiles		2	53	1887-1903
Foiles		4	431	1907-1916
Foiles		4	136	1907-1916
Foiles		1	69	1878-1887

CALHOUN COUNTY BIRTHS

Surname	Given Name	Book	Page	Year
Foiles		4	57	1907-1916
Foiles		1	52	1878-1887
Foiles		2	55	1878-1903
Foiles		1	55	1878-1887
Foiles		1	52	1878-1887
Foiles		2	34	1887-1903
Foiles		2	92	1887-1903
Foiles		2	61	1887-1903
Foiles		1	40	1878-1887
Foiles		4	547	1907-1916
Foiles		1	9	1878-1887
Foiles		3	245	1903-1915
Foiles	(Still Born)	3	265	1903-1915
Foiles	(Still Born)	3	268	1903-1915
Foiles	Anna C.	1	41	1878-1887
Foiles	Beatrice Leota	3	236	1903-1915
Foiles	Beulah	1	56	1878-1887
Foiles	Carl Leo	4	86	1907-1916
Foiles	Dennis W.	1	33	1878-1887
Foiles	Dora Eva	4	522	1878-1887
Foiles	Edith Vera	2	125	1887-1903
Foiles	Florence	3	148	1903-1915
Foiles	Frederick Jacob	2	106	1887-1903
Foiles	Gabriella	1	12	1878-1887
Foiles	Jeddie Lee	2	107	1887-1903
Foiles	Jesse	1	46	1878-1887
Foiles	John B.	3	8	1903-1915
Foiles	John Howard	2	88	1887-1903
Foiles	Joseph Frederick	2	32	1887-1903
Foiles	Kenneth B.	2	120	1887-1903
Foiles	Lawrence	4	316	1907-1916
Foiles	Lee	2	112	1887-1903
Foiles	Lidia	1	38	1878-1887
Foiles	Lilla Dell	1	10	1878-1887
Foiles	Luther Allen	4	121	1907-1916

CALHOUN COUNTY BIRTHS

Surname	Given Name	Book	Page	Year
Foiles	Mary Etta	1	16	1878-1887
Foiles	Mary Lucille	4	304	1907-1916
Foiles	Merrill Ellis	3	115	1903-1915
Foiles	Mertha J.	1	35	1878-1887
Foiles	Ora	1	25	1878-1887
Foiles	Orirn	1	25	1878-1887
Foiles	Shelby William	4	92	1907-1916
Foiles	Venton Leroy	4	182	1907-1916
Foiles	Vera Ione	3	156	1903-1915
Foiles	Willie T.	2	54	1887-1903
Foiles	Winnie Viola	2	99	1887-1903
Follis	Ethel Mae	2	121	1887-1903
Follis	Harriet Mandy Ellen	4	543	1907-1916
Follis	Rosalie	4	340	1907-1916
Fonck	Beulah Ione	2	50	1887-1903
Fonck	Christopher Columbus	2	89	1887-1903
Fonck	Harriet Ellen	2	77	1887-1903
Fonck	Lillian	3	100	1903-1915
Fonck	Marie Lucy	2	66	1887-1903
Ford	Vivian Marcella	3	223	1903-1915
Fortschneider		4	531	1907-1916
Fortschneider	Agnes Amelia	4	310	1907-1916
Fortschneider	Bernice	3	246	1903-1915
Fortschneider	Bertha	2	68	1887-1903
Fortschneider	Henry A.	2	109	1887-1903
Fortschneider	Sophia C.	1	9	1878-1887
Foster	Anna	4	35	1907-1916
Foster	Charles L.	2	111	1887-1903
Foster	Frances	4	204	1907-1916
Foster	Harold Lee	4	134	1907-1916
Foster	Lily	2	47	1887-1903
Foster	Lola May	4	501	1907-1916
Foster	Walter K.	4	464	1907-1916
Foster	Watson	4	217	1907-1916
Foval	Mable Ford	2	59	1907-1916

CALHOUN COUNTY BIRTHS

Surname	Given Name	Book	Page	Year
Foval	Mary Irene	2	115	1907-1916
Foval	Russell Joseph	4	17	1907-1916
Fowler		3	24	1903-1915
Fowler		4	9	1907-1916
Fowler	Alice	3	76	1903-1915
Fowler	Arthur Lyle	2	8	1887-1903
Fowler	Esther S.	4	131	1907-1916
Fowler	Eupel Lee	2	116	1887-1903
Fowler	Ray	2	97	1887-1903
Fowler	Rose	2	97	1887-1903
Fowler	Sarah Valera	2	45	1887-1903
Fox		2	99	1887-1903
Fox	Harry Virgil	3	190	1903-1915
Franck	Jerry	4	266	1907-1916
Franck	Tom	4	266	1907-1916
Frank		2	96	1887-1903
Frank	Albert Harrison	3	207	1903-1915
Frank	Della Maria	3	163	1903-1915
Frank	Esther	3	32	1903-1915
Frank	Henry A.	2	128	1887-1903
Frank	John	4	29	1907-1916
Frank	Lucille	4	28	1907-1916
Frank	Sterling Theodore	4	148	1907-1916
Franke		4	515	1907-1916
Franke		1	74	1878-1887
Franke	Charles A.H.	4	433	1907-1916
Franke	Clara F.E.	2	17	1887-1903
Franke	Elmer William Fred	2	108	1887-1903
Franke	Fredrick Ross	3	174	1903-1915
Franke	Harry Robert	4	192	1907-1916
Franke	Howard	3	170	1903-1915
Franke	John	2	6	1887-1903
Franke	Martha L.	4	402	1907-1916
Franke	Minnie Elizabeth	2	72	1887-1903
Franke	Nevada A.	4	189	1907-1916

CALHOUN COUNTY BIRTHS

Surname	Given Name	Book	Page	Year
Franke	Paul Fred	2	102	1887-1903
Franke	Ralph	3	31	1903-1915
Franke	Thelma Minnie A.	4	88	1907-1916
Franke	Vera Lesetta	4	13	1907-1916
Franke	William R.	3	73	1903-1915
Frederick		1	25	1878-1887
Frederickson	George	3	57	1903-1915
Freeman		1	29	1878-1887
Freesmeyer		2	77	1887-1903
Freesmeyer		2	46	1887-1903
Freesmeyer		2	2	1887-1903
Freesmeyer		2	85	1887-1903
Freesmeyer	Floyd	2	22	1887-1903
Freesmeyer	Frank R.	3	134	1903-1915
Freesmeyer	Hattie C.	1	63	1878-1887
Freesmeyer	Lorene Leota	2	99	1887-1903
Friedel	Albert William	2	5	1887-1903
Friedel	Alice Paulina	2	28	1887-1903
Friedel	Annie Agnes	2	75	1887-1903
Friedel	George Edward	2	47	1887-1903
Friedel	Mary Leona	1	62	1878-1887
Friedel	Norbert John	4	556	1907-1916
Friedel (Friedle)	John C	1	62	1878-1887
Friedel (Friedle)	Maria Appolomia	2	46	1887-1903
Friman	Alvera	4	20	1907-1916
Fritz	August	2	67	1887-1903
Fry		2	15	1887-1903
Fryman		4	528	1907-1916
Fryman	Clara	4	112	1907-1916
Fuhler	Margaretha	1	6	1878-1887
Fulkerson	Alfred L.	3	212	1903-1915
Fulkerson	Frank	2	7	1887-1903
Fulkerson	Harry G.	2	149	1887-1903
Fulkerson	Nellie W.	4	100	1907-1916
Fulkerson	William Orland	4	209	1907-1916

CALHOUN COUNTY BIRTHS

Surname	Given Name	Book	Page	Year
Fuller	Alonson Somers	4	79	1907-1916
Fuller	August	4	497	1907-1916
Fuller	Carlton Ethemer	2	104	1887-1903
Fuller	Clarence	4	592	1907-1916
Fuller	Dorothy Fay	4	323	1907-1916
Fuller	Goldy Irene	3	131	1903-1915
Fuller	James Douglas	1	11	1878-1887
Fuller	James Paul	4	301	1907-1916
Fuller	Kate	1	17	1878-1887
Fuller	Margaret Thelma	3	228	1903-1915
Funk		4	396	1907-1916
Funk		2	122	1887-1903
Funk	Doris Audrey	4	568	1907-1916
Funk	Dorothy Bernice	4	441	1907-1916
Funk	Georgia Leah	2	112	1887-1903
Funk	Gerald	4	544	1907-1916
Funk	Harold	4	544	1907-1916
Funk	Harry Carl	4	573	1907-1916
Funk	Henry	4	272	1907-1916
Funk	Pauline	3	109	1903-1915
Funk	Theodore Allen	3	210	1903-1915
Funk	William	2	29	1887-1903
Gambill	Donald Wilson	4	550	1907-1916
Gambill	Oren Bain	3	132	1903-1915
Gannis	August	2	4	1887-1903
Gannis	John G.	2	4	1887-1903
Ganse	Carl H.	3	103	1903-1915
Gansz	Albert William	2	127	1887-1903
Gansz	Clarence Leroy	4	314	1907-1916
Gansz	George August	3	20	1903-1915
Gansz	Luther	4	571	1907-1916
Gansz	Ora Ada	4	416	1907-1916
Gant	Herman Orlaand	4	508	1907-1916
Gant	Ida May	4	185	1907-1916
Gantz		4	175	1907-1916

CALHOUN COUNTY BIRTHS

Surname	Given Name	Book	Page	Year
Gardner		1	12	1878-1887
Gardner		2	68	1887-1903
Gardner	Enos B.	2	67	1887-1903
Gardner	Nanso Enis	4	552	1907-1916
Gardner	Nathaniel Lynn	4	390	1907-1916
Gasky		1	63	1878-1887
Gates	(Still Born)	3	279	1903-1915
Gates	Enos Wilson	4	381	1907-1916
Gates	George C.	2	39	1887-1903
Gates	Harrison Sherman	2	30	1887-1903
Gates	Nellie Rebeca	3	118	1903-1915
Gates	Winnie Delorttea	4	152	1907-1916
Geeding		1	66	1878-1887
Geeding		1	51	1878-1887
Geeding		1	35	1878-1887
Geeding	Iva Estella	1	23	1878-1887
Geers		3	194	1903-1915
Geers	Herman William	4	127	1907-1916
Geers	John Barney	4	15	1907-1916
Gehhausen	(Still Born)	3	275	1903-1915
Geisler	Grace Ida	2	120	1887-1903
Gennings	Peter	2	52	1887-1903
Gerber	Eugena A.	2	15	1887-1903
Gerecke	Arthur L.	2		1887-1903
Gerecke	Elizabeth Marie	2	76	1887-1903
Gerecke	Margerite	4	356	1907-1916
Gerecke	Raymond Charles	4	547	1907-1916
Gerkin		1	19	1878-1887
Gerstaker	George	2	8	1887-1903
Geske		2	97	1887-1903
Geske	Bessie Leona	4	114	1907-1916
Geske	Carl Frederick W.	1	43	1878-1887
Geske	Mary Rosa	2	41	1887-1903
Geske	Minnie	2	77	1887-1903
Geske	Sanuel	3	369	1903-1915

CALHOUN COUNTY BIRTHS

Surname	Given Name	Book	Page	Year
Geskie	Louis Abraham	2	52	1887-1903
Geskie	Minnie Louise	2	74	1887-1903
Geskie	Rosa Emma	2	65	1887-1903
Getz		4	273	1907-1916
Getz		2	127	1887-1903
Getz		2	127	1887-1903
Ghorley	Berdie Estella	3	168	1903-1915
Gianini	Assumta Julia	2	67	1887-1903
Gianinini	Giconda C.	2	82	1887-1903
Giannini	Amedeo	3	236	1903-1915
Giers	Beatrice	2	16	1887-1903
Gilbert		2	67	1887-1903
Gilbert	Blanche	2	50	1887-1903
Gilbert	Harry Franklin	2	52	1887-1903
Gilbert	Ray	4	120	1907-1916
Gilbert	Roscoe	2	118	1887-1903
Gilbert	Vera	2	85	1887-1903
Gill		1	15	1878-1887
Gill	Lettie E.	1	68	1878-1887
Gill	Maurice	4	493	1907-1916
Gilland	Oscar Jesse	1	35	1903-1915
Gillespie	Clemina V.	3	244	1903-1915
Gillett	Charles	2	3	1887-1903
Gilliam	Louis	4	450	1907-1916
Gisler		2	59	1887-1903
Gisler	Albert F.	4	149	1907-1916
Globe		4	24	1907-1916
Godar		4	583	1907-1916
Godar		4	351	1907-1916
Godar		2	83	1887-1903
Godar		1	33	1878-1887
Godar	Andrew	1	69	1878-1887
Godar	Antone	1	16	1878-1887
Godar	August	1	56	1878-1887
Godar	Benjamin Franklin	1	9	1878-1887

CALHOUN COUNTY BIRTHS

Surname	Given Name	Book	Page	Year
Godar	Bertha Theresa	1	78	1878-1887
Godar	Caroline	1	78	1878-1887
Godar	Charles	2	25	1887-1903
Godar	Dennis	1	3	1878-1887
Godar	Doretta A.	1	3	1878-1887
Godar	Elizabeth	1	17	1878-1887
Godar	Ellen	1	32	1878-1887
Godar	Florine Catherine	4	355	1907-1916
Godar	Irwin R.	3	143	1903-1915
Godar	James E.	1	46	1878-1887
Godar	Joseph	1	42	1878-1887
Godar	Julius Alfred	1	32	1878-1887
Godar	Lenora Lee	2	106	1878-1903
Godar	Marguerite Leonre	2	96	1887-1903
Godar	Mary Elizabeth	1	7	1878-1887
Godar	Mary Ernestine	2	65	1887-1903
Godar	Norbert Thomas	2	116	1887-1903
Godar	Raymond Arthur	2	49	1887-1903
Godar	Robert Francis	4	248	1907-1916
Godar	Rosalie	2	5	1887-1903
Godar	Zyprian Louis	2	46	1887-1903
Goetway	Otis Anton	2	38	1887-1903
Goetz	(Still Born)	3	277	1903-1915
Goetz	Florentine Ida	3	38	1903-1915
Goeway	Mabel	2	63	1887-1903
Goeway	Harold Franklin	4	343	1907-1916
Goltz		4	480	1907-1916
Goltz	Alta K.	3	189	1903-1915
Goltz	Charles	2	29	1887-1903
Goltz	Elza K.	4	53	1907-1916
Goltz	Herman	4	195	1907-1916
Goltz	Marie	4	317	1907-1916
Goltz	Roy L.	3	74	1903-1915
Goltz	Urban Ezra	4	191	1907-1916
Goodin	George Willis	4	298	1907-1916

CALHOUN COUNTY BIRTHS

Surname	Given Name	Book	Page	Year
Goodin	Leona Delores	4	225	1907-1916
Goodin	William W.	4	298	1907-1916
Gordon	Howard E.	2	2	1887-1903
Gordon		2	80	1887-1903
Gordon		1	26	1878-1887
Gordon		1	45	1878-1887
Gordon		4	543	1907-1916
Gordon	Benjamin M.	1	43	1878-1887
Gordon	Carl	1	79	1878-1887
Gordon	Clara Mertel	1	61	1878-1887
Gordon	Herbert Lee	2	41	1887-1903
Gordon	Hallie Mae	2	41	1887-1903
Gordon	Norman C.	1	56	1878-1887
Gordon	Stanley	2	39	1887-1903
Gordon	Thomas A.	2	71	1887-1903
Gose		3	224	1903-1915
Gosey	Dinah	2	25	1887-1903
Gottwey	Louis	2	7	1887-1903
Gotway	Beulah	2	101	1887-1903
Gotway		2	99	1887-1903
Gotway	Archie Anthony	4	67	1907-1916
Gotway	Blanche	2	87	1887-1903
Gotway	Charles Edward	1	54	1878-1887
Gotway	Cuba Tresa	2	56	1887-1903
Gotway	C.E.	4	467	1907-1916
Gotway	John William	3	204	1903-1915
Gotway	Julia Hanner	1	28	1878-1887
Gotway	Lena	3	22	1903-1915
Gotway	Norbert Leroy	4	336	1907-1916
Gotway	Pauline Weltha	3	83	1903-1915
Gotway	Zeta Mary	4	6	1907-1916
Gourley		4	451	1907-1916
Gourley	Freeda Florence	4	194	1907-1916
Gourley	Harry	2	123	1887-1903
Gourley	Mary L.	4	409	1907-1916

CALHOUN COUNTY BIRTHS

Surname	Given Name	Book	Page	Year
Gourley	Nellie Agnes	4	268	1907-1916
Grace	Ruby	2	86	1887-1903
Graham		3	188	1903-1915
Graham	Alma	4	121	1907-1916
Graham	Beatrice	4	426	1907-1916
Graham	Charles A.H.	4	467	1907-1916
Graham	Earl	3	232	1903-1915
Graham	Freda Irene	4	260	1907-1916
Graham	Martha	4	570	1907-1916
Graham	Ruth N.	4	323	1907-1916
Grall	Mary Jane	1	8	1878-1887
Gramer	Nancy Elizabeth	2	6	1887-1903
Grammer	Gussie Marie	4	509	1907-1916
Grammer	Lawrence Joseph	4	397	1907-1916
Grammer	William Dennis	1	65	1878-1887
Grandsiner	Eufa Loraine	3	6	1903-1915
Grandsinger		2	93	1887-1903
Grandsinger	Gertrude Lena	3	207	1903-1915
Grandsinger	Mary B.	2	55	1887-1903
Grassman	Beula Iola	2	12	1887-1903
Grassmann	Francis	1	71	1878-1887
Grassmann	Harry	2	43	1887-1903
Grassmann	Ione M.	3	138	1903-1915
Grassmann	Joseph Anton	2	122	1887-1903
Grassmann	Lucile	2	95	1887-1903
Grassmann	Rose	2	79	1887-1903
Grassmann	William A.	2	5	1887-1903
Gray		2	59	1887-1903
Gray		2	4	1887-1903
Gray		1	60	1878-1887
Gray		2	41	1887-1903
Gray	Elsie Melissa	4	451	1907-1916
Gray	Harold V.	4	408	1907-1916
Gray	Howard	4	162	1907-1916
Gray	Ima Francis	4	510	1907-1916

CALHOUN COUNTY BIRTHS

Surname	Given Name	Book	Page	Year
Gray	Vernia	2	21	1887-1903
Greathouse		4	105	1907-1916
Greathouse		2	87	1887-1903
Greathouse	Arthur B.	1	68	1878-1887
Greathouse	Charles B.	2	18	1887-1903
Greathouse	James William	2	128	1887-1903
Grecke		2	89	1887-1903
Green		4	259	1907-1916
Gregory		4	525	1907-1916
Gresham		2	57	1887-1903
Gresham		4	57	1907-1916
Gresham		4	525	1907-1916
Gresham	Barbara Jane	2	78	1887-1903
Gresham	Beatrice Irene	4	170	1907-1916
Gresham	Edna	4	557	1907-1916
Gresham	Harry	2	57	1887-1903
Gresham	Harry Logan	3	216	1903-1915
Gresham	Jospeh G.	2	16	1887-1903
Gresham	Nellie Frances	4	90	1907-1916
Gresham	Nina Maude	4	478	1907-1916
Gresham	Norma M.	4	305	1907-1916
Gresham	Raus	2	43	1887-1903
Gresham	Sadie May	3	38	1903-1915
Gresham	Silas Vernon	3	106	1903-1915
Gresham	Velma Lucile	4	436	1907-1916
Gresham	William McKinley	2	76	1887-1903
Gress		2	52	1887-1903
Gress		4	54	1907-1916
Gress		4	197	1907-1916
Gress		4	542	1907-1916
Gress	Cecelia	2	83	1887-1903
Gress	Edwin J.	2	104	1887-1903
Gress	Margaret	4	406	1878-1887
Griffen	Bertie (Twin)	1	37	1878-1887
Griffen	Bertha (Twin)	1	37	1878-1887

CALHOUN COUNTY BIRTHS

Surname	Given Name	Book	Page	Year
Grigsby	Charles R.	1	72	1878-1887
Grigsby	Helen G.	4	173	1907-1916
Grigsby	Myrtle E.	1	54	1878-1887
Grigsby	Ora Elizabeth	4	44	1907-1916
Grigsby	William	4	394	1907-1916
Grigsby	William Henry	2	57	1887-1903
Grover		4	575	1907-1916
Grover	Calvin	1	74	1878-1887
Grover	Clarene M.	4	281	1907-1916
Grover	Flossie H.	4	483	1907-1916
Grover	George Edward	4	280	1907-1916
Grover	John M.	1	53	1878-1887
Grover	Leonard A.	4	434	1907-1916
Grover	Marvin Hubert	4	225	1907-1916
Grover	Owen Edward	4	150	1907-1916
Grover	Sadie P.	4	37	1907-1916
Groves	Curtis Allen	2	106	1907-1916
Groves	Susan Sabina	3	54	1903-1915
Grueter	Rosa Helena	2	52	1887-1903
Grueter	Thomas			1907-1916
Guthrie		4	522	1907-1916
Guthrie	Cecil Clarence	3	26	1903-1915
Guthrie	Charles J.	1	34	1878-1887
Guthrie	Irene E.	1	33	1878-1887
Guthrie	Lester A.	3	143	1887-1903
Guthrie	Maggie M.	1	16	1878-1887
Guthrie	Roland (Twin)	2	75	1887-1903
Guthrie	Ralph Lee (Twin)	2	75	1887-1903
Guthrie	Vayne	4	169	1907-1916
Guthrie	Wardell Bartin	4	507	1907-1916
Hack	Gerald	4	424	1907-1916
Hadley		1	73	1878-1887
Hadley		1	59	1878-1887
Hadley	Edna Ione	2	73	1878-1887
Hadley	Fredus Guy	2	65	1878-1887

CALHOUN COUNTY BIRTHS

Surname	Given Name	Book	Page	Year
Hadley	Hazel Genelle	3	132	1887-1903
Hadley	Ruth Arlin	4	539	1907-1916
Hadley	William Albert	2	48	1887-1903
Hadley	Un-named Female	1	27	1878-1887
Hagen		4	495	1907-1916
Hagen		2	98	1887-1903
Hagen		1	59	1878-1887
Hagen		4	174	1907-1916
Hagen		4	495	1907-1916
Hagen		2	115	1887-1903
Hagen	(Still Born)	3	272	1903-1915
Hagen	Adolia Catherine	4	126	1907-1916
Hagen	Anna Sophia	2	89	1887-1903
Hagen	Bernard Henry	4	210	1907-1916
Hagen	Bridget	3	242	1903-1915
Hagen	Charles	2	74	1887-1903
Hagen	Christopher	2	77	1887-1903
Hagen	Clara Anna	1	57	1878-1887
Hagen	Clara Cecilia	3	63	1903-1915
Hagen	Dora	2	84	1887-1903
Hagen	Edward	4	129	1907-1916
Hagen	Gertrude	4	291	1907-1916
Hagen	Henry	1	76	1907-1916
Hagen	Henry Charles	2	62	1887-1903
Hagen	Henry Herman	4	301	1907-1916
Hagen	Jeanetta C.	3	28	1903-1915
Hagen	John A.	1	32	1907-1916
Hagen	Lulu Odessa	4	151	1907-1916
Hagen	Michael Robert	4	283	1907-1916
Hagen	Pauline Catherine	4	46	1907-1916
Hagen	Rachel Elizabeth	2	101	1887-1903
Hagen	Ray Gilbert	4	22	1907-1916
Hagen	Renard George	4	321	1907-1916
Hagen	Una V.	2	85	1887-1903
Hagen	Vincent Lawrence	4	577	1907-1916

Surname	Given Name	Book	Page	Year
Hagen	Walter Lee	3	16	1903-1915
Hagen	William Reuben	2	71	1887-1903
Hagen	Zelma Juanita	4	367	1907-1916
Hailey	Howard William	2	38	1887-1903
Haines	Anna Lucile	3	172	1903-1915
Haines	Lavina A.	3	61	1903-1915
Halemeyer		4	595	1907-1916
Halemeyer	Alice Anna	4	223	1907-1916
Halemeyer	August Robert	4	279	1907-1916
Halemeyer	Charles Fred	4	154	1907-1916
Halemeyer	Earnest	4	429	1907-1916
Hall		4	580	1907-1916
Hall	Nora Hattie May	4	101	1907-1916
Hall	Norman A.L.	4	207	1907-1916
Hallemeyer		4	87	1907-1916
Hallemeyer	John	3	247	1903-1915
Hallett	Palmer	2	27	1887-1903
Hallett	William L.	1	18	1878-1887
Hallford		3	134	1903-1915
Hamilton		1	14	1878-1887
Hamilton		1	3	1878-1887
Hamilton		1	37	1878-1887
Hamilton		1	77	1878-1887
Hamilton	Elias A.	1	46	1878-1887
Hamilton	Ervin Perry	4	448	1907-1916
Hamilton	Freda Irene	4	586	1907-1916
Hamilton	Gertrude	3	111	1903-1915
Hamilton	Ione Viola	2	51	1887-1903
Hamilton	Joseph	1	79	1878-1887
Hamilton	Julius Perry	1	79	1878-1887
Hamilton	Margaret K.	1	66	1878-1887
Hamilton	Mary Ann	2	109	1887-1903
Hamilton	Mary L.	1	36	1878-1887
Hammel	Homer	2	124	1887-1903
Hammer	Bernard Lee	4	277	1907-1916

CALHOUN COUNTY BIRTHS

Surname	Given Name	Book	Page	Year
Hancock	Robert W.	4	495	1907-1916
Hancock	Wilma E.	4	573	1907-1916
Hanks		4	39	1907-1916
Hanks	Elizabeth T.A.	4	106	1907-1916
Hanks	Eutha	4	174	1907-1916
Hanks	Thelma	4	536	1907-1916
Hannekan		4	87	1907-1916
Hannekan	Anna	3	169	1903-1915
Hanneken		4	336	1907-1916
Hanneken		2	118	1887-1903
Hanneken	Helen	4	284	1907-1916
Hanneken	John Rudolph	4	200	1907-1916
Hanneken	Katherine Hendrena	4	30	1878-1887
Hanneken	Theodore	1	10	1878-1887
Hanneken	William	2	127	1887-1903
Hannel	Hubert	1	52	1878-1887
Hannels		3	156	1903-1915
Hanson	Anna Mary	2	47	1887-1903
Haper	Nona	1	37	1878-1887
Haper	Vaughn	2	62	1887-1903
Hardesty		2	87	1887-1903
Hardesty	E.	3	30	1903-1915
Harlander	Paul Ward	3	139	1887-1903
Harlow		2	100	1887-1903
Harlow	(Still Born)	3	266	1887-1903
Harlow	Elsie Cleo	2	66	1887-1903
Harlow	Faye Eliza	2	117	1887-1903
Harrell		1	12	1878-1887
Harrell		2	80	1887-1903
Harrell	Clarence Edward	2	75	1887-1903
Harrell	James Pemberton	1	21	1878-1887
Harrell	James P.	1	32	1878-1887
Harrell	Smith A.	1	38	1878-1887
Harrison		1	41	1878-1887
Harrison	Edward Rollins	1	57	1878-1887

Surname	Given Name	Book	Page	Year
Harrison	George	2	34	1887-1903
Harrison	John G.	1	21	1878-1887
Harrison	Lettia Agnes	1	28	1878-1887
Harrison	Mary	1	39	1878-1887
Harrison	William Lawrence	1	10	1878-1887
Harrison	William S.			1907-1916
Hartman	Bertha Christina	3	179	1903-1915
Hartman	Mary Rachael	2	62	1887-1903
Hartman	Valentine J.	4	438	1907-1916
Hartman	William Henry	4	571	1907-1916
Haselhorst	Ella Elizabeth	3	201	1903-1915
Haselhorst	Veronica M.	2	49	1887-1903
Hasford	Arthur	4	578	1907-1916
Hasford	Russel	4	123	1907-1916
Hasselkuss	Golda	2	25	1887-1903
Hasselkuss	Oma	2	117	1887-1903
Hassen	Sarah A.	1	9	1878-1887
Hassenstaub		2	78	1887-1903
Hassenstaub	Maggie	2	62	1887-1903
Hasting		2	80	1887-1903
Hasty	Lucy M.	1	45	1878-1887
Hatfield		4	224	1907-1916
Hatfield	Christine Elizabeth	4	123	1907-1916
Hatfield	Harvey Kenneth	4	370	1907-1916
Hatfield	Lela V.	4	456	1907-1916
Hatfield	Roy	3	99	1903-1915
Hatteman	Matilda	1	73	1878-1887
Hattimer	Dena O.	3	160	1903-1915
Haubs	Daniel F.	2	62	1887-1903
Haubs	James Godfrey	2	110	1887-1903
Haubs	Margaret M.	4	449	1907-1916
Haufs	Ione Clare	3	66	1903-1915
Haug	Dorine Catherine Marie	2	85	1887-1903
Haug	Henrich W.	2	24	1887-1903
Haug	Henry Will Fred	2	29	1887-1903

CALHOUN COUNTY BIRTHS

Surname	Given Name	Book	Page	Year
Haug	Janisa	2	84	1887-1903
Haug	John Adam	2	123	1887-1903
Haug	Lawrence	2	126	1887-1903
Haug	Theresa Catherine	4	310	1907-1916
Haug	William Fred	4	125	1907-1916
Haugh	Mary	4	590	1907-1916
Hausmann		2	116	1887-1903
Hausmann		4	546	1907-1916
Hausmann		4	200	1907-1916
Hausmann		4	130	1907-1916
Hausmann	Henry Taylor	4	22	1907-1916
Hausmann	Lewis Fred Taylor	3	64	1903-1915
Hausmann	Ross Albert	4	70	1907-1916
Hayn		4	137	1907-1916
Hayn		4	380	1907-1916
Hayn	Carl Simon	3	118	1903-1915
Hayn	Edward Casper	4	541	1907-1916
Hayn	Elizabeth Anna	4	108	1907-1916
Hayn	Frank Joseph	4	307	1907-1916
Hayn	Freda Barbara	4	555	1907-1916
Hayn	Gertrude Louise	4	312	1907-1916
Hayn	Joseph	3	104	1903-1915
Hayn	Joseph Arthur	3	49	1903-1915
Hayn	Julia Anna	4	485	1907-1916
Haynes	Glen	4	503	1903-1915
Haynes	Vern Cyrus	4	378	1907-1916
Hays		3	6	1903-1915
Hays	Augusta Delitha	2	113	1887-1903
Hays	Florence Adna	4	365	1907-1916
Hays	Hobart	2	97	1887-1903
Hays	Nora Alberta	4	478	1907-1916
Hazelhorst	Anna	2	32	1887-1903
Hazelhorst	Mark Raymond	2	89	1887-1903
Hazelhorst	Martin	2	103	1887-1903
Hazelhorst	Nettie	2	30	1887-1903

CALHOUN COUNTY BIRTHS

Surname	Given Name	Book	Page	Year
Hazelhorst	Thresa	2	31	1887-1903
Hazelhorst	Mabel	3	111	1903-1915
Hazelwonder		4	233	1907-1916
Hazelwonder		4	304	1907-1916
Hazelwonder	(Still Born)	3	284	1903-1915
Hazelwonder	Guy	2	66	1887-1903
Hazelwonder	Lorraine	4	503	1907-1916
Hazelwonder	Margaret	2	95	1887-1903
Hazelwonder	Mary	2	81	1887-1903
Hazelwonder	Michael	2	121	1887-1903
Hazelwonder	Sadie	3	138	1903-1915
Hazelwonder	Thelma Irene	4	560	1907-1916
Hearst	Charles Edward	4	468	1907-1916
Hearst	Edna	4	5	1907-1916
Heavner		1	58	1878-1887
Heavner	Dorothy Irene	4	53	1907-1916
Heavner	Howard Orville	4	212	1907-1916
Heavner	Thomas	4	464	1907-1916
Heavner	Gilbert Leroy	1	36	1878-1887
Heavner	James Buford	1	46	1878-1887
Heavner	Oliver Jessie	4	508	1907-1916
Heffington		1	54	1878-1887
Heffington	Alice Lucile	4	15	1907-1916
Heffington	Emma Salees (Twin)	3	193	1903-1915
Heffington	George Pierce (Twin)	3	193	1903-1915
Heffington	Grace	2	15	1887-1903
Heffington	Joseph M.	3	237	1903-1915
Heffington	Marie Eliza	4	458	1907-1916
Heffington	Mary E.	4	74	1907-1916
Heffington	Rolland	1	12	1878-1887
Heffington	William Harrison	2	31	1878-1903
Heffner		4	481	1907-1916
Heffner	Sarah C.	1	44	1878-1887
Hefner	Howard H.	1	76	1878-1887
Hefner	Orpha Ruth	4	241	1907-1916

CALHOUN COUNTY BIRTHS

Surname	Given Name	Book	Page	Year
Hefner	Peral Alfred	1	44	1878-1887
Hegger	Harry John	4	165	1907-1916
Hegger	Mary Dora	3	174	1903-1915
Hegger	Robert Elmer	4	521	1907-1916
Heidenreich	Freda E.	3	104	1903-1915
Heidenreich	Frederick	2	11	1887-1903
Heidenreich	Charles	1	63	1878-1887
Heidenreich	Elizabeth M.	2	27	1887-1903
Heidenreich	John Henry	1	12	1878-1887
Heidenreich	Nona Marie	4	55	1907-1916
Heidenreich	Roland Edward	2	128	1887-1903
Heidenreich	Sophronia	1	47	1878-1887
Heidenreich	Clemens	1	33	1878-1887
Heimer	Anna Irene	4	388	1907-1916
Heimer	Dorothy Lucile	3	252	1903-1915
Heimer	Elizabeth	3	117	1903-1915
Heimer	Joseph Albert	4	235	1907-1916
Heimer	Martin E.	4	489	1907-1916
Held	Anna Irene	4	364	1907-1916
Held	Clarence	4	365	1907-1916
Held	Fred Edward	4	186	1907-1916
Held	Ida	2	55	1887-1903
Held	James Andrew	1	10	1878-1887
Held	Rose M.	2	123	1887-1903
Held	William	3	258	1903-1915
Helena		2	0	1887-1903
Helfrich	Matilda	2	112	1887-1903
Hemphill		1	61	1878-1887
Hemphill	Cora Marie	3	140	1903-1915
Hemphill	David V.	2	122	1887-1903
Hemphill	Dorothy Irene	4	53	1907-1916
Hemphill	Ray Melvin	2	60	1887-1903
Henderson	Royal	2	117	1887-1903
Hendricks	Gerhard McKinley	2	72	1887-1903
Hendricks	Guy Elmer	2	63	1887-1903

CALHOUN COUNTY BIRTHS

Surname	Given Name	Book	Page	Year
Hendricks	Margareth Pearl	2	90	1887-1903
Hendricks	Stewart Max	3	48	1903-1915
Hendricks	William E.	4	128	1907-1916
Hendrickson	Howard Clayton	4	242	1907-1916
Henricks	William Earl	2	70	1887-1903
Herkert		2	120	1887-1903
Herkert		3	64	1903-1915
Herkert	Annie Marie	2	92	1878-1887
Herkert	John	4	111	1907-1916
Herkert	Joseph Albert	4	8	1907-1916
Herkery	Bertha Theresa	3	168	1903-1915
Herrmann	Lily	4	418	1907-1916
Herrmann	Violet	2	36	1887-1903
Herron	Albert Victor	1	78	1878-1887
Herron	Charles Lester	2	14	1887-1903
Herron	Charles William	4	205	1907-1916
Herron	Charlotte Rachael	1	56	1878-1887
Herron	Harry	1	42	1878-1887
Herron	Howard	2	72	1887-1903
Herron	Lettie Elizabeth	2	14	1887-1903
Herron	Leveta Fern	4	432	1907-1916
Herron	Lily	1	17	1878-1887
Herron	Mary Elizabeth	4	243	1907-1916
Herron	Mary E.	4	452	1907-1916
Herron	Mina Frances	4	325	1907-1916
Herron	Pearley (Twin)	2	36	1887-1903
Herron	Virley (Twin)	2	36	1887-1903
Herron	Sara Myrtle	4	542	1907-1916
Herron	Sylvester M.	1	39	1878-1887
Herron	Wallace S.	2	15	1887-1903
Herter	Albert Henry	4	599	1907-1916
Herter	Flossie Ann	4	531	1907-1916
Herter	Paul Edward	4	354	1907-1916
Herter	Sherman J.	4	190	1907-1916
Herter	WilliamJ.	3	201	1903-1915

CALHOUN COUNTY BIRTHS

Surname	Given Name	Book	Page	Year
Hessen		4	176	1907-1916
Hesson	J. Edward	4	310	1907-1916
Hetzer		4	18	1907-1916
Hetzer	Ardella Ethel	4	166	1907-1916
Higgerson		2	75	1887-1903
Higgerson		2	7	1887-1903
Higgerson	Anna May	2	86	1887-1903
Higgerson	Sarah Margaret	1	29	1878-1887
Higham	Benjamin	1	65	1878-1887
Higham	Gertie Leona	2	44	1887-1903
Higham	John William	2	4	1887-1903
Higham	Mary Dallas	2	26	1887-1903
Higham	Nathan	1	72	1878-1887
Hildebrand	Dorah	2	29	1887-1903
Hilderbrand	Emma	1	22	1878-1887
Hill		2	42	1887-1903
Hill		2	62	1887-1903
Hill		4	413	1907-1916
Hill	Allie	2	121	1887-1903
Hill	Andrew F.	4	488	1907-1916
Hill	Carry May	2	70	1887-1903
Hill	Etta Letta	2	77	1887-1903
Hill	Geneva Catherine	4	319	1907-1916
Hill	George David	2	127	1887-1903
Hill	Julia Catherine	3	70	1903-1915
Hill	Leonard Rufus	1	66	1878-1887
Hill	Lillian	2	96	1887-1903
Hill	Lorina Alma	4	237	1907-1916
Hill	Marcus L.	4	329	1907-1916
Hill	Oliver J.	4	69	1907-1916
Hill	Oscar A.	1	56	1878-1887
Hill	Randolph Burl	3	243	1903-1915
Hill	Roy Raymond	4	512	1907-1916
Hill	Rufus L.	4	302	1907-1916
Hill	Sarah	1	47	1878-1887

CALHOUN COUNTY BIRTHS

Surname	Given Name	Book	Page	Year
Hill	Silas Frank	4	314	1907-1916
Hill	William Overston	4	192	1907-1916
Hillen	Agnes	3	34	1903-1915
Hillen	Anna	2	26	1887-1903
Hillen	Bernard A.	4	407	1907-1916
Hillen	Clement Mark	3	240	1903-1915
Hillen	Estella Catherine	4	274	1907-1916
Hillen	Frank	3	62	1903-1915
Hillen	Ida Margaret	3	221	1903-1915
Hillen	Irene Rosiana	4	135	1907-1916
Hillen	John	3	62	1903-1915
Hillen	Loretta Mary	4	287	1907-1916
Hillen	William	2	118	1887-1903
Hillerby	Marti Leon	4	63	1907-1916
Hinkle	Julia Josephine	3	79	1903-1915
Hirst	Joseph William	4	107	1907-1916
Hodson	Rebecca C. (Twin)	2	100	1887-1903
Hodson	Henrietta (Twin)	2	100	1887-1903
Hoemen	Aloysius	4	154	1887-1903
Hoemen	Emma Elizabeth	4	287	1907-1916
Hoemen	Mary Emma	4	16	1907-1916
Hoghn	Roy Francis	2	53	1887-1903
Holderfield	James William	1	29	1878-1887
Hollmeier	Johanna	1	2	1878-1887
Hollmeier	Wilhelmina	1	2	1878-1887
Holmes	Lillian C.	4	409	1907-1916
Holterfield	George Henry	2	33	1887-1903
Holterfield	Irene Pansy	4	396	1907-1916
Holtzworth	Lena Ruth	3	205	1903-1915
Holtzworth	Lucy F.	3	204	1903-1915
Holtzworth	William Edward	3	145	1903-1915
Holzwarth	Harry Earl	2	121	1887-1903
Holzworth	Margaret L.	2	115	1887-1903
Holzworth	Walter Benjamin	3	204	1903-1915
Hoots		2	87	1887-1903

CALHOUN COUNTY BIRTHS

Surname	Given Name	Book	Page	Year
Hoots	Clide Romen	1	68	1878-1887
Hopper		2	36	1887-1903
Horkey		1	13	1878-1887
Horman	Catherine Marie	4	84	1907-1916
Horts	Sarah Alice	1	16	1878-1887
Hosey		1	14	1878-1887
Hosey	Ethel May	3	121	1903-1915
Houseman		4	110	1907-1916
Housman		1	66	1878-1887
Housman	Bernice	4	341	1907-1916
Housmann		2	94	1887-1903
Housmann		4	445	1907-1916
Housmann		4	282	1907-1916
Housmann		4	356	1907-1916
Housmann		4	19	1907-1916
Howard		1	32	1878-1887
Howard	Floyd	2	4	1887-1903
Howdashell	Lavina	3	242	1903-1915
Howdeshell		3	161	1903-1915
Howdeshell	(Still Born)	3	284	1903-1915
Howdeshell	(Still Born)	3	276	1903-1915
Howdeshell	Ernest A.	4	403	1907-1916
Howdeshell	Marlin	4	389	1907-1916
Howdeshell	Mildred Elizabeth	3	254	1903-1915
Howdeshell	Owen Kiel	4	225	1907-1916
Howdyshell		3	92	1903-1915
Howland		2	53	1887-1903
Howland	Cora Ann	2	99	1887-1903
Howland	Dorothy May	4	238	1907-1916
Howland	Edna Wilene	4	87	1907-1916
Howland	Eliza Edmond	4	326	1907-1916
Howland	Harvey	2	5	1887-1903
Howland	Lewis Franklin	4	379	1907-1916
Howland	Marion A.	4	360	1907-1916
Howland	Mildred Louise	4	124	1907-1916

CALHOUN COUNTY BIRTHS

Surname	Given Name	Book	Page	Year
Howland	Vernon Earl	4	235	1907-1916
Howland	Warren	3	215	1903-1915
Hubbard		1	75	1878-1887
Hubbard		2	40	1887-1903
Hubbard		1	62	1887-1903
Hubbard		3	256	1903-1915
Hubbard		1	41	1878-1887
Hubbard		1	16	1878-1887
Hubbard	Charles Isaac	1	50	1878-1887
Hubbard	Dorothy	2	118	1887-1903
Hubbard	Mary E.	1	31	1878-1887
Hubbard	Mildred Geneva	4	381	1907-1916
Hubbard	Nora Lucile	4	208	1907-1916
Huff	Guy Arnold	1	9	1878-1887
Huffstuter	Ethel M.	2	6	1887-1903
Huffstuter	Margaret G.	1	16	1878-1887
Hughes	Edmond Thomas	4	327	1907-1916
Hughes	Harry	2	89	1887-1903
Hughes	John Joseph	4	415	1907-1916
Hughes	Margaret B.	4	489	1907-1916
Hughes	Minnie Lou Etta	2	84	1887-1903
Hughey		2	116	1887-1903
Humphrey	Adeline Jane	1	70	1878-1887
Humphrey	Adolph Stephen	2	92	1887-1903
Humphrey	Alta May	2	33	1887-1903
Humphrey	Goldie Elizabeth	2	72	1887-1903
Humphrey	Joseph William	2	49	1887-1903
Humphrey	Katy E.	2	14	1887-1903
Hunt		1	52	1878-1887
Hunt		1	28	1878-1887
Hunt	Capitola I.	1	52	1878-1887
Hunt	Goldie	3	62	1903-1915
Hunt	Homer Lafay	2	95	1887-1903
Hunter		4	315	1907-1916
Hunter		1	42	1878-1887

CALHOUN COUNTY BIRTHS

Surname	Given Name	Book	Page	Year
Hunter		4	466	1907-1916
Hunter		4	579	1907-1916
Hunter	(Still Born)	3	282	1903-1915
Hunter	Alberta	4	477	1907-1916
Hunter	Charles C.	2	16	1887-1903
Hunter	Howard C.	4	422	1907-1916
Hunter	Louis Jackson	4	369	1907-1916
Hunter	William Archie	1	13	1878-1887
Hurst	Naoma Edith	4	232	1907-1916
Husman	Dorothy	4	406	1907-1916
Husman	Mary Frances	2	16	1887-1903
Husman	Veronia	4	198	1907-1916
Hussman	Emily Pheloneia	3	69	1903-1915
Hutchens	Sadie I.	3	19	1903-1915
Hutchins	Martha Jane	2	109	1887-1903
Hutchins	Mary Matilda	4	255	1907-1916
Hutchins	William Henry	4	92	1907-1916
Iepper		2	73	1887-1903
Ikemeyer	Theresia	1	9	1878-1887
Imming		4	190	1907-1916
Imming	Clara	2	67	1887-1903
Imming	Mary Dolores	4	596	1907-1916
Ingersoll		1	64	1878-1887
Ingersoll		1	25	1878-1887
Ingersoll	Ferol Beulah	4	347	1907-1916
Ingersoll		4	478	1907-1916
Ingersoll	Earl C.	3	5	1903-1915
Ingersoll	Lilly	3	222	1903-1915
Ingersoll		4	588	1907-1916
Ingersoll		4	467	1907-1916
Ingersoll	Adrian Aloys	4	542	1907-1916
Ingersoll	Beulah	2	33	1887-1903
Ingersoll	Charles Wesley	1	26	1878-1887
Ingersoll	Harry Gilbert	2	125	1887-1903
Ingersoll	Cora Edna	1	41	1878-1887

CALHOUN COUNTY BIRTHS

Surname	Given Name	Book	Page	Year
Ingersoll	Flora Ogal	1	41	1878-1887
Ingersoll	Frances Opal	4	250	1907-1916
Ingersoll	Gladys Virginia	4	250	1907-1916
Ingersoll	Joseph Edward	4	255	1907-1916
Ingersoll	Lena Coralie	4	372	1907-1916
Ingersoll	Perry N.	1	52	1878-1887
Ingersoll	Ralph Lee	2	45	1887-1903
Ingersoll	Robert C.	2	8	1887-1903
Ingle	Alice Pearl	2	53	1887-1903
Ingle	Alma Alice	2	3	1887-1903
Ingle	Dorothy	4	29	1907-1916
Ingle	Esther May	4	13	1907-1916
Ingle	Eva Violet	2	9	1887-1903
Ingle	Irene	4	601	1907-1916
Ingle	Joseph William	2	109	1887-1903
Ingle	Josie Ettel	1	77	1878-1887
Ingle	Leo Ray	4	191	1907-1916
Ingle	Naomi Ruth	2	62	1887-1903
Ingle	Pearl Clifford	2	112	1887-1903
Ingle	William Otis	2	53	1887-1903
Ingle	Gracie	2	38	1887-1903
Inman		1	22	1878-1887
Inman	Allen Dail	4	519	1907-1916
Inman	Lyman Julius	4	31	1907-1916
Inman	L. Elizabeth	1	67	1878-1887
Inman	Mabel Marie	4	212	1907-1916
Irvin	George	1	12	1878-1887
Irvin	John Oscar	1	51	1878-1887
Irwing		4	177	1907-1916
Isringhausen	William Arthur	4	563	1907-1916
Ivers	Hubert C.	4	458	1907-1916
Jackens		1	55	1878-1887
Jackson	Samuel	2	129	1887-1903
Jackson	Virgil W.	2	77	1887-1903
Jacobs		2	3	1887-1903

CALHOUN COUNTY BIRTHS

Surname	Given Name	Book	Page	Year
Jacobs	(Still Born)	3	275	1903-1915
Jacobs	Clarence	2	73	1887-1903
Jacobs	Cleve	2	1	1887-1903
Jacobs	Dallas Frances	3	180	1903-1915
Jacobs	Freda Leona	4	163	1907-1916
Jacobs	Henry	4	18	1907-1916
Jacobs	Howard Gilbert	3	202	1903-1915
Jacobs	John	1	18	1878-1887
Jacobs	Lester Dietrich	4	599	1907-1916
Jacobs	Mary	4	416	1907-1916
Jacobs	Nona V.	4	43	1907-1916
Jacobs	Opal Pauline	3	48	1903-1915
Jacobs	Rosa Lucinda	4	111	1907-1916
Jacobs	Susan	1	66	1878-1887
Jacobs	Viola	4	569	1907-1916
Jacobs	Winnie Eola	3	101	1903-1915
Jacobsmeyer	Elizabeth	1	14	1878-1887
Jamison	Maude Velma	2	110	1887-1903
Jansson	Thomas Lewis	1	70	1878-1887
Jennings		1	33	1878-1887
Jennings	Althea	4	313	1907-1916
Jennings	Erma Mary	4	198	1907-1916
Jennings	Harry Lee	1	54	1878-1887
Jewsbury	Velma Martha	4	13	1907-1916
Johndrow	Clyde Lester	4	363	1907-1916
Johndrow	Floyd Ramond	4	220	1907-1916
Johnes	Carlean Agnes	3	72	1903-1915
Johnes	John	1	44	1878-1887
Johnes	Paul Herman	3	200	1903-1915
Johns		1	68	1878-1887
Johns		1	27	1878-1887
Johns	Allan	1	57	1878-1887
Johns	Artie Velma	3	3	1903-1915
Johns	Lena	1	56	1878-1887
Johns	Mary	2	48	1887-1903

CALHOUN COUNTY BIRTHS

Surname	Given Name	Book	Page	Year
Johns	Mary E.	1	46	1878-1887
Johns	Walter Lee	2	46	1887-1903
Johnson		2	75	1887-1903
Johnson		2	104	1887-1903
Johnson		2	95	1887-1903
Johnson		4	345	1907-1916
Johnson		2	4	1887-1903
Johnson		1	53	1887-1887
Johnson		2	6	1887-1903
Johnson		4	101	1907-1916
Johnson		1	76	1878-1887
Johnson	Allen W.	1	53	1878-1887
Johnson	Alma Olive	2	40	1887-1903
Johnson	Barbara Alice	4	136	1907-1916
Johnson	Benjamin (Twin)	2	47	1887-1903
Johnson	Irvin (Twin)	2	47	1887-1903
Johnson	Bertha Leona	2	109	1887-1903
Johnson	Carrie	1	8	1903-1915
Johnson	Charles C.	2	58	1887-1903
Johnson	Charles Wesley	4	125	1887-1903
Johnson	Charles W.	1	447	1887-1887
Johnson	Elmer Lawrence	4	208	1907-1916
Johnson	Harley Calvin	3	121	1903-1915
Johnson	Henry C.	1	53	1878-1887
Johnson	Howard	1	33	1878-1887
Johnson	Inez Louisa	4	377	1907-1916
Johnson	Isaac Abner	4	253	1907-1916
Johnson	John Wesley	1	11	1878-1887
Johnson	Lola Lucille	4	564	1907-1916
Johnson	Lorina Alma	2	13	1887-1903
Johnson	Louisa	2	122	1887-1903
Johnson	Nellie	1	19	1878-1887
Johnson	Otta Orville	1	53	1878-1887
Johnson	Percy Clement	3	57	1903-1915
Johnson	Robert Ford	4	2	1907-1916

CALHOUN COUNTY BIRTHS

Surname	Given Name	Book	Page	Year
Johnson	Roy Lorenzo	1	35	1878-1887
Johnson	Susie G.	3	237	1903-1915
Johnson	Wanda Lotus	4	461	1907-1916
Johnson	William Henry	1	3	1878-1887
Johnston		2	19	1887-1903
Johnston	Clara D.	4	336	1907-1916
Johnston	Henry Donald	4	434	1907-1916
Johnston	Laura Amelia	4	52	1907-1916
Johnston	Lewis	4	229	1907-1916
Johnston	Maolia	3	43	1903-1915
Johnston	Minnie Melvina Rebecca	4	126	1907-1916
Johnston	Theodore Isaac	3	177	1903-1915
Jones		4	72	1907-1916
Jones		2	82	1887-1903
Jones		2	30	1887-1903
Jones		3	150	1903-1915
Jones	(Still Born)	3	285	1903-1915
Jones	Adrian	4	576	1907-1916
Jones	Artie Alma	2	46	1887-1903
Jones	Charles Cleveland	4	369	1907-1916
Jones	Frederick	4	352	1907-1916
Jones	Freeda Marion	2	58	1887-1903
Jones	Herman Oden	3	195	1903-1915
Jones	Joseph David	4	536	1907-1916
Jones	Lee Armond	2	101	1887-1903
Jones	Lela Fern	3	4	1903-1915
Jones	Lloyd Comador	2	120	1887-1903
Jones	Lois Louise	3	66	1903-1915
Jones	Lulu Estella	3	187	1903-1915
Jones	Manerva	1	21	1878-1887
Jones	Paul	2	13	1887-1903
Jones	Paul Harley	4	413	1907-1916
Jones	Ralph Henry	4	141	1907-1916
Jones	Ruby	2	117	1887-1903
Joy	Avada	1	15	1878-1887

CALHOUN COUNTY BIRTHS

Surname	Given Name	Book	Page	Year
Joy	Edith	2	16	1887-1903
Joy	Mary Alma	1	38	1878-1887
Joy	Raymond S.	2	52	1887-1903
Joy	Paul	2	54	1887-1903
Kaibel	Adolph Frederick	4	215	1907-1916
Kaibel	Rose	4	97	1907-1916
Kaibel		3	239	1903-1915
Kaibel	Grace Viola	2	116	1887-1903
Kaibel	Walter John	3	99	1903-1915
Kamp		2	83	1887-1903
Kamp		4	33	1907-1916
Kamp		1	76	1878-1887
Kamp		2	88	1887-1903
Kamp		4	233	1907-1916
Kamp		3	238	1903-1915
Kamp	Aloise M.	4	297	1907-1916
Kamp	Arthur Frank	2	69	1887-1903
Kamp	Delight Antoinette	4	215	1907-1916
Kamp	Emmaline Mary	4	591	1907-1916
Kamp	Josephine Frances	4	49	1907-1916
Kamp	Katherine	2	119	1887-1903
Kamp	Mary Magdalena	2	112	1887-1903
Kamp	Muriel Catherine	3	231	1903-1915
Kanellakan	Georgianna	3	247	1903-1915
Kanellakan	Josephine	4	222	1907-1916
Kanellakan	Meinard	4	76	1907-1916
Kary	Thedore	3	197	1903-1915
Kasinger	Grace Marie	3	29	1903-1915
Keach	James Thomas	1	26	1878-1887
Keating	Blanche	1	57	1878-1887
Keech	France Rosella	1	7	1878-1887
Keehner	Clarence	4	364	1907-1916
Keehner	Esther Mary Caroline	4	147	1907-1916
Keehner	Fay	4	273	1907-1916
Keehner	Kermit	4	591	1907-1916

CALHOUN COUNTY BIRTHS

Surname	Given Name	Book	Page	Year
Keeney	Louis	2	59	1887-1903
Keeting	Anna Iona	3	70	1903-1915
Keeton		2	68	1887-1903
Keeton	Chester Leroy	1	72	1878-1887
Keeton	John Matthew	1	21	1878-1887
Keeton	Lora Irene	2	111	1903-1915
Keeton	Viola May	3	181	1903-1915
Keightley		1	67	1878-1887
Keightley	Ann Rebecca	1	26	1878-1887
Keightley	John	2	19	1903-1915
Keil	Julia Mary	4	448	1907-1916
Keim		3	128	1903-1915
Keim		3	241	1903-1915
Keim	Helena Louise	1	40	1878-1887
Keim	Lena Regina	4	420	1907-1916
Keim	Louise	3	29	1903-1915
Keim	Tresa Louisa	2	113	1887-1903
Kellenberger		1	9	1878-1887
Kelley	Marvin E.	2	97	1887-1903
Kelley	Mary A.	2	110	1887-1903
Kelley	Robert Perry	3	206	1903-1915
Kelly	William Antone	3	123	1903-1915
Kennedy	Gilbert William	3	27	1903-1915
Kennedy	Stella Fay	2	34	1887-1903
Kent	(Still Born)	3	278	1903-1915
Kent	Earl Layfayette	2	101	1887-1903
Kent	Ruby Hazel	2	82	1887-1903
Kerkoff	Helena	2	41	1887-1903
Kerkoff	Raymond Bernard	4	568	1907-1916
Kerns		2	97	1887-1903
Kerns		2	62	1887-1903
Kerns	Harry Richard	2	85	1887-1903
Ketchum		4	335	1907-1916
Ketchum		2	17	1887-1903
Ketchum	Charles R.	1	10	1878-1887

CALHOUN COUNTY BIRTHS

Surname	Given Name	Book	Page	Year
Ketchum	Verloria	4	516	1907-1916
Kiel	Albert Herman	4	109	1907-1916
Kiel	Bernard	2	3	1887-1903
Kiel	Edward John	4	281	1907-1916
Kiel	Emma Helena	0	0	1887-1903
Kiel	Frances Mary	2	107	1887-1903
Kiel	Frances Mary	2	108	1887-1903
Kiel	Leonard Barney	4	139	1907-1916
Killebrew		2	111	1887-1903
Killebrew		2	88	1887-1903
Killebrew		1	5	1878-1887
Killebrew		4	152	1907-1916
Killebrew	Harold Leo	3	239	1903-1915
Killebrew	Clarence Herman	2	78	1887-1903
Killebrew	Cordia Blanche	2	70	1887-1903
Killebrew	Douglas S.	3	59	1903-1915
Killebrew	Edna Mary	2	90	1887-1903
Killebrew	Evelyn Zandree	4	382	1907-1916
Killebrew	Harold	3	128	1903-1915
Killebrew	John M. Forrest	2	73	1887-1903
Killebrew	Margaret Florence	3	160	1903-1915
Killebrew	Mary Jane	2	100	1887-1903
Killebrew	Paul John	2	124	1887-1903
Killebrew	Thomas	1	76	1878-1887
Kimberley	Nona Alfa	1	10	1878-1887
Kimberly	Alice Alma	1	61	1878-1887
Kinder		3	286	1903-1915
Kinder		4	198	1907-1916
Kinder	(Still Born)	3	264	1903-1915
Kinder	August Louis	2	24	1903-1915
Kinder	Caroline Louise	4	32	1907-1916
Kinder	Clara Charlotte Emma	3	153	1903-1915
Kinder	Elmer O.	4	33	1907-1916
Kinder	Elvier Kermit	3	257	1903-1915
Kinder	Emma F.	4	355	1907-1916

CALHOUN COUNTY BIRTHS

Surname	Given Name	Book	Page	Year
Kinder	Fae	4	513	1907-1916
Kinder	Fred Herman	3	103	1903-1915
Kinder	Frederick A.	2	24	1887-1903
Kinder	Frederick H.H.	2	24	1887-1903
Kinder	Henrietta J.	4	511	1907-1916
Kinder	Henry	2	23	1887-1903
Kinder	Henry	4	179	1907-1916
Kinder	Henry Charles (Twin)	2	69	1887-1903
Kinder	John F. (Twin)	2	69	1887-1903
Kinder	Herman	2	29	1887-1903
Kinder	Luella	4	158	1907-1916
Kinder	Mae	4	513	1907-1916
Kinder	Mina	2	30	1887-1903
Kinder	Paul Clemmons	4	132	1907-1916
Kinder	Richard H.	4	429	1907-1916
Kinder	Robert Vaughn	3	155	1903-1915
Kingery		3	187	1903-1915
Kingery		2	45	1887-1903
Kingsley		4	186	1907-1916
Kinkade	Amelia J.	1	8	1878-1887
Kinkade	Howard Evert	2	73	1887-1903
Kinman	Josephine Otilla	3	113	1903-1915
Kinscherff	Lillian C.	2	100	1887-1903
Kinsel		3	51	1903-1915
Kinsel	Clarence Franklin	2	123	1887-1903
Kirn		3	149	1903-1915
Kirn	Grace Alice	4	124	1907-1916
Kirn	Julie Kathartina (Twin)	3	253	1903-1915
Kirn	Susanna Margareth (Twin)	3	253	1903-1915
Kitson		2	42	1887-1903
Kitson		1	10	1878-1887
Kitson		2	21	1887-1903
Kitson		1	76	1878-1887
Kitson		3	124	1903-1915
Kitson		1	65	1878-1887

Surname	Given Name	Book	Page	Year
Kitson		2	11	1887-1903
Kitson	Bertha E.	1	42	1878-1887
Kitson	Beulah Nola	4	37	1907-1916
Kitson	Clide William	4	38	1907-1916
Kitson	Jesse Raymond	1	46	1878-1887
Kitson	Lora Blanch	3	159	1903-1915
Kitson	Mamie Elsie	2	60	1887-1903
Kitson	Noah Ralph	1	34	1878-1887
Kitson	Oneeta Eileen	4	576	1907-1916
Kitson	Sarah Mabel	2	70	1887-1903
Kitson	Susan	1	69	1878-1887
Kitson	William	1	18	1878-1887
Kitson	William R.	3	25	1903-1915
Kitson	Wilmer Andrew	2	119	1887-1903
Klaas	Fred T.	3	226	1903-1915
Klaas	Anna Techla	3	229	1903-1915
Klaas	Charles	4	88	1907-1916
Klaas	Charley	2	103	1887-1903
Klaas	Elizabeth	1	29	1878-1887
Klaas	Emil Bernard	4	259	1907-1916
Klaas	Emil W.	4	407	1907-1916
Klaas	John O.	4	471	1907-1916
Klaas	Lawrence John	4	564	1907-1916
Klaas	Louis	3	13	1903-1915
Klaas	Raymond Herman	4	337	1907-1916
Klemme	Howard C.	4	111	1907-1916
Klemme	Mary	4	188	1907-1916
Klocka	Joseph	3	253	1903-1915
Klocka	Myrtle Frances	4	234	1907-1916
Klocke	Agnes	4	85	1907-1916
Klockee	Edward	2	91	1887-1903
Klocken	Charles Frank	3	152	1903-1915
Klockenkemper	Frank	2	57	1887-1903
Klockenkemper	John George	2	127	1887-1903
Klockenkemper	John Julius	4	221	1907-1916

CALHOUN COUNTY BIRTHS

Surname	Given Name	Book	Page	Year
Klockenkemper	L.	4	459	1907-1916
Klockenkemper	Rapheal	4	138	1907-1916
Klocker	Henry	2	76	1887-1903
Klunk		3	228	1903-1915
Klunk		4	539	1907-1916
Klunk		2	115	1887-1903
Klunk		2	93	1887-1903
Klunk		4	541	1907-1916
Klunk		2	89	1887-1903
Klunk	Adam	2	42	1887-1903
Klunk	Alfred P.	3	178	1903-1915
Klunk	Anna	2	7	1887-1903
Klunk	Antone H.	3	108	1903-1915
Klunk	Catherine L.	2	54	1887-1903
Klunk	Charles Michael	2	45	1887-1903
Klunk	Harold Francis	4	99	1907-1916
Klunk	Lena	3	32	1887-1903
Klunk	Mary Lisey	2	64	1887-1903
Klunk	Michael	2	28	1887-1903
Klunk	Peter Lawrence	2	100	1887-1903
Klunk	Ray J.	4	396	1907-1916
Klunk	Theresa C.	3	254	1903-1915
Klunk	Theresa C.	4	294	1907-1916
Klunk	Valentine C.	3	18	1903-1915
Klunk	Walter	2	89	1887-1903
Klunk	William	2	55	1887-1903
Knallekan	Josephine	2	120	1887-1903
Knese	Annie Catherine	1	6	1878-1887
Knese	Elizabeth Adeline	3	44	1903-1915
Knese	Margaret	1	78	1878-1887
Knese	Mary Caroline	2	47	1887-1903
Knight		4	57	1907-1916
Knight		2	36	1887-1903
Knight		4	206	1907-1916
Knight	Arthur	4	370	1907-1916

CALHOUN COUNTY BIRTHS

Surname	Given Name	Book	Page	Year
Knight	Edward	4	164	1907-1916
Knight	Edward Antone	4	326	1907-1916
Knight	Ellia Lewis	4	422	1907-1916
Knight	John D.	4	473	1907-1916
Knight	Valley	2	11	1887-1903
Knowlton	Bertha A.	1	31	1878-1887
Knowlton	Lora Lee	2	17	1887-1903
Koenig	Charles	3	64	1903-1915
Koenig	Elizabeth	4	558	1907-1916
Koenig	Joseph Louis	2	104	1887-1903
Koenig	Mary Katherine	2	90	1887-1903
Kohn	Clara	2	78	1887-1903
Kramer		2	91	1887-1903
Kramer	Jack	4	266	1907-1916
Kramer	Octavy D.	2	102	1887-1903
Kramer	Thomas Estes	3	37	1903-1915
Krause	August F.M.	2	126	1887-1903
Krause	Lillie	3	209	1903-1915
Krause	Mary	2	59	1887-1903
Kraut	Charles Levi	3	219	1903-1915
Kraut	Curtis Ervin	4	199	1907-1916
Kraut	Freda Junita	2	113	1887-1903
Kraut	Harold John	4	406	1907-1916
Kraut	Herman E.	4	119	1907-1916
Kraut	Herman F.	1	391	1878-1887
Kraut	Myrtle Valeria	4	563	19071916
Kraut	Ross Levi	4	237	1907-1916
Kraut	Sophia M.M.	4	118	1907-1916
Kreamer	John E.	4	502	1907-1916
Kreid	Viola Ethelyene	4	71	1907-1916
Kremer	Eileen Helen	4	557	1907-1916
Kremple	John Barney	1	72	1878-1887
Kremple	Thomas	2	7	1887-1903
Kress	Albert Elmer	3	221	1903-1915
Kress	Charlotte Wionna	4	245	1907-1916

CALHOUN COUNTY BIRTHS

Surname	Given Name	Book	Page	Year
Kress	Fay L.	4	454	1907-1916
Kress	Isaac A.	3	14	1903-1915
Kress	Lulu	2	37	1887-1903
Kress	Perry M.	4	247	1907-1916
Kress	Raymond John M.	4	415	1907-1916
Kritz	Alta May	2	43	1887-1903
Kritz	Laura Catherine	2	67	1887-1903
Kritz	Mable Elizabeth	4	276	1907-1916
Kritz	Minnie Louisa	3	212	1903-1915
Kroeschel	Catherine	1	54	1878-1887
Kroeschel	Pearl Kenneth	4	374	1907-1916
Kroeschel	Stella Mae	4	393	1907-1916
Kroeschell	Raymond Lee	4	585	1907-1916
Kroeshell	Charles James	4	261	1907-1916
Kronable	Alvira	4	496	1907-1916
Kronable	Edward John	4	512	1907-1916
Kronable	Robert William	4	274	1907-1916
Kronable	Wilhelmina K.	4	394	1907-1916
Kronable	William Joseph	4	275	1907-1916
Kroschell	Rose Ellen	4	520	1907-1916
Kroshell		1	4	1878-1887
Kuck	Christian Carl	4	56	1907-1916
Kuck	Irene Etta	4	349	1907-1916
Kuhn	Katie	2	27	1887-1903
Kulp	Alma	2	24	1887-1903
Kulp	Alma Dora Magdalina	2	23	1887-1903
Kulp	Frederick	2	56	1887-1903
Kulp	Herman	2	24	1887-1903
Kulp	Lillie	3	119	1903-1915
Kulp	Sullivan William	2	23	1887-1903
Kulp	William	2	24	1887-1903
Kurtz		1	18	1878-1887
Kurtz	Bertha May	2	27	1887-1903
Kurtz	Francis Stephen	2	40	1887-1903
Labbee		1	21	1878-1887

CALHOUN COUNTY BIRTHS

Surname	Given Name	Book	Page	Year
Lackey	Price	4	395	1907-1916
Lahurey	Frank Lewis	2	70	1887-1903
Laird		2	84	1887-1903
Laird	Clara Opal	2	111	1887-1903
Laird	James W.	1	7	1878-1887
Laird	Joseph Roy	4	288	1907-1916
Laird	Levi Taylor	3	175	1903-1915
Laird	Lilian Cephrona	4	31	1907-1916
Laird	Nellie	4	204	1907-1916
Laird	Rebecca Emeline	4	35	1907-1916
Laird	Rosa Lee	3	122	1903-1915
Lakin	Aretta Marie	4	166	1907-1916
Lamar	Charles Frederick	1	69	1878-1887
Lamar	Gertrude Ellen	2	31	1887-1903
Lamar	Jospeh Cyprien	2	13	1887-1903
Lamar	Leonia Marie	1	74	1878-1887
Lamar	Lucy Elizabeth	4	335	1907-1916
Lamar	Sarah	1	45	1878-1887
Lammy		2	40	1887-1903
Lammy	Elia Jane	1	44	1878-1887
Lammy	Ethel Hannah	1	30	1878-1887
Lammy	John Earl	2	105	1887-1903
Lammy	Mary	3	91	1903-1915
Lammy	Raymond Levi	2	79	1887-1903
Lammy	Sarah Estella	2	60	1887-1903
Lammy	William H.	1	62	1878-1887
Lancaster		2	94	1887-1903
Lancaster	Lingene	2	17	1887-1903
Landon	Ralph E.	2	72	1887-1903
Lane	Albert Washington	3	134	1903-1915
Lane	Andrew O. R.	2	109	1887-1903
Lane	Benjamin	2	31	1887-1903
Lane	John Harrison	2	23	1887-1903
Lane	Katie Elizabeth	1	5	1878-1887
Lappie	Bessie M.	4	202	1907-1916

CALHOUN COUNTY BIRTHS

Surname	Given Name	Book	Page	Year
Lard		2	93	1887-1903
Larrison	Linley	2	19	1887-1903
Larrison	Marion Homer	2	8	1887-1903
Lawson	Charles Evert	1	4	1878-1887
Lawson	Golda May	2	64	1887-1903
Lawson	Mary Jane	1	42	1878-1887
Lawson	Raymond	3	138	1903-1915
Lawson	Trent Taft	4	114	1907-1916
Lawson	Walter	1	69	1878-1887
Lawson	William	1	16	1878-1887
Layne	John M.	3	250	1903-1915
Legrand	Mary Maria	1	37	1878-1887
Lehr		2	78	1887-1903
Lehr		4	97	1907-1916
Lehr	(Still Born)	3	277	1903-1915
Lehr	William H.	2	99	1887-1903
Leistrich		2	81	1887-1903
Leistritz		2	106	1887-1903
Leistritz		2	19	1887-1903
Leistritz	Ernest Miller	4	181	1907-1916
Leistritz	Harold Luther	3	247	1903-1915
Leistritz	Hazel Lorraine	3	4	1903-1915
Lessig		4	159	1907-1916
Lessig		1	77	1878-1887
Lessig	Bertha	4	81	1907-1916
Lessig	Fred	2	31	1887-1903
Lessig	Helnea Inez	4	572	1907-1916
Lessig	Melvin C. Jr.	4	230	1907-1916
Lessig	Solomon	2	29	1887-1903
Leuis	Fred	3	144	1903-1915
Lewis		2	126	1887-1903
Lewis		3	196	1903-1915
Lewis	Carl Frederick	4	589	1907-1916
Lewis	Paul Howard	4	589	1907-1916
Lewis	Ray	2	75	1887-1903

CALHOUN COUNTY BIRTHS

Surname	Given Name	Book	Page	Year
Likes	James L.	2	17	1887-1903
Likes		2	106	1887-1903
Likes	George Roscoe	3	231	1903-1915
Likes	Russell Richard	3	52	1903-1915
Lind	Edward F.	1	17	1878-1887
Lind	John Nicholas Joseph	1	2	1878-1887
Lind	Leo C.	1	59	1878-1887
Linderman	Hilda	4	45	1907-1916
Linderman	Inez	4	138	1907-1916
Linkogle		2	96	1887-1903
Linkogle		2	44	1887-1903
Linkogle	Capitola R.	1	41	1878-1887
Linkogle	Elizabeth Irene	2	39	1887-1903
Linkogle	Elsie Ottilla	2	69	1887-1903
Linkogle	Fred Earl	2	45	1887-1903
Linkogle	Harriet Mildred	2	96	1887-1903
Linkogle	Hazel Marion	2	88	1887-1903
Linkogle	John E.J.S.	1	71	1878-1887
Linkogle	Joseph A.	3	35	1903-1915
Linkogle	Leslie Allen	2	58	1887-1903
Linkogle	Romeo Clemmens	2	90	1887-1903
Linkogle	William	2	91	1887-1903
Lock	Ruth	2	50	1887-1903
Logsden	Helen Irene	3	128	1903-1915
Loney	Gertrude	3	142	1903-1915
Long		1	14	1878-1887
Long		2	80	1887-1903
Long	Anna May	3	174	1903-1915
Long	Anna Violet	4	464	1907-1916
Long	Charles Morrison	4	256	1907-1916
Long	Dorothy Inez	4	578	1907-1916
Long	Ellen Marguerite	4	415	1907-1916
Long	Emma Arta	1	76	1878-1887
Long	Ethel Willis	2	122	1887-1903
Long	Floyd Wilson	2	56	1887-1903

CALHOUN COUNTY BIRTHS

Surname	Given Name	Book	Page	Year
Long	Freddie Lee	2	35	1887-1903
Long	Grace Margaret	4	151	1907-1916
Long	Grover Cleveland	1	60	1878-1887
Long	Henry Newton	2	18	1887-1903
Long	Hilda Marie	4	161	1907-1916
Long	Hollis Vernon	4	346	1907-1916
Long	Hibert O.	4	386	1907-1916
Long	Jessie	4	52	1907-1916
Long	Jessie	1	36	1878-1887
Long	John Floyd	4	220	1907-1916
Long	Jospeh Barnet	2	34	1887-1903
Long	Mary Alma	1	20	1878-1887
Long	Mary Leona	4	465	1907-1916
Long	Newton Clay	1	38	1878-1887
Long	Spencer Vaughan	3	203	1903-1915
Long	Thomas Luther	2	102	1887-1903
Looper		4	155	1907-1916
Looper	Cleo Edward	2	122	1887-1903
Looper	Lee Owen	2	100	1887-1903
Lorsbach	Adaline	2	51	1887-1903
Lorsbach	Adaline Christina	3	23	1903-1915
Lorsbach	Adalaide Marie	4	393	1907-1916
Lorsbach	Albert	4	526	1907-1916
Lorsbach	Charles Franklin	2	83	1887-1903
Lorsbach	George William	2	37	1907-1916
Lorsbach	Henry	1	2	1878-1887
Lorsbach	Izella Mary	4	563	1907-1916
Lorsbach	Paul O.	4	124	1907-1916
Lorsbach	William	2	171	1887-1903
Lorsbach	William Francis	3	203	1903-1915
Lowe	Clarence Eugene	2	33	1887-1903
Lowe	John W. H.	1	18	1878-1887
Luff	Charles	4	307	1907-1916
Lumley		1	50	1878-1887
Lumley		3	108	1903-1915

CALHOUN COUNTY BIRTHS

Surname	Given Name	Book	Page	Year
Lumley		1	58	1878-1887
Lumley		2	13	1887-1903
Lumley	(Still Born)	3	273	1903-1915
Lumley	Alma May	1	6	1878-1887
Lumley	Elba Turner	3	20	1903-1915
Lumley	Elza R.	1	61	1878-1887
Lumley	George Alva	1	78	1878-1887
Lumley	Marvin Turner	1	48	1878-1887
Lumley	Nona Z.	1	24	1878-1887
Lumley	Orville	3	203	1903-1915
Lumley	Rosivel E.	1	37	1878-1887
Lumley	Thomas M.	2	25	1887-1903
Lumley	Velma Roselle	4	554	1907-1916
Lumley	Vera Irene	4	435	1907-1916
Lumley	Zoda D.	1	44	1878-1887
Lunn	Francis W.	1	21	1878-1887
Luper		4	170	1907-1916
Lynn		1	40	1878-1887
Lynn	Louis Murph	1	7	1878-1887
Lynn		1	51	1878-1887
Lyons	Helen Lucille	4	149	1907-1916
Maag		3	197	1903-1915
Maag	John E.	4	77	1907-1916
Maag	Mabel Irene	3	11	1903-1915
Maag	Raymond Wesley	4	285	1907-1916
Mackeldon	Junita	2	124	1887-1903
Mackey		2	94	1887-1903
Mackey		2	99	1887-1903
Mackey	Everett Lee	2	119	1887-1903
Madison		1	56	1878-1887
Madison		1	74	1878-1887
Madison		2	12	1887-1903
Madison	Clara	4	427	1907-1916
Madison	Cora May	2	26	1887-1903
Madison	Elizabeth	4	454	1907-1916

CALHOUN COUNTY BIRTHS

Surname	Given Name	Book	Page	Year
Madison	Mary Edith	4	519	1907-1916
Mager		4	375	1907-1916
Mager		4	376	1907-1916
Mager	Bernice Catherine	4	581	1907-1916
Mager	Catherine	2	17	1887-1903
Mager	Elma Lorain	2	95	1887-1903
Mager	Fred Carl	2	129	1887-1903
Mager	George Henry	1	59	1878-1887
Mager	Leslie Raymond	2	72	1887-1903
Mager	Louis George	2	61	1887-1903
Mager	Wilhelm	1	44	1878-1887
Maines	Marzella Rose	3	30	1903-1915
Maines		4	75	1907-1916
Maines	Opal Josephine	4	93	1907-1916
Mallett		1	12	1878-1887
Malone		3	136	1903-1915
Malone	Loraine	2	116	1887-1903
Malone	Maudie Marie	2	92	1887-1903
Manker	Marion Schley	2	124	1887-1903
Manley	Osa Ruth	4	566	1907-1916
Manning		1	29	1878-1887
Manning	Oliver Winfield	1	50	1878-1887
Mappen		2	102	1887-1903
Mappin	Lela	3	32	1903-1915
March	Eleta Mae	4	66	1907-1916
Marine		3	49	1903-1915
Marion		3	227	1903-1915
Marion	Bulah M.	1	60	1878-1887
Marshall	Iva May	4	34	1907-1916
Marshall	Jane	2	121	1887-1903
Marshall	Odie	3	152	1903-1915
Martin		2	2	1887-1903
Martin		1	62	1878-1887
Martin		2	63	1887-1903
Martin		1	19	1878-1887

CALHOUN COUNTY BIRTHS

Surname	Given Name	Book	Page	Year
Martin		4	101	1907-1916
Martin		3	211	1903-1915
Martin	Alma Lucile	3	191	1903-1915
Martin	Charles Phil	4	345	1907-1916
Martin	Claud	2	126	1887-1903
Martin	Clemma Veta	4	185	1907-1916
Martin	Dorothy Isola	4	280	1907-1916
Martin	Flora Edith	4	449	1907-1916
Martin	Gladys Alice	3	186	1903-1915
Martin	Irvin	4	346	1907-1916
Martin	John Porter	4	365	1907-1916
Martin	John Porter	4	586	1907-1916
Martin	Juanita	4	426	1907-1916
Martin	Judith Irene	3	112	1903-1915
Martin	Lela Ruth	3	16	1903-1915
Martin	Lillian Louise	4	405	1907-1916
Martin	Margaret Elizabeth	1	31	1878-1887
Martin	Maude E. (Twin)	1	31	1878-1887
Martin	Mary M. (Twin)	1	31	1878-1887
Martin	Melvin	4	507	1907-1916
Martin	Minnie Rose	1	14	1878-1887
Martin	Thomas O.	4	482	1907-1916
Martin	William Leslie	2	124	1887-1903
Massey		1	24	1878-1887
Massey	Bertha Alma	2	92	1887-1903
Massey	Julia Magdalena	2	120	1887-1903
Mathews		2	95	1887-1903
Mathews	Beulah Irene	4	382	1907-1916
Mathews	Vernice Ray	4	481	1907-1916
Matthews	Goldie Leveta	3	169	1903-1915
Matthews	Velma May	2	117	1887-1903
Mattison	Herbert Evert	3	111	1903-1915
Maxey		2	118	1887-1903
Maxfield	Adelia Helen	4	252	1907-1916
Maxfield	Eugene	4	348	1907-1916

CALHOUN COUNTY BIRTHS

Surname	Given Name	Book	Page	Year
Mcauley	Everett Fowler	3	214	1903-1915
Mcauley	Robert Fowler	4	36	1907-1916
McBride		2	58	1887-1903
McBride	Cora	2	72	1887-1903
McBride	Mary	2	69	1887-1903
McCafferty	John Warren	1	18	1878-1887
McCarthy	Adaline Leone	4	69	1907-1916
McCarthy	Margaret	4	241	1907-1916
McCartney		1	8	1878-1887
McCartney	Aga.M.	1	19	1878-1887
McCartney	Mary	4	461	1907-1916
McCartney	Tony H.	4	584	1907-1916
McCinny	George	1	75	1878-1887
McClemens	William H.	2	34	1887-1903
McClimens	Emily	2	6	1887-1903
McClimens	George R.	2	98	1887-1903
McClimens	Grigsay	2	51	1887-1903
McClimens	Jane	2	124	1887-1903
McClimens	Robert Nelson	2	13	1887-1903
McClimens	Charles C.	1	67	1878-1887
McClure	George	2	29	1887-1903
McConnell		1	71	1878-1887
McConnell	Guy A.	1	22	1878-1887
McConnell	Marie Naomi	2	66	1887-1903
McConnell	Nellie	1	42	1878-1887
McConnell	Robert A.	1	49	1878-1887
McConnell	Sarah F.	1	15	1878-1887
McCoy	David	2	15	1887-1903
McCoy	Obie L.	2	35	1887-1903
McCoy	Virtie	1	76	1878-18887
McDonald	Alta Nora Catherine	4	302	1907-1916
McDonald	Charles Joseph	4	545	1907-1916
McDonald	Charles J.	2	14	1887-1903
McDonald	Charles Edgar	1	46	1878-1887
McDonald	Clara Agnes	1	35	1878-1887

CALHOUN COUNTY BIRTHS

Surname	Given Name	Book	Page	Year
McDonald	Clarence T.	1	24	1878-1887
McDonald	Frank S.	4	484	1907-1916
McDonald	Ida L. (Still Born)	3	271	1903-1915
McDonald	James	1	10	1878-1887
McDonald	Leo	2	1	1887-1903
McDonald	Majarie E.L.	4	491	1907-1916
McFarland		4	582	1907-1916
McFarland	Lexie M.	4	444	1907-1916
McGee		3	249	1903-1915
McGee	Albert Thomas	3	186	1903-1915
McGee	Carl August	4	286	1907-1916
McGee	Celin Josephine	4	510	1907-1916
McGee	George Dewey	2	128	1887-1903
McGee	Isaac Paul	3	183	1903-1915
McGee	Luella Catherine	3	90	1903-1915
McGee	Mary Alire	3	132	1903-1915
McGee	Robert William	4	338	1907-1916
McGee	Vera Sabine	3	99	1903-1915
McGee	William Henry	4	180	1907-1916
McGregor	Laura L.	2	32	1887-1903
McGruder	William Dee	2	98	1887-1903
McGuire		3	81	1903-1915
McGuire	Charles Thomas	4	533	1907-1916
McGuire	John Louis	2	45	1887-1903
McGuire	Mary Helen	2	71	1887-1903
McGuire	Mildred Lion	3	245	1903-1915
McGuire	William Earl	4	133	1907-1916
McIntire		2	53	1887-1903
McIntire		3	234	1903-1915
McIntire		1	19	1878-1887
McIntire	(Still Born)	3	276	1903-1915
McIntire	Harry Allen	4	483	1907-1916
McIntire	Mary Olive	4	73	1907-1916
McIntire	Minerva Josephine	4	555	1907-1916
McIntire	Paul Elbie	4	257	1907-1916

CALHOUN COUNTY BIRTHS

Surname	Given Name	Book	Page	Year
McIntire	Pearl	1	48	1878-1887
McLaughlin		1	13	1878-1887
McLaughlin	Thorld C.	2	122	1887-1903
McLester	Biddie Bell	2	15	1887-1903
McNabb	Lawrence Edward	4	545	1907-1916
McNabb	Rosalie	4	366	1907-1916
McNelly	Juanita	4	353	1907-1916
McNelly	Phlennie A (Twin)	1	70	1878-1887
McNelly	Wren A. (Twin)	1	70	1878-1887
McNelly	Raymond W.	4	483	1907-1916
McWaters	Albert W.	1	3	1878-1887
McYfee	Robert William	4	122	1907-1916
Meehan	Thomas P.	1	33	1878-1887
Meesz	George W.	1	2	1878-1887
Meier	Emma	2	23	1887-1903
Meier	John	2	29	1887-1903
Meier	Josaphina	2	23	1887-1903
Meinsinger		2	106	1887-1903
Meisenhamer	Carrie	1	7	1878-1887
Meisenheimer	Lulu M.	1	20	1878-1887
Menke		4	88	1907-1916
Menke	Catherine	3	268	1903-1915
Menke	John	2	55	1887-1903
Menke	William Joseph	3	15	1903-1915
Merida	Junitia	3	126	1903-1915
Merida	Samuel Jackson	2	129	1887-1903
Meseke	Bertha Marie	3	244	1903-1915
Meseke	George William	3	117	1903-1915
Meseke	Louis A.	2	118	1887-1903
Meseke	Oscar	4	201	1907-1916
Meseke	Otto	4	362	1907-1916
Mest	Maria C.	1	20	1878-1887
Metts	Beulah	2	1	1887-1903
Metts	Mary Malissa	1	31	1878-1887
Mettz	Edith V.	1	21	1878-1887

CALHOUN COUNTY BIRTHS

Surname	Given Name	Book	Page	Year
Meyer		1	21	1878-1887
Meyer	Alvina Clara	4	525	1907-1916
Meyer	Asil Orville	3	233	1903-1915
Meyer	Charles	4	285	1907-1916
Meyer	Frank Otto	1	15	1878-1887
Meyer	Henry	3	81	1903-1915
Meyer	Henry Martin	3	209	1903-1915
Meyer	Homer	3	33	1903-1915
Meyer	John Gevert	4	66	1907-1916
Meyer	Joseph Myron	4	76	1907-1916
Meyer	Leonard Garret	3	202	1903-1915
Meyer	Mall Raymond	4	142	1907-1916
Meyer	Martin Jr.	4	146	1907-1916
Meyer	Meta	4	227	1907-1916
Meyer	Walter	1	15	1878-1887
Meyer	Walter (Twin) Possible	4	519	1907-1916
Meyer	Christian (Twin) Possible	4	519	1907-1916
Meyers		1	71	1878-1887
Meyers	Clarence Joseph	3	258	1903-1915
Meyers	Julia	3	10	1903-1915
Meyers	Leland L.	3	129	1903-1915
Meyers	Zelia	4	469	1907-1916
Mielke		4	175	1907-1916
Mielke	Joanna	2	93	1887-1903
Mielke	Arthur	2	83	1887-1903
Mielke	Clara Leone	2	24	1887-1903
Mielke	Francis M.	2	50	1887-1903
Mielke	Josie Edward	1	5	1878-1887
Mielke	Mary Elizabeth	2	90	1887-1903
Mielke	Mary E.	1	74	1878-1887
Mielke	Mary Irene	4	241	1907-1916
Mielke	Nancy Jane	2	60	1887-1903
Mikus	Ida Dora	1	38	1878-1887
Mikus	Joseph Anton	2	101	1887-1903
Mikus	Leonard	4	95	1907-1916

CALHOUN COUNTY BIRTHS

Surname	Given Name	Book	Page	Year
Mikus	Rosa Wilhelmina	2	68	1887-1903
Milkie	William A.	1	21	1878-1887
Miller		2	67	1887-1903
Miller		4	25	1907-1916
Miller		2	38	1887-1903
Miller		2	38	1887-1903
Miller	Ames	2	82	1887-1903
Miller	Ann Elizabeth	1	50	1878-1887
Miller	Curtis L.	4	459	1907-1916
Miller	Elvira M.	1	18	1878-1887
Miller	Emma V.	1	37	1878-1887
Miller	Joseph Antone	2	10	1878-1903
Miller	Joseph Edward	2	65	1887-1903
Miller	Julia Augustine	1	20	1878-1887
Miller	Julius C.	1	63	1878-1887
Miller	Laura	2	18	1887-1903
Miller	Marie Ione	2	113	1887-1903
Miller	Mary S.	1	39	1878-1887
Miller	May E.	1	46	1878-1887
Miller	Pearl Catharine	2	28	1887-1903
Miller	Peter Albert	2	22	1887-1903
Miller	Peter W.	2	1	1887-1903
Miller	Raymond	3	150	1903-1915
Miller	Samuel Harvey	4	491	1907-1916
Miller	Sarah Jane	1	49	1878-1887
Miller	Victor	2	53	1887-1903
Miner		3	235	1903-1915
Miner		2	63	1887-1903
Miner	George A.	4	156	1907-1916
Miner	James A.	2	116	1887-1903
Miner	Lela May	4	320	1907-1916
Mitchell	Irven Lafayette	3	210	1903-1915
Mitchell	Lawrence Clarence	2	46	1887-1903
Mitchell	Thomas O.	2	123	1887-1903
Moenning	Elmer Frederick	4	232	1907-1916

CALHOUN COUNTY BIRTHS

Surname	Given Name	Book	Page	Year
Moffett	Myrtle O.	4	81	1907-1916
Moffit		2	123	1887-1903
Moffit	John H.	4	306	1907-1916
Moffit	Lee	4	306	1907-1916
Moffit	Valeria	4	305	1907-1916
Monroe	Hilda	2	2	1887-1903
Moore	Anthy Leona	2	108	1887-1903
Moore	Guy Royal	1	51	1878-1887
Moore	Margaret	1	25	1878-1887
Moorman		4	205	1907-1916
Morhan	John	4	61	1907-1916
Morris	Bert	3	26	1903-1915
Morris	Cecil Leroy	2	111	1887-1903
Morrison		2	110	1887-1903
Mortland		1	79	1878-1887
Mortland		1	78	1878-1887
Mortland	Albert Ernst	1	26	1878-1887
Mortland	Bertha	1	45	1878-1887
Mortland	Bruce Millar	3	1	1903-1915
Mortland	Charles L.	1	46	1878-1887
Mortland	Dorothy Lucile	2	105	1878-1903
Mortland	George	4	6	1907-1916
Mortland	Goldie E.S.	1	59	1878-1887
Mortland	Herbert E.	1	13	1878-1887
Mortland	Isabella	1	9	1878-1887
Mortland	James A.	1	63	1878-1887
Mortland	Mable E.	1	46	1878-1887
Mortland	Robert F.	4	443	1907-1916
Mortland	Sarah Ann	1	68	1878-1887
Mortland	Thomas Gardner	1	43	1878-1887
Mortland	Thomas L.	4	373	1907-1916
Mortland	Wilson N.	2	55	1887-1903
Mortland	William U. Jr.	4	95	1907-1916
Morton		3	261	1903-1915
Morton	Mehala Twichell	4	40	1907-1916

CALHOUN COUNTY BIRTHS

Surname	Given Name	Book	Page	Year
Morton	Ray Dow	4	158	1907-1916
Morton	Ray Howe	4	159	1907-1916
Morton	Walter G.	4	443	1907-1916
Moses		2	58	1887-1903
Moses	Gerald	4	530	1907-1916
Moss		1	42	1878-1887
Moss	Jesse W.	1	36	1878-1887
Moss	Leroy (Twin)	1	72	1878-1887
Moss	Francis (Twin)	1	72	1878-1887
Mossman	Bernice Mary	4	598	1907-1916
Mossman	Frank	4	417	1907-1916
Mossman	Mary Ann	2	124	1887-1903
Mottaz		4	471	1907-1916
Mottaz		2	22	1887-1903
Mottaz	Francis H.	2	13	1887-1903
Mottaz	George Alexis	2	41	1887-1903
Mottaz	Harvey Sharp	2	43	1887-1903
Mottaz	Maud	2	8	1887-1903
Mottaz	Nellie Beatrice	2	8	1887-1903
Mottaz	Sophia	1	46	1878-1887
Moultrie	Robert Logan	2	105	1887-1903
Mower		4	242	1907-1916
Mozier	Delia Lee Mae	3	144	1903-1915
Mozier	Ruby	4	603	1907-1916
Mueller	Martha Agatha	4	394	1907-1916
Mueller	Walter Alfred	4	561	1907-1916
Mulkey		1	38	1878-1887
Mulky	Grant Dewey	2	107	1887-1903
Naber	Gennenvive Adaline	4	558	1907-1916
Nachand	Eva Agnes	2	97	1887-1903
Nachand	John R.	2	44	1887-1903
Nachand	Roscoe A.	2	87	1887-1903
Nairn	John A.	2	89	1887-1903
Naland	Clarence W.	2	58	1887-1903
Narrop	Charles M.	2	23	1887-1903

CALHOUN COUNTY BIRTHS

Surname	Given Name	Book	Page	Year
Narrup	Clifford Henry	4	234	1907-1916
Narrup	Mary Jane	1	70	1878-1887
Narup		2	35	1887-1903
Narup	Carl H.	3	158	1903-1915
Narup	Everett	4	334	1907-1916
Narup	Mathes	1	15	1878-1887
Narup	Richard	4	529	1907-1916
Narup	Robert	4	597	1907-1916
Narup	Sarah	4	532	1907-1916
Narup	Sarah Lorraine	4	363	1907-1916
Narup	Viola Regina	4	262	1907-1916
Narup	William Lawrence	4	155	1907-1916
Narup	Zita A.	4	284	1907-1916
Navarre	Joseph M.	3	103	1903-1915
Neal	William McKinley	2	118	1887-1903
Nelson		3	137	1903-1915
Nelson	Jennie C.	1	67	1878-1887
Nelson	Mary	3	5	1903-1915
Nelson	Perry Ernest	2	33	1887-1903
Nelson	William Jasper	2	10	1887-1903
Nevius	Ova	4	309	1907-1916
Nevius	Veda Zeroba	2	80	1887-1903
Nevius		2	64	1887-1903
Nevius	Marguerite Velma	3	55	1903-1915
Nevius	Frances Elaine	3	252	1903-1915
Nevius	George T.	1	30	1878-1887
Nevius	Harlen A.	3	198	1903-1915
Nevius	Ova	2	35	1887-1903
Nevius	Ova R.	1	9	1878-1887
Nevius	Verbena C.	3	159	1903-1915
Nevius	Anna Selma	4	70	1907-1916
Nevius		4	567	1907-1916
Newman	Claude C.	4	143	1907-1916
Newman	Freda Myotta	4	71	1907-1916
Nicholas		1	64	1907-1916

CALHOUN COUNTY BIRTHS

Surname	Given Name	Book	Page	Year
Nicholas		2	86	1887-1903
Nicholas	Luly Floy	1	72	1878-1887
Nicholas	nellie Alice	2	34	1878-1887
Nicholas	Obie Claude	1	73	1887-1903
Nicholas	Ora Camille	2	83	1878-1887
Nicholas	Wilson Ross	2	33	1887-1903
Nimerick		3	278	1903-1915
Nimerick	Margaret	4	86	1907-1916
Nodbush	Mary Christina	1	7	1878-1887
Noe	Netta (Twin)	1	24	1878-1887
Noe	Etta (Twin)	1	24	1878-1887
Nold	Frederick	3	246	1903-1915
Nolle		4	201	1907-1916
Nolle	Emma Otte	3	184	1903-1915
Nolte		3	223	1903-1915
Nolte	Curtis	4	18	1907-1916
Nolte	Henry K.	4	354	1907-1916
Nolte	Jospeh	1	23	1878-1887
Nolte	Robert M.	4	177	1907-1916
Nolten	Bertie A.	1	52	1878-1887
Norris		3	44	1903-1915
Norris		3	209	1903-1915
Norris	Charles	4	219	1907-1916
Northcut	Chetty G.	1	49	1878-1887
Norton		2	87	1887-1903
Norton	Neta Ann	4	12	1907-1916
Norton	Vernia Alice	2	60	1887-1903
Norton	Wayne Cecil	3	2	1903-1915
Oberjohann		3	114	1887-1903
Oberjohann	Henry F.	3	20	1903-1915
Oberjohann	Loren George	4	209	1907-1916
Oberjohann	Otto Luther	3	164	1903-1915
Oberjohann	William	4	47	1907-1916
Oberjohn	Johanna K.	4	442	1907-1916
Oden		1	14	1878-1887

CALHOUN COUNTY BIRTHS

Surname	Given Name	Book	Page	Year
Oden		3	170	1903-1915
Oden	Charlotta	4	276	1907-1916
Oden	Jessie Pearl	1	67	1878-1887
Oden	Loren Willard	4	537	1907-1916
Oden	Merrill	3	119	1903-1915
Oden	Morland	4	391	1907-1916
Oettle		4	505	1907-1916
Oettle		2	93	1887-1903
Oettle	Anna Florence	4	340	1907-1916
Oettle	Bertha Aledith	4	48	1907-1916
Oettle	Edith Marie	2	95	1887-1903
Oettle	Emil F.	4	498	1907-1916
Oettle	Forrest O.	4	412	1907-1916
Oettle	Frederick W.	1	31	1878-1887
Oettle	Harry Norbert	2	128	1887-1903
Oettle	Hester E.	3	142	1903-1915
Oettle	Isaac Monroe	3	102	1903-1915
Oettle	Keith Robert	4	40	1907-1916
Oettle	Kenneth	4	149	1907-1916
Oettle	Oscar	3	10	1903-1915
Oettle	Ralph	2	130	1887-1903
Oettle	Raymond	3	113	1903-1915
Oettle	Roy F.	2	90	1887-1903
Oettle	Russel William	4	239	1907-1916
Oettle	Viola Katherine	4	244	1907-1916
Oettle	Walter William	2	105	1887-1903
Ogden	Elsie Mable	2	78	1887-1903
Ogden	Ernest S.	4	112	1907-1916
Ohearm		2	86	1887-1903
Ontis	John	3	157	1903-1915
Orthwerth	Bernice	4	420	1907-1916
Orthwerth	Loretta A.	4	128	1907-1916
Ortlee	George Lee	1	28	1878-1887
Ortwell	Herman	2	59	1887-1903
Osborn	Robert	4	529	1907-1916

CALHOUN COUNTY BIRTHS

Surname	Given Name	Book	Page	Year
Osborne	Eli	1	64	1878-1887
Osterman	Anna Edith	3	55	1903-1915
Osterman	Charlotte	4	577	1907-1916
Osterman	Herman John	4	277	1907-1916
Osterman	Martha Elizabeth	4	277	1907-1916
Osterman	Mary E.	2	123	1887-1903
Osterman	Minnie (Twin)	4	83	1907-1916
Osterman	Mamie (Twin)	4	83	1907-1916
Osterman	William Tilford	3	192	1903-1915
Otte	Carl H.	1	22	1878-1887
Ottwell	(Still Born)	3	265	1903-1915
Ottwell	Beatrice M.	3	185	1903-1915
Ottwell	Effie Adaline	2	34	1887-1903
Ottwell	Mary	3	30	1903-1915
Ottwell	Mary U.	4	410	1907-1916
Ottwell	Tressa	4	470	1907-1916
Otwell		4	191	1907-1916
Otwell	Marvin Leslie	4	74	1907-1916
Otwell	Zona Armona	4	315	1907-1916
Owens	John	1	5	1878-1887
Owens	Laura E.	2	9	1887-1903
Owens	Mary E.	1	22	1878-1887
Owings	Roy A.	2	119	1887-1903
Pace		14	308	1907-1916
Pace	Frank Arthur	4	226	1907-1916
Pach	Mary	2	104	1887-1903
Painlaloux	Ray V.	2	73	1887-1903
Palmer	Bertha	1	53	1878-1887
Parker		2	103	1887-1903
Parker	Harry Mortimer	2	8	1887-1903
Parker	Kenneth Ray	4	240	1907-1916
Parker	Stephen M.	2	130	1887-1903
Parriott		3	274	1903-1915
Patney	Caroline	1	12	1878-1887
Patrick		2	118	1887-1903

CALHOUN COUNTY BIRTHS

Surname	Given Name	Book	Page	Year
Patrick	Ross Annel	1	73	1878-1887
Patterson	Anna M.	2	19	1887-1903
Paucket	Alice	4	333	1907-1916
Pavlick	Ralph A.	2	31	1887-1903
Peacock	Beatrice	2	65	1887-1903
Peacock	Jesse Luther	1	50	1878-1887
Peacock	John Orville	4	153	1907-1916
Peacock	Lorney Edward	4	4	1907-1916
Pearson	(Still Born)	3	262	1903-1915
Pearson	Darrell	4	579	1907-1916
Pearson	Harry Wood	3	177	1903-1915
Peeler	Francis Marion	3	180	1903-1915
Peeler	Freemont	2	85	1887-1903
Peeler	Howard Edward	4	560	1907-1916
Peeler	James Irvin	1	67	1878-1887
Peeler	Malissa Cloe	4	387	1907-1916
Peeler	Martha	1	14	1878-1887
Peeler	Raymond Warren	4	248	1907-1916
Peeler	Tracy A.	2	63	1887-1903
Pehm	Fred Augustus	4	181	1907-1916
Pehm	Herman Joseph	3	210	1903-1915
Pehm	Josephine	4	300	1907-1916
Peisker	William H.	4	502	1907-1916
Pelican		2	89	1887-1903
Pelican	Gladys Leona	4	425	1907-1915
Pelican	John Francis	1	47	1878-1887
Pelikaan	Carl Roland	3	220	1903-1915
Pellican	Lamberton	2	125	1887-1903
Pellican	Stephen F.	2	21	1887-1903
Pellikaan	Maude M.	1	73	1878-1887
Pellikan	Harold Roscoe	2	92	1887-1903
Pellikan	Ray Lewellyn	4	523	1907-1916
Pence		4	450	1907-1916
Penny	James W.	1	23	1878-1887
Pepper	Alfred Lewis	4	150	1903-1915

CALHOUN COUNTY BIRTHS

Surname	Given Name	Book	Page	Year
Peppers		4	479	1907-1916
Percentena	Lucy	1	32	1878-1887
Percenteni	Asunta Percille	1	62	1878-1887
Percentina		2	45	1887-1903
Percentina		2	21	1887-1903
Percentina	Bartholomew	2	65	1887-1903
Percentina	Gicondo	2	39	1887-1903
Percentina	Peter B.	2	1	1887-1903
Perry		1	75	1878-1887
Perry		1	33	1878-1887
Perry		1	6	1878-1887
Perry	Nellie Amanda	1	49	1878-1887
Peters	August Newton	2	103	1887-1903
Peters	Lenore Elizabeth	4	247	1907-1916
Peters	Lucille Martha	4	502	1907-1916
Peters	Myria	4	470	1907-1916
Peters	Robert	2	110	1887-1903
Peterson		4	437	1907-1916
Peterson	Thelma	3	19	1903-1915
Petre		4	214	1907-1916
Petre	Mark T.	4	39	1907-1916
Peuterbaugh		4	91	1907-1916
Peuterbaugh		4	86	1907-1916
Peuterbaugh		3	282	1903-1915
Peuterbaugh		2	79	1887-1903
Peuterbaugh	Daisy Evelyn	3	164	1903-1915
Peuterbaugh	Eliza	3	263	1903-1915
Peuterbaugh	Homer	2	115	1887-1903
Peuterbaugh	Lizzie Ray	2	12	1887-1903
Peuterbaugh	Violet	4	295	1907-1916
Peuterbaugh	William Allen	4	535	1907-1916
Philips	Violet Lucille	4	263	1907-1916
Philips	William K.	4	173	1907-1916
Phillipps		1	28	1878-1887
Phillips	Perry L.	4	296	1907-1916

CALHOUN COUNTY BIRTHS

Surname	Given Name	Book	Page	Year
Phillips		4	44	1907-1916
Phillips	Casey Milow	2	73	1887-1903
Phillips	Meta	3	74	1903-1915
Phillips	Ruth Frances	4	163	1907-1916
Phillips	Samuel	4	557	1907-1916
Phillips	William Arnold	2	84	1887-1903
Phillips	Arnold Doety	4	328	1907-1916
Pichardt	Fred Edward	4	304	1907-1916
Pickett		1	20	1878-1887
Pickett	Juranda Kizaeh	1	45	1878-1887
Piper		2	7	1887-1903
Piper	Edga A.	1	35	1878-1887
Piper	Nina	1	20	1878-1887
Piper	Wilma V.	2	79	1887-1903
Pistoe		2	45	1887-1903
Plainer	Frederick Tobias	2	61	1887-1903
Pliester		1	33	1878-1887
Pluester		1	68	1878-1887
Pluester	Barney	2	26	1887-1903
Plummer		1	40	1878-1887
Plummer		4	67	1907-1916
Plummer	Abram	1	11	1878-1887
Plummer	Carl Otto	2	17	1887-1903
Plummer	Clara A.	1	22	1878-1887
Plummer	Clifford O.	3	36	1903-1915
Plummer	Dorthy M.	4	503	1907-1916
Plummer	Elsie A.	2	59	1887-1903
Plummer	Estella	2	82	1887-1903
Plummer	Fredrick I.	3	8	1903-1915
Plummer	James Paul	4	511	1907-1916
Plummer	Jasper Cleveland	1	56	1878-1887
Plummer	Lillian	3	167	1903-1915
Plummer	Lulu Abagail	1	5	1878-1887
Plummer	May	2	82	1887-1903
Plummer	Nellie Edith	3	37	1903-1915

CALHOUN COUNTY BIRTHS

Surname	Given Name	Book	Page	Year
Plummer	Nora Edith	2	35	1887-1903
Plummer	Nora Pearl	2	71	1887-1903
Plummer	Oletha Beatrice	4	167	1907-1916
Plummer	Orville	1	3	1878-1887
Plummer	Paul	4	8	1907-1916
Plummer	Robert K.	4	399	1907-1916
Plummer	Rosa A.	1	69	1878-1887
Plummer	Rosco Earl	3	89	1903-1915
Plummer	Sarah Helena	2	45	1887-1903
Plummer	Sarah Helena	2	47	1887-1903
Plummer	William Harrison	4	68	1907-1916
Plummer	Stephen S.	1	3	1878-1887
Pluster	John	1	18	1878-1887
Pluster	Wilhelmina	2	5	1887-1903
Pohl		2	101	1887-1903
Pohlman		4	41	1907-1916
Pohlman	(Still Born)	3	272	1903-1915
Pohlman	Alva	3	97	1903-1915
Pohlman	Anna C.	1	4	1878-1887
Pohlman	Annie	2	111	1887-1903
Pohlman	Antone Edward	4	341	1907-1916
Pohlman	Bernard Herman	4	240	1907-1916
Pohlman	Carl Baromey	3	109	1903-1915
Pohlman	Carl H.	4	531	1907-1916
Pohlman	Frederick William	4	77	1907-1916
Pohlman	George Tobias	4	354	1907-1916
Pohlman	Jospeh John	2	101	1887-1903
Pohlman	Lawrence	1	27	1878-1887
Pohlman	Lawrence	4	178	1907-1916
Pohlman	Leander	4	371	1907-1916
Pohlman	Leo	4	419	1907-1916
Pohlman	Leo Herman Andrew	4	127	1907-1916
Pohlman	Louis Herman	3	237	1903-1915
Pohlman	Marie Elizabeth	4	345	1907-1916
Pohlman	Martin William	4	336	1907-1916

Surname	Given Name	Book	Page	Year
Pohlman	Nicholas	2	109	1887-1903
Pohlman	Robert H.	4	490	1907-1916
Pohlman	Robert Joseph	3	195	1903-1915
Pohlman	William J.	1	63	1878-1887
Pohlman	Wilma	4	598	1907-1916
Ponsalot	Ernest C.	3	71	1903-1915
Pontero		4	82	1907-1916
Pontero		1	41	1878-1887
Pontero	Lewis Abner	3	225	1903-1915
Pontice	Ione Neomi	4	504	1907-1916
Poor		3	251	1903-1915
Poor		3	176	1903-1915
Poor		4	132	1907-1916
Poor		4	152	1907-1916
Poor	Capitola	1	34	1878-1887
Poor	Donald W.	4	456	1907-1916
Poor	Goldie	4	267	1907-1916
Poor	James E.	1	52	1878-1887
Poor	Margaret	4	585	1907-1916
Poor	Margarette	4	470	1907-1916
Poor	William Irena	4	575	1907-1916
Poore	Abner	4	10	1907-1916
Poore	Henry Franklin	1	31	1878-1887
Poore	Marie	3	176	1903-1915
Poore	Thomas	4	453	1907-1916
Pope		2	98	1887-1903
Potter		3	264	1903-1915
Powell		2	81	1887-1903
Powell		2	94	1887-1903
Powell		2	69	1887-1903
Powell	Delbert	3	81	1887-1903
Powell	Ernest	4	213	1907-1916
Powell	George G.	2	57	1887-1903
Powell	James Howard	2	67	1887-1903
Powell	Mary Ellen	2	48	1887-1903

CALHOUN COUNTY BIRTHS

Surname	Given Name	Book	Page	Year
Powell	Ruth	4	22	1907-1916
Powell	Willena	4	136	1907-1916
Powers		2	3	1887-1903
Powers	Vera V.	1	58	1878-1887
Pranger	George Garret	2	8	1887-1903
Praul		2	98	1887-1903
Praul	Zetta Irma	2	102	1887-1903
Pregalden	Charles Victor	2	16	1887-1903
Pregalden	Andrew Jackson	2	28	1887-1903
Pregalden	Anton Joseph	2	28	1887-1903
Pregalden	Beatrice Mary	2	93	1887-1903
Pregalden	Judith S.	2	45	1887-1903
Pregalden	Mary Louisa	1	3	1878-1887
Presley		1	40	1878-1887
Presley		1	40	1878-1887
Presley	Ethel M.	4	358	1907-1916
Presley	Furman Marrin	4	347	1907-1916
Presley	Geneva Iola	4	139	1907-1916
Presley	George G.	4	380	1907-1916
Presley	Harry Isaac Leon	4	541	1907-1916
Presley	Inez Iola	4	300	1907-1916
Presley	Laura Erma	4	224	1907-1916
Presley	Perry Lamont	4	469	1907-1916
Presley	Virgil W.	3	14	1903-1915
Presse	Elizabeth Caroline	2	7	1887-1903
Pressey		4	555	1907-1916
Pressley		2	63	1887-1903
Pressley	Arthur	4	374	1907-1916
Pressley	George R.	1	59	1878-1887
Pressley	George Marin	2	49	1887-1903
Pressley	John Samuel	2	4	1887-1903
Pressley	Laura E.	1	19	1878-1887
Pressley	Pearl A.	4	230	1907-1916
Pressley	Phillip R.	3	192	1903-1915
Preston		1	22	1878-1887

CALHOUN COUNTY BIRTHS

Surname	Given Name	Book	Page	Year
Preston		2	46	1887-1903
Prewitt		3	241	1903-1915
Pruitt	Loren	4	281	1907-1916
Puterbaugh	Floyd	1	17	1878-1887
Puterbaugh	Wilma L.	4	494	1907-1916
Quiller		1	46	1878-1887
Quiller	John Peter	1	78	1878-1887
Quiller	Minnie E.	1	61	1878-1887
Quiller	Ray	3	3	1903-1915
Quiller	Vera	4	476	1907-1916
Quiller	Vernelle Estelene	4	481	1907-1916
Quinn	John W.	1	44	1878-1887
Raker	Jospeh	2	23	1887-1903
Ramirez	Myrl B.	4	472	1907-1916
Ramsey		1	55	1878-1887
Ramsey	Archey Earnest	1	73	1878-1887
Ramsey	Chauncey E.	1	41	1878-1887
Ramsey	Christopher L.	1	53	1878-1887
Ramsey	Cyrus Edwin	4	386	1907-1916
Ramsey	Geneva	4	553	1907-1916
Ramsey	Ida May	4	72	1907-1916
Ramsey	John Thomas	1	60	1878-1887
Ramsey	Lucy Irene	4	352	1907-1916
Ramsey	Opal Vernola	4	362	1907-1916
Ramsey	Orland Ludwell	4	551	1907-1916
Ramsey	Robert Lafayette	4	507	1907-1916
Ramsey	Rose Esther	4	84	1907-1916
Raney	John Herbert	1	29	1878-1887
Rap		3	283	1903-1915
Rap		4	457	1907-1916
Rapp		4	121	1907-1916
Rapp		4	188	1907-1916
Rapp		4	588	1907-1916
Rapp		4	140	1907-1916
Rapp	Irene Bertha	4	273	1907-1916

CALHOUN COUNTY BIRTHS

Surname	Given Name	Book	Page	Year
Ray	Allison B.	4	433	1907-1916
Ray	Lawrence O.	3	25	1903-1915
Ray	Mary Leota	4	385	1907-1916
Ray	Mildred Marie	4	184	1907-1916
Raymond	Joseph	3	151	1903-1915
Read		2	3	1887-1903
Red	Aetna Aurelia	1	5	1878-1887
Reed		4	330	1907-1916
Reed		1	57	1878-1887
Reed		1	43	1878-1887
Reed		1	16	1878-1887
Reed		1	14	1878-1887
Reed		2	66	1887-1903
Reed		2	120	1887-1903
Reed		1	62	1878-1887
Reed		1	29	1878-1887
Reed		2	60	1887-1903
Reed		1	37	1878-1887
Reed	Allie	2	38	1887-1903
Reed	Arthur	2	19	1887-1903
Reed	Arthur	1	29	1878-1887
Reed	Arthur	2	126	1887-1903
Reed	James W.	1	32	1878-1887
Reed	Lela Gladis	4	279	1907-1916
Reed	Manuel	2	60	1887-1903
Reed	Oval	3	75	1903-1915
Reed	Philip	4	264	1907-1916
Reed	William Thomas	3	75	1903-1915
Reeves		1	26	1878-1887
Reeves		1	17	1878-1887
Reeves	Albert Sidney	2	88	1887-1903
Reeves	Orphia Estella	2	96	1887-1903
Reeves	Osca R.	1	24	1878-1887
Reeves	William A.	1	35	1878-1887
Reimenschneider		2	35	1887-1903

CALHOUN COUNTY BIRTHS

Surname	Given Name	Book	Page	Year
Reimenschneider	Charles John	2	35	1887-1903
Reimenschneider	Edward John	2	90	1887-1903
Reimenschneider	Roy	2	125	1887-1903
Reinsocker	Caroline E.	1	70	1878-1887
Reinsocker	Caroline Margaret	1	59	1878-1887
Reinsocker	Henry W.	1	45	1878-1887
Reiss	Lila Helena	4	55	1907-1916
Reiss	Carl	3	125	1903-1915
Ren		1	10	1878-1887
Renoad	Alma Pearl	2	71	1887-1903
Renoad	Bessie Marie	2	81	1887-1903
Rentz		2	93	1887-1903
Rentz		2	125	1887-1903
Rentz	Adele Mary	3	107	1903-1915
Retzer		4	297	1907-1916
Retzer		2	68	1887-1903
Retzer		2	106	1887-1903
Retzer		2	91	1887-1903
Retzer	Albert M.	2	79	1887-1903
Retzer	Frank William	2	494	1907-1916
Retzer	John L.	4	193	1907-1916
Retzer	Katherine B.	4	431	1907-1916
Retzer	Otto John	4	348	1907-1916
Retzer	Ruth Mary	4	504	1907-1916
Retzer	Samuel Stark	2	57	1887-1903
Rexrote		4	1	1907-1916
Rhinesocker	George Franklin	2	18	1887-1903
Rice		4	564	1907-1916
Richards	Beatrice	4	445	1907-1916
Richards	Cecil Forrest	4	263	1907-1916
Richards	John R.	3	217	1903-1915
Richards	Mamie Viola	4	102	1907-1916
Richards	Mary Ellen (Still Born)	3	281	1903-1915
Richardson		1	16	1878-1887
Richey	Alice Myrtle	1	26	1878-1887

CALHOUN COUNTY BIRTHS

Surname	Given Name	Book	Page	Year
Richey	Amanda May	4	158	1907-1916
Richey	Henry O.	1	35	1878-1887
Richey	Howard M.	1	47	1878-1887
Richey	Lulu Melissa	1	8	1878-1887
Richey	Luther Orville	2	129	1887-1903
Richey	Raymond	2	115	1887-1903
Richie		2	63	1887-1903
Richter		4	265	1907-1916
Richter	Frederick	2	80	1887-1903
Richter	Katie	2	19	1887-1903
Richter	Lena	2	65	1887-1903
Richter	Margaret	1	55	1878-1887
Richter	Marvin	4	567	1907-1916
Richter	Merlin W.	4	81	1907-1916
Richter	Nellie Leota	3	255	1903-1915
Richter	Orville	4	183	1907-1916
Richter	Zoda Kasper	4	261	1907-1916
Riemenschneider	Matilda Frances	2	71	1887-1903
Ringhausen		4	39	1907-1916
Ringhausen	Arthur Jerome	4	423	1907-1916
Ringhausen	Charles Clifford	2	22	1887-1903
Ringhausen	Christian Louis	2	11	1887-1903
Ringhausen	Christian (Twin)	2	129	1887-1903
Ringhausen	Christina (Twin)	2	129	1887-1903
Ringhausen	Clarence Paul	2	70	1887-1903
Ringhausen	Edna Margaret	4	238	1907-1916
Ringhausen	Edward L.	2	9	1887-1903
Ringhausen	Elsie Irene	3	165	1903-1915
Ringhausen	Frances Effie	2	40	1887-1903
Ringhausen	Frieda Louise	4	102	1907-1916
Ringhausen	Harry William	2	37	1887-1903
Ringhausen	James A.	2	121	1887-1903
Ringhausen	Jesse Christopher	2	86	1887-1903
Ringhausen	John C.	4	491	1907-1916
Ringhausen	Louis E.	1	42	1878-1887

CALHOUN COUNTY BIRTHS

Surname	Given Name	Book	Page	Year
Ringhausen	Louis William (Possible Twin)	3	120	1903-1915
Ringhausen	Possible Twin	3	120	1903-1915
Ringhausen	Mary Agnes	2	92	1887-1903
Ringhausen	Paul	2	96	1887-1903
Ringhausen	Stephen	2	49	1887-1903
Ringhausen	Sucie	3	105	1903-1915
Ringhausen	Theodore	4	68	1907-1916
Ritter		3	21	1903-1915
Ritter		4	260	1907-1916
Ritter	Anna Kamp	2	92	1887-1903
Ritter	Arthur J.	2	96	1987-1903
Ritter	Eugene Otto	4	252	1907-1916
Ritter	John	2	86	1887-1903
Ritter	Joseph Adam	4	103	1907-1916
Ritter	Lucille E.	2	119	1887-1903
Ritter	Phillip Adam	4	49	1907-1916
Ritter	Thelma L.	3	162	1903-1915
Rivard	Mariette	1	33	1878-1887
Roach	Florence Ester	3	135	1903-1915
Roach	Harold Kenneth	4	346	1907-1916
Roach	John Paul	4	26	1907-1916
Roach	Marilla	1	6	1878-1887
Roach	Pearl	2	119	1887-1903
Roach	William H.C.	3	176	1903-1915
Robbins	Evart W.	3	159	1903-1915
Robbins	George Leslie	4	341	1907-1916
Robbins	Ila Beatrice	4	104	1907-1916
Robeen	Andrew	2	5	1887-1903
Robeen	Catherine Gertrude	2	69	1887-1903
Robeen	Ceceila Pauline	4	416	1907-1916
Robeen	Josephine Marguerite	4	77	1907-1916
Robeen	Louis A.	4	592	1907-1916
Robeen	Robert Raymond	4	333	1907-1916
Robertson	Carl Paul	4	27	1907-1916
Robertson		2	89	1887-1903

CALHOUN COUNTY BIRTHS

Surname	Given Name	Book	Page	Year
Robertson	Elba A.	2	105	1887-1903
Robertson	Henry Edwin	2	125	1887-1903
Robertson	Lawrence Don	3	163	1903-1915
Robertson	Mary Etta	4	145	1907-1916
Robinson		1	6	1878-1887
Robinson		3	63	1903-1915
Rodaker		2	61	1887-1903
Rodgers	Alice	2	45	1887-1903
Rodgers	Sade	2	81	1903-1915
Roehl	(Still Born)	3	273	1903-1915
Roehl	Felena Hermoine	4	535	1907-1916
Roehl	Francis J.	1	69	1878-1887
Roentz		2	84	1887-1903
Roentz	John Louis	2	54	1887-1903
Roentz	Lena	2	26	1887-1903
Rogers	Morris Jerome	4	260	1907-1916
Rogers	Thomas	2	2	1887-1903
Rogers	Zelie	2	27	1887-1903
Rohe	Catherina	1	4	1878-1887
Rosa	(Still Born)	3	285	1903-1915
Rosa	Anna Elizabeth	2	73	1887-1903
Rosa	Carl L.	2	72	1887-1903
Rosa	Clair Allen	4	289	1907-1916
Rosa	Hettie M.	2	14	1887-1903
Rosa	Loraine Freda	2	46	1887-1903
Rosa	Lulu Ethel	2	32	1887-1903
Rosa	Mamie Oslea	2	43	1887-1903
Rosa	Margie Ruth	2	64	1887-1903
Rosa	Nina May	3	84	1903-1915
Rosa	Roy Elder	2	33	1887-1903
Rosa	William Henry	2	5	1887-1903
Rose		1	64	1878-1887
Rose		2	14	1887-1903
Rose		2	32	1887-1903
Rose		2	2	1887-1903

CALHOUN COUNTY BIRTHS

Surname	Given Name	Book	Page	Year
Rose		1	55	1878-1887
Rose		4	129	1907-1916
Rose	Anton Joseph	4	98	1907-1916
Rose	Arvella L.	2	44	1887-1903
Rose	Cecelia	4	297	1907-1916
Rose	Elizabeth Anna	4	19	1907-1916
Rose	Gladys Anne	2	101	1887-1903
Rose	Guy D.	1	77	1878-1887
Rose	Harry Armstrong	2	83	1887-1903
Rose	Henry John	4	130	1907-1916
Rose	Herman William	4	418	1907-1916
Rose	Lester Blevens	2	55	1887-1903
Rose	Milan M. (Twin)	3	226	1903-1915
Rose	Minnie	2	32	1887-1903
Rose	Minnie M. (Twin)	3	227	1903-1915
Rose	Otis	2	42	1887-1903
Rose	Raus Cecil	4	117	1907-1916
Rose	Raymond B.	4	528	1907-1916
Rose	William Bryan	2	130	1887-1903
Rose	William H.	4	166	1907-1916
Rose	John	2	85	1887-1903
Ross		2	111	1887-1903
Roth		3	105	1903-1915
Roth		2	85	1887-1903
Roth		4	518	1907-1916
Roth		2	93	1887-1903
Roth		3	108	1903-1915
Roth		2	81	1887-1903
Roth		1	37	1878-1887
Roth		2	110	1887-1903
Roth	Anna Mary	2	48	1887-1903
Roth	Catharina Anna	2	42	1887-1903
Roth	Cecilia Bethildas	4	523	1907-1916
Roth	Charles John	2	65	1887-1903
Roth	Edmond Leo	4	371	1907-1916

CALHOUN COUNTY BIRTHS

Surname	Given Name	Book	Page	Year
Roth	Edward Adam	4	421	1907-1916
Roth	Frances Mary	4	516	1907-1916
Roth	Frank A.	1	42	1878-1887
Roth	Joseph	2	43	1887-1903
Roth	Joseph Thomas	2	72	1887-1903
Roth	Mabel May	3	236	1903-1915
Roth	Mary Catherine	2	9	1887-1903
Roth	Mathias	2	81	1887-1903
Roth	Nicholas Adam	1	50	1878-1887
Roth	Noah M.	2	40	1887-1903
Roth	Rosa A.	4	287	1907-1916
Roth	Stepehn William	2	49	1887-1903
Roundcount	Francis Helena	4	561	1907-1916
Roundcount	Henry A.	2	27	1887-1903
Roy	Jame Orland	3	216	1903-1915
Royal	Norma Ernestine	2	102	1887-1903
Ruetz		3	107	1903-1915
Rule	Jessie	2	50	1887-1903
Rullon	(Still Born)	3	267	1903-1915
Rulon		1	51	1878-1887
Rulon		1	27	1878-1887
Rulon	Erma Mary	4	575	1907-1916
Rulon	James Leo	4	207	1907-1916
Rumpel		2	82	1887-1903
Runde	Kenneth R.	3	3	1903-1915
Runde	Marjel Elizabeth	3	104	1903-1915
Rupley	William Edward	4	199	1907-1916
Russell	Alice	2	9	1887-1903
Russell	Grace Myrtle	2	58	1887-1903
Russell	Mabel E.	1	13	1878-1887
Russell	Maud Alice	1	30	1878-1887
Russell	Ray Lester	2	117	1887-1903
Rustemeyer		3	114	1903-1915
Rustemeyer	Anna Gertrude Kora	2	12	1887-1903
Rustemeyer	Maria Anna	1	60	1878-1887

CALHOUN COUNTY BIRTHS

Surname	Given Name	Book	Page	Year
Rustemeyer	Uvo Edward	1	24	1878-1887
Ruyle		1	55	1878-1887
Ruyle		2	16	1887-1903
Ruyle		1	73	1878-1887
Ruyle		1	11	1878-1887
Ruyle		1	50	1878-1887
Ruyle		4	408	1907-1916
Ruyle		3	225	1903-1915
Ruyle		2	61	1887-1903
Ruyle		2	28	1887-1903
Ruyle	Arthur	1	28	1878-1887
Ruyle	Bessie	4	189	1907-1916
Ruyle	Clarence William	4	137	1907-1916
Ruyle	Clifford	2	32	1887-1903
Ruyle	Donald	3	98	1903-1915
Ruyle	Dorothy	2	103	1887-1903
Ruyle	Edna Earl	4	2	1907-1916
Ruyle	Effie Anna	1	13	1878-1887
Ruyle	Flossie	2	79	1887-1903
Ruyle	George	3	45	1903-1915
Ruyle	Henry Lee	2	44	1887-1903
Ruyle	Herley Noland	4	84	1907-1916
Ruyle	James Douglas	4	35	1907-1916
Ruyle	John F.	1	42	1878-1887
Ruyle	Joseph Etta	4	390	1907-1916
Ruyle	Lester Earl	2	65	1887-1903
Ruyle	Lillian Anna Belle	3	100	1903-1915
Ruyle	Mildred Lucile	4	24	1907-1916
Ruyle	Mossie Elizabeth	3	73	1903-1915
Ruyle	Nona Myria	3	50	1903-1915
Ruyle	Orland Harold	4	316	1907-1916
Ruyle	Roy Samuel	2	93	1887-1903
Ruyle	Stanley	2	67	1887-1903
Ruyle	Virginia Helen	4	414	1907-1916
Ruyle	Walter	4	105	1907-1916

CALHOUN COUNTY BIRTHS

Surname	Given Name	Book	Page	Year
Ryne		2	86	1887-1903
Sackman	Alice Ottelia	2	38	1887-1903
Sackman	Eyle Paul	2	71	1887-1903
Sackman	Francis	1	52	1878-1887
Sackman	Frederick	2	11	1887-1903
Sackman	Lucy Otllia	3	114	1903-1915
Sackman	Martin Edward	1	57	1878-1887
Sackman	Michael	1	66	1878-1887
Sackman	Paul Albert	2	120	1887-1903
Sackman	William Efford	2	10	1887-1903
Sager	Edgar Freegmar Flatt	2	98	1887-1903
Sagez	George Franklin	2	16	1887-1903
Sagez	Hester	2	114	1887-1903
Sagez	Mary Louisa	1	72	1878-1887
Sampson		1	47	1878-1887
Sampson	Leona Dorothy	2	125	1887-1903
Sampson	Mary Oval	2	21	1887-1903
Sancamper	George R.	4	471	1907-1916
Sanders	Edward Evert	2	112	1887-1903
Sanders	Martha	3	35	1903-1915
Sanders	Margeret E.	3	34	1903-1915
Sanders	Mary Ann	2	47	1887-1903
Sanford	Philip Sheridan	2	7	1887-1903
Saunders		2	85	1887-1903
Saunders	Harriette Belle	2	98	1887-1903
Saunders	Mason	3	2	1903-1915
Savidge		1	34	1878-1887
Savidge	Alice	1	21	1878-1887
Schaffer		3	238	1903-1915
Schaffer	Doras Marie	4	350	1907-1916
Schleeper		4	428	1907-1916
Schleeper		1	53	1878-1887
Schleeper		1	72	1878-1887
Schleeper	Albert Mathias	3	133	1903-1915
Schleeper	Archie Paul	3	106	1903-1915

CALHOUN COUNTY BIRTHS

Surname	Given Name	Book	Page	Year
Schleeper	Catherine	1	13	1878-1887
Schleeper	Charles L. (Twin)	2	19	1887-1903
Schleeper	Catherine (Twin)	2	19	1887-1903
Schleeper	Dorothy Mary	4	569	1907-1916
Schleeper	Elmer Carl	4	179	1907-1916
Schleeper	Frances A.	4	139	1907-1916
Schleeper	John Jr.	4	486	1907-1916
Schleeper	John Paul	2	78	1887-1903
Schleeper	Lena	1	66	1878-1887
Schleeper	Leonard John	4	70	1907-1916
Schleeper	Marian A.	4	487	1907-1916
Schleeper	Marvin Albert			1907-1916
Schleeper	Mary	2	99	1887-1903
Schleeper	Mary Catherine	1	78	1878-1887
Schleeper	Mildred Gertrude	3	257	1903-1915
Schleeper	Raymond Harry	4	255	1907-1916
Schleeper	Robert George	4	338	1907-1916
Schleeper	Theodore	2	55	1903-1915
Schleeper	Viola Sloane	1	60	1878-1887
Schlieper		4	325	1907-1916
Schlieper		4	26	1907-1916
Schlieper	Arthur James	4	389	1907-1916
Schlieper	Dale	2	119	1887-1903
Schlieper	Florence Marie	4	357	1907-1916
Schlieper	Howard Arthur	4	553	1907-1916
Schlieper	Marvin Henry	4	256	1907-1916
Schlieper	Nellie Mae	4	134	1907-1916
Schlieper	Nellie Marie	2	84	1907-1916
Schlieper	Ocie Viola	4	579	1907-1916
Schlieper	Orval Ray	2	111	1887-1903
Schlieper	Paul Arthur	3	256	1903-1915
Schlieper	Paul (Twin)	4	133	1907-1916
Schlieper	Pauline (Twin)	4	133	1907-1916
Schlinker	Alma	4	419	1907-1916
Schmeider	Joseph	1	55	1878-1887

CALHOUN COUNTY BIRTHS

Surname	Given Name	Book	Page	Year
Schmeider	Teresa Dora	2	128	1887-1903
Schmidt	Dorothy Nancy	3	42	1903-1915
Schmidt	Frank H.	2	128	1887-1903
Schmidt	Jerome Henry	4	309	1907-1916
Schmidt	Masie Adeline	4	270	1907-1916
Schmidt	Pauline	4	334	1907-1916
Schmidt	Rachel	4	303	1907-1916
Schmidt	William Henry Taylor	4	7	1907-1916
Schmidtz	Cecelia	3	61	1903-1915
Schmieder	Charles Alfred	4	599	1907-1916
Schmitz	Margaret Mary	1	64	1878-1887
Schmitz	Mary Francis	3	185	1903-1915
Schneider		2	27	1887-1903
Schneider	Charles J.	1	64	1878-1887
Schneider	Katy Lizy	2	20	1887-1903
Schneider	Lizzie M.	2	55	1887-1903
Schneider	Mary	1	43	1878-1887
Schneider	Peter	1	66	1878-1887
Schobernd	Gerhard	2	59	1887-1903
Schoetker	Theodore Williard	3	184	1903-1915
Schopper	Walter Edward	2	55	1887-1903
Schroggins	Margaret O'Fane	2	119	1887-1903
Schulte	Henry W.	4	596	1907-1916
Schulte	Irene	4	527	1907-1916
Schultz		4	60	1907-1916
Schulze		3	117	1903-1915
Schulze		3	98	1903-1915
Schulze	Lillie	2	120	1887-1903
Schuman		3	47	1903-1915
Schuman	Alexander	2	37	1887-1903
Schuman	Frank Joseph	2	11	1887-1903
Schuman	Minnie Cora	2	34	1887-1903
Schuman	Minnie C.	2	43	1887-1903
Schumann		3	188	1903-1915
Schumann	Arthur Henry	2	89	1887-1903

CALHOUN COUNTY BIRTHS

Surname	Given Name	Book	Page	Year
Schumann	Francis	1	50	1878-1887
Schumann	Verna Helen	4	125	1907-1916
Schuster	Sophia Sarah	4	274	1907-1916
Scleeper		1	53	1878-1887
Sconce	August	1	70	1878-1887
Sconce	Mary J.	1	35	1878-1887
Sconce	Racheal Anna	4	250	1907-1916
Sconce	Ruby	2	22	1887-1903
Scott	Harry	2	28	1887-1903
Scoville	Mary Mabel	1	79	1878-1887
Scroggins	Mary E.	2	94	1887-1903
Scroggins	George A.	3	166	1903-1915
Seby	Alice	3	195	1903-1915
Seetz	Lilly May	1	7	1878-1887
Seibanman		3	17	1903-1915
Seidler		4	548	1907-1916
Seidler		4	597	1907-1916
Seidler	Earl Alfred	4	142	1907-1916
Seidler	Elmer James George	3	149	1903-1915
Seidler	Freda	4	343	1907-1916
Seidler	Grace	4	1	1907-1916
Seidler	Lucinda Illene	3	103	1903-1915
Seidler	Mary C.	4	453	1907-1916
Seidler	Obie	2	108	1887-1903
Seidler	William R.	4	372	1907-1916
Seimer	Paul Henry	4	453	1907-1916
Selby	Lenore	2	37	1887-1903
Senate	Sarah Emma	1	4	1878-1887
Sepper		2	88	1887-1903
Sergent		2	106	1887-1903
Severe		4	171	1907-1916
Sevier		2	129	1887-1903
Sevier		2	46	1887-1903
Sevier	Arthur	2	108	1887-1903
Sevier	Charles Raymond	3	155	1903-1915

CALHOUN COUNTY BIRTHS

Surname	Given Name	Book	Page	Year
Sevier	Edna	4	58	1907-1916
Sevier	Hallie Mae	4	584	1907-1916
Sevier	Harry Otis	4	509	1907-1916
Sevier	Joseph Albert	4	414	1907-1916
Sevier	Martha Elizabeth	2	117	1887-1903
Sevier	Minnie P.	3	17	1903-1915
Sevier	Nola Sarah	4	493	1907-1916
Sevier	Olive Leona	4	183	1907-1916
Sevier	Roy C.	4	473	1907-1916
Sevier	Tillie May	4	324	1907-1916
Sevier	Winnie Lucille	4	517	1907-1916
Shandrow		4	363	1907-1916
Shandrow		4	75	1907-1916
Shandrow		2	126	1887-1903
Shandrow	Doris Blossom	4	527	1907-1916
Shandrow	Ella Ann	2	46	1887-1903
Shandrow	Lucy Bell (Twin)	2	45	1887-1903
Shandrow	George (Twin)	2	45	1887-1903
Shanks		2	111	1887-1903
Shanks		2	111	1887-1903
Shanks	Dora May	4	383	1907-1916
Shannon	Abigal May	2	36	1887-1903
Shannon	Clara	1	77	1887-1887
Shannon	James H.	1	23	1878-1887
Shannon	Lucy	1	59	1878-1887
Shannon	Myrtle	1	43	1878-1887
Shannon	Sarah J.	2	16	1887-1903
Shaw		2	115	1887-1903
Shaw	Clarence Everett	3	229	1903-1915
Shaw	Ervin	4	150	1907-1916
Shea	Catherine	3	127	1903-1915
Shea	Mary	3	220	1903-1915
Sheff	Chester Nelson	4	505	1907-1916
Sheridan		4	532	1907-1916
Sheridan	Rose A.	4	284	1907-1916

Surname	Given Name	Book	Page	Year
Sherman	Effie	2	96	1887-1903
Sherman	Iantha Ora	2	62	1887-1903
Sherman	Lauretta H.	2	121	1887-1903
Sherman	Lester	4	529	1907-1916
Shireman		4	484	1907-1916
Shireman	Charles S.	2	39	1887-1903
Shireman	Clarence Woodrow	4	492	1907-1916
Shireman	Frank	2	36	1887-1903
Shireman	Jesse Francis	4	222	1907-1916
Shireman	Martin Henry	4	122	1907-1916
Shireman	Mary Marie	2	53	1887-1903
Shireman	Nellie Leona	2	25	1887-1903
Shireman	William Obie	3	136	1903-1915
Shive	Charles Roland	3	53	1903-1915
Shive	Daisy R.F.	2	115	1887-1903
Shobernd	Mary Josephine	3	78	1903-1915
Shook	Ralph Marion John	4	582	1907-1916
Shopper		3	137	1903-1915
Show	Clara S.	2	19	1887-1903
Show	Herschell Allen	4	585	1907-1916
Show	Theresa Catherine	2	125	1887-1903
Sibernman		4	412	1907-1916
Sibernman		4	411	1907-1916
Sibley		1	51	1878-1887
Sibley		1	58	1878-1887
Sibley	Elizabeth	4	583	1907-1916
Sibley	Florence	4	272	1907-1916
Sibley	Forrest O.	4	520	1907-1916
Sibley	George Wilson	4	3	1907-1916
Sibley	Katherine	4	94	1907-1916
Sibley	Marie	4	3	1907-1916
Sibley	Thelma	4	94	1907-1916
Sibley	Virginia Lorraine	4	392	1907-1916
Sidler		3	24	1903-1915
Sidwell		3	161	1903-1915

CALHOUN COUNTY BIRTHS

Surname	Given Name	Book	Page	Year
Sidwell	Bertha Ardela	1	36	1878-1887
Sidwell	Clarence A.	3	25	1903-1915
Sidwell	Claude O.	2	16	1887-1903
Sidwell	Dorothea Winona	4	226	1907-1916
Sidwell	Edwin Elsworth	1	56	1878-1887
Sidwell	Ernest Lee	2	3	1887-1903
Sidwell	Esther May	4	273	1907-1916
Sidwell	Floy Grace	2	67	1887-1903
Sidwell	Kenneth Gerold	4	51	1907-1916
Sidwell	Mary Florence	2	65	1887-1903
Sidwell	Orval Floyd	2	50	1887-1903
Sidwell	Otto	4	156	1907-1916
Sidwell	Raymond	2	11	1887-1903
Sidwell	Ronald Orsen	3	232	1903-1915
Sidwell	Vernita Jewel	4	352	1907-1916
Sidwell	William Frances	4	38	1907-1916
Siebanmann	Wallace Edward	3	199	1903-1915
Siebenmann		3	107	1903-1915
Sieberman	Georgian Arleigh	4	263	1907-1916
Siebus	Gustave	2	29	1887-1903
Siedler	(Twin)	3	240	1903-1915
Siedler	(Twin)	3	240	1903-1915
Siedler	Charles A.	4	486	1907-1916
Siemer	(Still Born)	3	272	1903-1915
Siemer	Edward Minard	2	101	1887-1903
Siemer	Herbert Mernard	4	303	1907-1916
Siemer	Irene	4	291	1907-1916
Siemer	Johnie	2	29	1887-1903
Siemer	Leo Herman	4	59	1907-1916
Siemer	Leonard	4	99	1907-1916
Siemer	Loretta Rosina	4	217	1907-1916
Siemer	Paul Henry	4	495	1907-1916
Siemer	Raymond	3	190	1903-1915
Siemer	Roselia Ida	4	373	1907-1916
Siemer	Verna M.	4	292	1907-1916

CALHOUN COUNTY BIRTHS

Surname	Given Name	Book	Page	Year
Sievers	Barney	4	463	1907-1916
Sievers	Carl	3	221	1903-1915
Sievers	Genevieve	4	384	1907-1916
Sievers	Henry	3	69	1903-1915
Sievers	Herman Albert	4	40	1907-1916
Sievers	John Barney	2	65	1887-1903
Sievers	Joseph	4	135	1907-1916
Sievers	Lawrence Anton	4	218	1907-1916
Sievers	Leo	2	124	1887-1903
Simon		4	367	1907-1916
Simon		2	8	1887-1903
Simon	Anna	2	68	1887-1903
Simon	Karl	2	37	1887-1903
Simon	Mary Adalena	4	302	1907-1916
Simon	Mildred Helen	4	487	1907-1916
Simon	William	2	17	1887-1903
Simonds	Andrew	2	54	1887-1903
Simons		1	44	1878-1887
Simons	Anna T.	4	167	1907-1916
Simpson		1	367	1878-1887
Simpson		1	25	1878-1887
Simpson	Alice Harriett	4	569	1907-1916
Simpson	Benjamin H.	2	6	1887-1903
Simpson	Omer Lloyd	2	114	1887-1903
Simpson	William McKinley	2	53	1887-1903
Sitton	William L.	2	15	1887-1903
Skirven		1	75	1878-1887
Skirvin	Charles Vinton	4	298	1907-1916
Skirvin	Willard Clyde	4	238	1907-1916
Slavin		3	33	1903-1915
Sleeper	George William	1	43	1878-1887
Sleeper	John Edward	1	7	1878-1887
Slinker	Herald (Twin)	4	203	1907-1916
Slinker	Louisa (Twin)	4	203	1907-1916
Slyter	Adda Girtrude	2	3	1887-1903

CALHOUN COUNTY BIRTHS

Surname	Given Name	Book	Page	Year
Smith		1	39	1878-1887
Smith		4	58	1907-1916
Smith		4	208	1907-1916
Smith		3	7	1903-1915
Smith		4	193	1907-1916
Smith		2	93	1887-1903
Smith		1	24	1878-1887
Smith		1	39	1878-1887
Smith	(Still Born)	3	274	1903-1915
Smith	August Woodrow	4	510	1907-1916
Smith	Becker	2	37	1887-1903
Smith	Birdie Lee	2	20	1887-1903
Smith	Cary A.	3	10	1903-1915
Smith	Charles	1	28	1878-1887
Smith	Charles	1	63	1878-1887
Smith	Charles Wesley	4	306	1907-1916
Smith	Charmian Elvira	4	177	1907-1916
Smith	Cora	1	27	1878-1887
Smith	C. Ethel	1	67	1878-1887
Smith	Della Irena	2	55	1887-1903
Smith	Ethel	2	75	1887-1903
Smith	Flossie Jane	2	110	1887-1903
Smith	George Edgar	2	114	1887-1903
Smith	George James	4	565	1907-1916
Smith	Georgia Lee	2	7	1887-1903
Smith	George Andrew	4	275	1907-1916
Smith	George Wesley	4	451	1907-1916
Smith	James F.	4	408	1907-1916
Smith	Kitty	1	10	1878-1887
Smith	Lee Nora	2	49	1887-1903
Smith	Logan	3	92	1903-1915
Smith	Louis E.	4	603	1907-1916
Smith	Louis Harrison	2	26	1887-1903
Smith	Martha E.	3	27	1903-1915
Smith	Mary Rosa	1	71	1878-1887

CALHOUN COUNTY BIRTHS

Surname	Given Name	Book	Page	Year
Smith	Melroy	2	44	1887-1903
Smith	Merle Leonard	4	63	1907-1916
Smith	Nancy Jane	4	424	1907-1916
Smith	Orio	1	27	1878-1887
Smith	O.T.	3	181	1903-1915
Smith	Robert B.	2	128	1887-1903
Smith	Ryman Otis	4	232	1907-1916
Smith	Stanley Allen	2	21	1887-1903
Smith	Stephen	1	10	1878-1887
Smith	Stephen	1	6	1878-1887
Smith	Theresa Marie	2	85	1887-1903
Smith	Walter Willard	4	357	1907-1916
Smyth	Amy Theresa	1	65	1878-1887
Smyth	John Herman	2	34	1887-1903
Smyth	Mary Gertrude	1	55	1878-1887
Smythe	Dee Lawrence	2	39	1887-1903
Snider		2	93	1887-1903
Snider	Allen D.	1	77	1878-1887
Snider	Daisy Leonora	3	68	1903-1915
Snider	Elmer T.	2	104	1887-1903
Snider	Everett Earl	2	98	1887-1903
Snider	Flora Temple	2	11	1887-1903
Snider	George Harrison	2	39	1887-1903
Snider	Ida Magdaline	4	347	1907-1916
Snider	James William	1	76	1878-1887
Snider	John Leonard	2	91	1887-1903
Snider	Lecty Mytle	2	18	1887-1903
Snider	Nancy Eva	4	197	1907-1916
Snider	Opel F.	4	475	1907-1916
Snider	Theodore R.	2	104	1887-1903
Snider	Viola Sloane	4	407	1907-1916
Snow	Andrew J.	1	60	1878-1887
Snow	Letha Maxine	4	517	1907-1916
Snow	Lillie Opal	4	296	1907-1916
Snow	Olin	2	48	1887-1903

CALHOUN COUNTY BIRTHS

Surname	Given Name	Book	Page	Year
Snow	Oma A.	2	1	1887-1903
Snyder		2	12	1887-1903
Snyder	Albert Marion	3	71	1903-1915
Snyder	Clarence A.	4	116	1907-1916
Snyder	Edward Marion	1	75	1878-1887
Snyder	Hendrenna	1	11	1878-1887
Snyder	Jerome Harry	3	91	1903-1915
Snyder	John	2	57	1887-1903
Snyder	Joseph Alfred	2	58	1887-1903
Snyder	Joseph A.	2	15	1887-1903
Snyder	Josephine	2	38	1887-1903
Snyder	Lillian	3	230	1903-1915
Snyder	Rebecca A.	1	61	1878-1887
Snyder	Vincent Otto	4	534	1907-1916
Snyder	Wilhelm	1	74	1878-1887
Snyders	Anna Marcella	4	210	1907-1916
Snyders	Annie	2	31	1887-1903
Snyders	August Antone	1	20	1878-1887
Snyders	Cyril	4	573	1907-1916
Snyders	Harry John	4	211	1907-1916
Snyders	Homer Rob	4	231	1907-1916
Snyders	Hubert Henry	4	375	1907-1916
Snyders	Jacob	2	108	1887-1903
Snyders	James Marvin	4	51	1907-1916
Snyders	John Paul	2	127	1887-1903
Snyders	Margierite Dorma	4	401	1907-1916
Snyders	Mary F.	2	19	1887-1903
Snyders	Paul Spencer	4	14	1907-1916
Snyders	Robert Leo	3	218	1903-1915
Snyders	Rosa	2	27	1887-1903
Sommer	Joseph	2	28	1887-1903
Southworth	Ethel E.	1	21	1878-1887
Spang		4	428	1907-196
Spang		4	543	1907-1916
Spanger	Charles Francis	1	30	1878-1887

CALHOUN COUNTY BIRTHS

Surname	Given Name	Book	Page	Year
Spencer	Virginia E.	4	196	1907-1916
Springer	Harry Mortland	1	63	1878-1887
Springstun	Ruby Lillian	2	120	1887-1903
Sprong	Dorothy Marie	3	60	1903-1915
Sprong	Waltman S.	4	268	1907-1916
Squier		1	38	1878-1887
Squier		3	53	1903-1915
Squier	Maud Brown	1	8	1878-1887
Squier	Ora Elizabeth	4	246	1907-1916
Staats		4	213	1907-1916
Stafford	Anizi	2	121	1887-1903
Stahl	Cecilia Anna	4	202	1907-1916
Stahl	Mary	3	60	1903-1915
Stahl	Rosaline	4	419	1907-1916
Starer	Dinah (Twin)	2	23	1887-1903
Starer	Dorah (Twin)	2	23	1887-1903
Starer	Sarah	2	23	1887-1903
Starkey		3	234	1903-1915
Starkey	Mabel	2	120	1887-1903
Starkey	Wesley	4	104	1907-1916
Stearns	Henry Jackson	4	185	1907-1916
Stearns	Pauline F.	4	404	1907-1916
Stearns	Paul	4	405	1907-1916
Steed	Martha Myrtle	2	108	1887-1903
Steinberg		3	239	1903-1915
Steinberg	Alice Elizabeth	4	100	1907-1916
Steinberg	Casper	4	385	1907-1916
Steinberg	Edith	4	269	1907-1916
Steinberg	Gladys	3	96	1903-1915
Stelbrink	(Still Born)	3	287	1903-1915
Stelbrink	Cecila	4	5	1907-1916
Stelbrink	John Alfred	2	78	1887-1903
Stelbrink	Joseph A.	2	121	1887-1903
Stelbrink	William A.	2	100	1887-1903
Stemmons	Helen Elizabeth	3	183	1903-1915

CALHOUN COUNTY BIRTHS

Surname	Given Name	Book	Page	Year
Stephens	Erna Marie	4	246	1907-1916
Sternes	Flossie Marie	2	94	1887-1903
Sternes	Thomas P.	3	28	1903-1915
Stewart		3	2	1903-1915
Stilbrink	Jerome	4	484	1907-1916
Stiles		4	468	1907-1916
Stiles		4	432	1907-1916
Stiles		2	42	1887-1903
Stiles	(Twin)			1887-1903
Stiles	Daisy M.	2	82	1887-1903
Stiles	Earl (Twin)	4	432	1907-1916
Stiles	Edith Irene	2	41	1887-1903
Stillbrink	Edward	3	113	1903-1915
Stimmon	Virgil Harold	3	199	1903-1915
Stinett	Harriett Marie	4	221	1907-1916
Stinneth	Virgell	4	47	1907-1916
Stinneth	(Still Born)	3	274	1903-1915
Stinneth	William Gordon	3	179	1903-1915
Stone		1	47	1878-1887
Stone		2	48	1887-1903
Stone	Helena Cornell	2	7	1887-1903
Stone	Milton A.	2	27	1887-1903
Struman	Georgia Irene	2	127	1887-1903
Stumbaugh	Minnie L.	2	54	1887-1903
Stumpf	Agnes Josephine	4	313	1907-1916
Stumpf	Albert	4	30	1907-1916
Stumpf	Andrew Rueben	2	26	1887-1903
Stumpf	Elsie Marie Elizabeth	4	168	1907-1916
Stumpf	Erma L.	4	549	1907-1916
Stumpf	George	2	48	1887-1903
Stumpf	Pauline A.	2	124	1887-1903
Styers	Ralph	2	115	1887-1903
Sudbrack	Florence	2	51	1887-1903
Suhling		2	60	1887-1903
Suhling		1	48	1887-1887

Surname	Given Name	Book	Page	Year
Suhling	Clarence John	4	258	1907-1916
Suhling	Dorothy Jeannette	4	79	1907-1916
Suhling	Gordon	1	63	1878-1887
Suhling	John Peter	1	63	1878-1887
Sum	Dennis	1	41	1878-1887
Summ	Francis	1	20	1878-1887
Summy	Pearl Maria	3	226	1903-1915
Surbeck	Frances Levina	4	131	1907-1916
Surgeon		2	27	1887-1903
Surgeon	Ames Boyd	2	68	1887-1903
Surgeon	Charles W.	1	36	1878-1887
Surgeon	Harry Claude	4	548	1907-1916
Surgeon	James Eussell	2	2	1878-1887
Surgeon	John Douglas	2	43	1878-1887
Surgeon	J. William	3	220	1903-1915
Surgeon	Kenneth Lamont	4	178	1907-1916
Surgeon	Martha M.	2	91	1878-1887
Surgeon	Myrtle E.	1	67	1903-1915
Sutter		1	88	1903-1915
Sutter		2	101	1887-1903
Sutter	John B.	3	166	1903-1915
Sutton	Anna Margaret	4	540	1907-1916
Sutton	Arnold Edward	4	508	1907-1916
Sutton	Bitha Arnold	4	182	1907-1916
Sutton	Carl Fred	4	52	1907-1916
Sutton	Edward Logan	2	124	1887-1903
Sutton	Flora Alma	3	147	1903-1915
Sutton	Frances Emmert	4	425	1907-1916
Sutton	Joseph Lee	4	549	1907-1916
Sutton	Lettie	4	305	1907-1916
Sutton	Mary Malinda	1	19	1878-1887
Sutton	Nola Erma	3	191	1903-1915
Sutton	Viola	4	460	1907-1916
Sutton	Zola Charles	4	56	1907-1916
Swan		4	402	1907-1916

CALHOUN COUNTY BIRTHS

Surname	Given Name	Book	Page	Year
Swan	Charles	3	222	1903-1915
Swan	Charles William	2	36	1887-1903
Swan	Douglass Harry	4	318	1907-1916
Swan	James Andrew	2	97	1887-1903
Swan	Mary Elizabeth	4	244	1907-1916
Swan	Mildred Ethel	4	201	1907-1916
Swan	Rose A.	3	12	1903-1915
Swarnes	Annie May	2	50	1887-1903
Swarnes	Jackson	2	12	1887-1903
Swearingin		4	45	1907-1916
Swearingin		4	465	1907-1916
Swearingin		4	11	1907-1916
Swearingin	Emil Vernon	4	161	1907-1916
Swearingin	Golda May	2	79	1887-1903
Swearingin	Harry M.	2	63	1887-1903
Swearingin	Herman	3	55	1903-1915
Swearingin	Howard Allen	4	358	1907-1916
Swearingin	James Allen	4	171	1907-1916
Swearingin	Lilly May	2	119	1887-1903
Swearingin	Nellie	3	263	1903-1915
Swearingin	Oloy Monrow	2	67	1887-1903
Sweeden		2	69	1887-1903
Sweeney		4	442	1907-1916
Sweeney	Andrew Stillman	4	601	1907-1916
Sweeney	Irene Alice	4	600	1907-1916
Sweeney	Mariah	1	36	1878-1887
Sweeney	Mary M.	2	1	1887-1903
Sweeten		2	95	1887-1903
Sweeten	Bessie May	3	57	1903-1915
Sweeten	Mary Irene	2	105	1887-1903
Sweeten		2	82	1887-1903
Sweeten	Bridges	2	74	1887-1903
Sweetman	Alfred Abraham	2	103	1887-1903
Sweetman	Everett James	3	166	1903-1915
Sweetman	Fay Edna	4	103	1907-1916

CALHOUN COUNTY BIRTHS

Surname	Given Name	Book	Page	Year
Sweetman	Florence Irene	2	129	1887-1903
Sweetman	Ford R.	4	602	1907-1916
Sweetman	Howard C.	2	110	1887-1903
Sweetman	Mary Anna	3	168	1903-1915
Sweetman	Racheal Ellen	2	78	1887-1903
Swift		2	61	1887-1903
Swift	George William	3	153	1903-1915
Swift	William	2	44	1887-1903
Synn	Louis Murph	1	7	1878-1887
Tadlock	Bessie M.	3	11	1903-1915
Tadlock	Thelma Leona	4	271	1907-1916
Taipon	Joseph Paul	2	51	1887-1903
Talbert		4	254	1907-1916
Talbert	Dora Luvina	4	90	1907-1916
Talbert	Mary Bernice	4	43	1907-1916
Talbort	Marion Lislee August	3	146	1903-1915
Talbot	Frances Otilla	4	9	1907-1916
Talley	Frances	2	37	1887-1903
Tannehill	George E.	1	49	1878-1887
Tapin	Anna Maria	1	75	1878-1887
Tavanah	Nellie V.	2	14	1887-1903
Tavener		4	398	1907-1916
Tavener	Edward	1	64	1878-1887
Tavenier	Dorothy	3	35	1903-1915
Tavenier	Ida May	2	31	1887-1903
Tavenier	Ione Cecil	3	199	1903-1915
Tavenier	Louis Theodore	1	56	1878-1887
Tavenier	Stella Irene	2	97	1887-1903
Tavernier		3	276	1903-1915
Tavernier	Louis Francis	2	105	1887-1903
Taviner	Stephen J.	1	35	1878-1887
Taylor		2	72	1887-1903
Taylor		2	73	1887-1903
Taylor	Lola (Twin)	3	39	1903-1915
Taylor	Lorie (Twin)	3	39	1903-1915

CALHOUN COUNTY BIRTHS

Surname	Given Name	Book	Page	Year
Tayon		1	75	1878-1887
Tayon	Clara Joannes	2	41	1887-1903
Tayon	Joseph Paul	2	51	1887-1903
Tayon	William Jasper	2	5	1887-1903
Telkamp	(Still Born)	3	271	1903-1915
Telkamp	Catherine	2	56	1887-1903
Telkamp	Catherine	2	68	1887-1903
Telkamp	Henry Barney	3	31	1903-1915
Telkamp	Matias Joseph	2	99	1887-1903
Telkamp	Rosa Ann	4	148	1907-1916
Telkamp	Theodore Joseph	1	59	1878-1887
Telkamp	Veronica	3	51	1903-1915
Temple		4	139	1907-1916
Temple	Alberta	3	32	1903-1915
Temple	Arthur	4	120	1907-1916
Temple	Charles Beverly	3	238	1903-1915
Tepen	Edwin Herman	4	548	1907-1916
Tepen	Elmer John	4	430	1907-1916
Tepen	Frederick Burnett	4	291	1907-1916
Tepen	Freieda Elizabeth	3	43	1903-1915
Tepen	Herman Lucas	4	56	1907-1916
Tepen	John William	2	31	1887-1903
Tepen	Katherine	2	33	1887-1903
Tepen	Leonard John	4	64	1907-1916
Tepen	Mary Katherine	3	133	1903-1915
Tepen	Paul T.	4	264	1907-1916
Tepen	Rose	3	141	1903-1915
Tepen	William Bernard	4	556	1907-1916
Tepen	William Lucas	4	339	1907-1916
Teppen		2	128	1887-1903
Teppen	Teresa	2	114	1887-1903
Terneus		4	431	1907-1916
Terneus	George Allen	4	204	1907-1916
Terneus	Myrtle	4	325	1907-1916
Terpin	Louis	1	5	1878-1887

CALHOUN COUNTY BIRTHS

Surname	Given Name	Book	Page	Year
Terry	Wilard	2	90	1887-1903
Tharp		1	58	1878-1887
Tharp	Bessie Mildred	3	162	1903-1915
Tharp	Claude Francis	1	68	1878-1887
Tharp	Cora Effie	2	2	1887-1903
Tharp	Francis Marcellus	1	58	1878-1887
Tharp	James Bryan	2	77	1887-1903
Tharp	Nancy A.	1	25	1878-1887
Tharp	Oscar J.	1	31	1878-1887
Thatcher	Mary C.	2	5	1887-1903
Thias	Charles William	1	68	1878-1887
Thomas	(Still Born)	3	278	1903-1915
Thomas	Donald	3	58	1903-1915
Thomas	Frederick Frank	2	103	1887-1903
Thomas	Hubert Ray	2	21	1887-1903
Thomas	James Clyde	4	474	1907-1916
Thomas	Jesse Raymond	3	95	1903-1915
Thomas	William Edward	4	18	1907-1916
Thompson	Maggie	2	18	1887-1903
Thurston		2	125	1887-1903
Tilley	E. Ruby	3	45	1903-1915
Tillotson	Phillis Katherine	4	332	1907-1916
Tilly	Harold William	2	129	1887-1903
Titus	Harry	4	497	1907-1916
Titus	Helen Lucille	3	46	1903-1915
Titus	Raymond	3	200	1903-1915
Todd	Fred	3	65	1903-1915
Todd	Herbert	3	206	1903-1915
Todd	James Edward	1	24	1887-1903
Todd	Quincy Ben	2	74	1887-1903
Todd	Raymond Macaraine	2	46	1887-1903
Todd	Ruby Lee	2	98	1887-1903
Todd	Stephen Hillman	4	238	1907-1916
Tolbert	Anna Irene	4	506	1907-1916
Tolbert	Emial Amelious	2	61	1887-1903

CALHOUN COUNTY BIRTHS

Surname	Given Name	Book	Page	Year
Tolbert	Evert V.	2	44	1887-1903
Tolbert	Herman William	4	353	1907-1916
Tolbert	Opal Pauline	3	50	1903-1915
Tolbert	Royal Bluford	1	28	1887-1903
Tolbert	William Kenneth	4	574	1907-1916
Toles		1	2	1878-1887
Toll	Guy Leroy	3	160	1903-1915
Toll	James Parker	3	234	1903-1915
Townsend		1	61	1878-1887
Tozier		2	100	1887-1903
Tozier	Ray Becker	2	81	1887-1903
Traufler		4	282	1907-1916
Traufler	Mary	2	42	1887-1903
Traufler	Peter	2	20	1887-1903
Tribble	Edith Alice	2	26	1887-1903
Tribble	Fester C.	3	13	1903-1915
Tribble	Mary Jane	4	16	1907-1916
Trobridge		2	91	1887-1903
Trobridge		1	55	1878-1887
Trobridge		2	98	1887-1903
Trobridge		2	105	1887-1903
Trowbridge		1	11	1878-1887
Trowbridge	Edna	4	21	1907-1916
Trowbridge	Norman Elmer	4	224	1907-1916
Trowbridge	Raymond S.	3	61	1903-1915
Trunnek	Evelena	1	23	1878-1887
Turnbeaugh	Essie Samantha	1	22	1878-1887
Turnbull	(Still Born)	3	275	1903-1915
Turnbull	Benjamin Ralph	4	12	1907-1916
Turnbull	Martin Hubert	3	63	1903-1915
Turnbull	Mildred E.	4	264	1907-1916
Turner		1	27	1878-1887
Turner		4	388	1907-1916
Turner	Charles L.	2	26	1887-1903
Turner	Isaac Marion	2	4	1887-1903

CALHOUN COUNTY BIRTHS

Surname	Given Name	Book	Page	Year
Turner	John Somers	2	33	1887-1903
Turner	Juanita	4	299	1907-1916
Turner	Sarah Bain	1	6	1878-1887
Turner	William Ernest	2	44	1887-1903
Turner	William Elmer	2	8	1887-1903
Turner	William F.	4	458	1907-1916
Turpin	Winnie Margaret	4	513	1907-1916
Twichell		1	39	1878-1887
Twichell		1	67	1878-1887
Twichell	Alonza	1	32	1878-1887
Twichell	Amy Pearl	2	75	1887-1903
Twichell	Clara Edna	3	186	1903-1915
Twichell	Donald Querin	2	123	1887-1903
Twichell	Edna Dorothy	2	19	1887-1903
Twichell	Flora Mae	1	16	1878-1887
Twichell	Joseph E.	1	72	1878-1887
Twichell	Leonard	2	49	1887-1903
Twichell	Lonnie E.	1	73	1878-1887
Twichell	Marjorie Maebella	4	16	1907-1916
Twichell	Maud Lee	1	66	1878-1887
Twichell	Maud Lee	1	60	1878-1887
Twichell	Oscar	2	28	1887-1903
Twichell	Overton	1	20	1878-1887
Twichell	Ross Ernest	2	130	1887-1903
Twichell	Sharon E.	3	141	1903-1915
Twitchell	Serilda Ann	1	19	1878-1887
Twitchell	Lyman E.	4	211	1907-1916
Twitchell	Othmer Carrol	4	322	1907-1916
Twitchell	Valeria Ione	4	441	1907-1916
Twitchell	Walter V.	2	3	1887-1903
Tyon	Gevert	2	18	1887-1903
Tyon	James Olvier	1	62	1878-1887
Ufer	Arthur	2	59	1887-1903
Ufer	William Herman	2	92	1887-1903
Ulery		3	245	1903-1915

CALHOUN COUNTY BIRTHS

Surname	Given Name	Book	Page	Year
Ulery		1	41	1878-1887
Ulery		4	236	1907-1916
Ulery	Dorothy Mae	4	517	1907-1916
Ulery	Edna Marie	4	249	1907-1916
Ulery	George W.	1	28	1878-1887
Ulery	Joseph G.	4	324	1907-1916
Ulery	Linley Lee	3	218	1903-1915
Ulery	Nellie Marie	4	25	1907-1916
Ulery	Noah Marion	2	84	1887-1903
Ulery	Osie Amanda	4	264	1907-1916
Ulery	Peter W.	4	545	1907-1916
Ulshoefer	Barbara Louisa	2	30	1887-1903
Underwood		4	427	1907-1916
Underwood		4	30	1907-1916
Underwood		1	65	1878-1887
Underwood	Flossie Louisiana	4	197	1907-1916
Underwood	Stephen D.	2	6	1887-1903
Vanarsdale	Charles Edward Augustus	4	59	1907-1916
Vanarsdale	Stephen Calvin	4	59	1907-1916
Vaughan	Robert E. Lee	2	85	1887-1903
Vaughn	Margaret	4	487	1907-1916
Vermillion		1	49	1878-1887
Vetter		4	48	1907-1916
Vetter		4	109	1907-1916
Vetter		3	193	1903-1915
Vetter		4	349	1907-1916
Vetter		2	106	1887-1903
Vetter		3	2	1903-1915
Vetter	(Still Born)	3	279	1903-1915
Vetter	(Still Born)	3	261	1903-1915
Vetter	(Still Born)	3	264	1903-1915
Vetter	Christian J.	1	32	1878-1887
Vetter	Gertie Sylva	2	113	1887-1903
Vetter	Goldie Freda	3	76	1903-1915
Vetter	Joseph	1	70	1878-1887

CALHOUN COUNTY BIRTHS

Surname	Given Name	Book	Page	Year
Vetter	Olin Joseph	4	440	1907-1916
Vetter	Ruby Rose	4	570	1907-1916
Vetter	Sebert E.	3	102	1903-1915
Vetter	William F.	4	493	1907-1916
Vetter	William Harrison	4	294	1907-1916
Vickroy	Charles Densmore	2	101	1878-1903
Vickroy	Clarence Wilbert	2	87	1887-1903
Vier	Anna Pearl	3	22	1903-1915
Vogal	Leonard Lawrence	4	217	1907-1916
Vogelpohl	Emma Mary	4	113	1907-1916
Voyles		3	129	1903-1915
Wagener	Henry	2	107	1887-1903
Waggle		2	46	1887-1903
Waggoner	Howard E.	2	88	1887-1903
Wagner		4	532	1907-1916
Wagner		2	107	1887-1903
Wagner	Amos Clemens	2	106	1887-1903
Wagner	Bernice Catherine	4	364	1907-1916
Wagner	Elma Lorain	2	95	1887-1903
Wagner	Ema Louie	2	104	1887-1903
Wagoner	Eckert	4	514	1907-1916
Wagoner	John	4	515	1907-1916
Wagoner	Loretta	4	383	1907-1916
Wagoner	Mary	2	14	1887-1903
Wahoff		1	39	1878-1887
Waldheuser		2	87	1887-1903
Waldheuser		2	83	1887-1903
Waldheuser	Harry William	2	16	1887-1903
Waldheuser		2	26	1887-1903
Walford		3	185	1903-1915
Walkinson	Nancy Ann	1	4	1878-1887
Wall		3	192	1903-1915
Wall	Faye Lotus	4	312	1907-1916
Wall	Ray	4	312	1907-1916
Wallace	Mary Elizabeth	2	27	1887-1903

CALHOUN COUNTY BIRTHS

Surname	Given Name	Book	Page	Year
Wallendoff	Marion Jospeh	4	92	1907-1916
Wallendorf	Cordelia Lusetta	2	57	1887-1903
Wallendorf	Luvena Bush	3	78	1903-1915
Wallendorf	Mary Ann	1	13	1878-1887
Wallendorff		3	139	1903-1915
Wallendorff	(Still Born)	3	279	1903-1915
Wallendorff	Doris	4	270	1907-1916
Wallendorff	Gilbert P.	4	1	1907-1916
Wallendorff	Hortense	3	116	1903-1915
Wallendorff	Ida	1	27	1878-1887
Wallendorff	John August	4	93	1907-1916
Wallendorff	Lucille	2	114	1887-1903
Wallendorff	Lymon C.	4	187	1907-1916
Walls	Arnold W.	4	400	1907-1916
Walls	Edna Elene	4	447	1907-1916
Walls	Gladys Mae	4	533	1907-1916
Walls	Larned Alfred	2	119	1887-1903
Walls	Mildred Etta	2	105	1887-1903
Walton	Earl	2	73	1887-1903
Ward		1	20	1878-1887
Ward	Alta May	1	72	1878-1887
Ward	Charles Allen	1	4	1878-1887
Ward	George Oliver	4	216	1907-1916
Ward	Mary Inez	2	37	1887-1903
Ward	Mary J.	2	116	1887-1903
Warner		4	583	1907-1916
Waters		4	587	1907-1916
Waters		4	423	1907-1916
Waters	(Still Born)	3	284	1903-1915
Waters	Iva Arvilla	4	344	1907-1916
Waters	Verney Edward	4	251	1907-1916
Watson		1	61	1878-1887
Watson		4	587	1907-1916
Watson		4	584	1907-1916
Watson	Amanda	2	10	1887-1903

CALHOUN COUNTY BIRTHS

Surname	Given Name	Book	Page	Year
Watson	Arleigh Francis	2	11	1887-1903
Watson	Arleigh F.	2	14	1887-1903
Watson	Earl Francis	1	69	1878-1887
Watson	Elva Peggy	4	120	1907-1916
Watson	Gerald B.	4	444	1903-1915
Watson	Herbert E.	3	58	1903-1915
Watson	Hobert Roy	2	76	1887-1903
Watson	Isabella	3	143	1903-1915
Watson	Leslie A.	2	1	1887-1903
Watson	Mary Viola	4	460	1907-1916
Watson	Maxine	4	240	1907-1916
Watson	Melbourne	4	242	1907-1916
Watson	Odessa Fern	3	171	1903-1915
Watson	Rhoda Alberta	4	428	1907-1916
Watson	Viola Bernice	2	113	1887-1903
Watters	Lidda E.	1	9	1878-1887
Watts		4	22	1907-1916
Watts		3	21	1903-1915
Watts		2	41	1887-1903
Watts	Charles Henry	2	38	1887-1903
Watts	Earl Lee	2	79	1887-1903
Watts	Etta Olive	1	79	1878-1887
Watts	Lena Viola	2	22	1887-1903
Watts	Leroy	2	10	1887-1903
Watts	Lucille	4	446	1907-1916
Watts	Mary Luerna	2	7	1887-1903
Wease	Arthur	2	112	1887-1903
Wease	Emmaline	2	34	1887-1903
Weaver		2	37	1887-1903
Weaver	John William	2	38	1887-1903
Weaver	Joseph	2	74	1887-1903
Webb		2	42	1887-1903
Webb	Edna Lavina	4	151	1907-1916
Webb	Elma Loraine	4	329	1907-1916
Webb	Henrietta	3	251	1903-1915

CALHOUN COUNTY BIRTHS

Surname	Given Name	Book	Page	Year
Webb	Lorraine	4	319	1907-1916
Webb	Millicent Beatrice	4	344	1907-1916
Webb	Orville Skeel	3	82	1903-1915
Webb	William	4	494	1907-1916
Webster		4	205	1907-1916
Webster	Allen Paul	4	492	1907-1916
Webster	Beulah M.	4	371	1907-1916
Webster	Christopher David	4	523	1907-1916
Webster	Daisy	4	65	1907-1916
Webster	Elizabeth Martha	4	237	1907-1916
Webster	Francis M.	2	60	1887-1903
Webster	George	1	24	1878-1887
Webster	George A.A.	1	75	1878-1887
Webster	Harey A.	4	474	1907-1916
Webster	Herman	3	71	1903-1915
Webster	Irene	4	351	1907-1916
Webster	James R.	2	121	1887-1903
Webster	Noah	2	46	1887-1903
Webster	Ralph Theodore	4	42	1907-1916
Webster	Sylva Ellen	1	5	1878-1887
Webster	William	2	14	1887-1903
Weigand	Henry W.	1	30	1878-1887
Weigand	Ruby Olive	1	51	1878-1887
Weigel	(Still Born)	3	280	1903-1915
Weigel	Elda	4	472	1907-1916
Weigel	Emma Mary	4	47	1907-1916
Weigel	Emma Mary	4	592	1907-1916
Weigel	Jacob	1	2	1878-1887
Weigel	Lucile	4	128	1907-1916
Weigel	Robert	4	202	1907-1916
Weigel	Vera	4	452	1907-1916
Weigel	William Edward	4	361	1907-1916
Weiner	Ella Marie	2	110	1887-1903
Weir	Lora Florence	3	165	1903-1915
Weir	M. Blanche	2	50	1887-1903

CALHOUN COUNTY BIRTHS

Surname	Given Name	Book	Page	Year
Weishaar		4	595	1907-1916
Weishaar		3	41	1903-1915
Weishaar	Annie C.	1	15	1878-1887
Weishaar	Catherina M.	4	192	1907-1916
Weishaar	Clara	4	572	1907-1916
Weishaar	E.J.	4	343	1907-1916
Weishaar	Henry Carl	4	99	1907-1916
Weishaar	Leo August	4	307	1907-1916
Weishaar	Mary	2	118	1887-1903
Weishaupt	Agnes F.	2	106	1887-1903
Weishaupt	Albert Charles	4	332	1907-1916
Weishaupt	Beulah May	4	400	1907-1916
Weishaupt	Emmie Rosina	3	233	1903-1915
Weishaupt	Frank	3	121	1903-1915
Weishaupt	Henry	1	67	1878-1887
Weishaupt	Lola M.	4	477	1907-1916
Weishaupt	Loretta Katherine	4	157	1907-1916
Weishaupt	Rosine	2	9	1887-1903
Welch		1	61	1878-1887
Welch	Roy	2	35	1887-1903
Welling		4	562	1907-1916
Wells	Katie May	1	25	1878-1887
Welsh	William Cleo	1	74	1878-1887
Welty	(Still Born)	3	281	1903-1915
Wheeler		1	27	1878-1887
Wheeler	Charles	1	64	1878-1887
Wheeler	Clayton	2	1	1887-1903
Whisman		4	148	1907-1916
Whisman		2	94	1887-1903
Whisman		4	95	1907-1916
Whisman		3	68	1903-1915
Whisman	Clay	4	339	1907-1916
Whisman	Delbert G.	4	559	1907-1916
Whisman	Jennitta	3	17	1903-1915
Whisman	Odessa Alice	3	161	1903-1915

CALHOUN COUNTY BIRTHS

Surname	Given Name	Book	Page	Year
Whisman	Raymond Louis	2	66	1887-1903
Whisman	Sethil Tressa	2	77	1887-1903
Whisman	Velma	4	348	1907-1916
Whisman	Vera V.	4	540	1907-1916
Whisman	Verna I.	4	539	1907-1916
White		2	21	1887-1903
White		2	83	1887-1903
White	Clifford Lee	2	110	1887-1903
White	Dorothy Azuba	3	178	1903-1915
White	Fanny Elizabeth	1	4	1878-1887
White	Fay	3	155	1903-1915
White	Howard	1	23	1878-1887
White	Luda A.	1	19	1878-1887
White	Mary Alice	4	29	1907-1916
White	Ralph	2	127	1887-1903
White	Roland Dalton	3	130	1903-1915
White	John Oliver	2	72	1887-1903
Whitten		1	52	1878-1887
Whitten	Lee Clark	3	241	1903-1915
Whitten	Virgil Gordon	3	97	1903-1915
Whitton		1	38	1878-1887
Whitton	Arthur C.	1	18	1878-1887
Wiegand		1	71	1878-1887
Wiegand		1	74	1878-1887
Wiegand	Charles Clinton	2	9	1887-1903
Wiegand	Effie	1	53	1878-1887
Wiegand	Essie Estella	1	71	1878-1887
Wiegand	Mary Augusta	2	53	1887-1903
Wieneke		4	76	1907-1916
Wieneke		3	42	1903-1915
Wieneke	Anna Ellen	3	93	1903-1915
Wieneke	Charles Henry	3	196	1903-1915
Wieneke	Pearl	2	55	1887-1903
Wieneke	Rosa	2	30	1887-1903
Wieneke	William Charley	2	30	1887-1903

CALHOUN COUNTY BIRTHS

Surname	Given Name	Book	Page	Year
Wiener	Anna Barbara	4	103	1907-1916
Wiener	Clarence	3	14	1903-1915
Wiener	Ernst Jr.	4	377	1907-1916
Wiener	William C.	3	67	1903-1915
Wier	Harold Alvin	3	165	1903-1915
Wildhagen		2	52	1887-1903
Wildhagen	Fred	3	29	1903-1915
Wildhagen	James Arthur	2	77	1887-1903
Wilkinson		1	36	1878-1887
Wilkinson		1	53	1878-1887
Wilkinson	Arizona Florence	2	34	1887-1903
Wilkinson	Claude	2	44	1887-1903
Wilkinson	Floyd E.	1	64	1878-1887
Wilkinson	Francis C.	2	43	1887-1903
Wilkinson	Francis Herol	2	63	1887-1903
Wilkinson	Harry	2	41	1887-1903
Wilkinson	James Richard	2	105	1887-1903
Wilkinson	Lucy	2	80	1887-1903
Wilkinson	Natie Lee	2	62	1887-1903
Wilkinson	Rula	3	107	1903-1915
Wilkinson	Ruth Lenora	2	35	1887-1903
Wilkinson	Stella	1	14	1878-1887
Wilkinson	Stella A.	3	12	1907-1916
Wilkinson	Thelma L.	3	11	1903-1915
Willard	Claud Estil	4	392	1907-1916
Willenburg	Albert August Heinric	3	28	1903-1915
Willenburg	Edith Ida Johanna	3	201	1903-1915
Willenburg	Viola C.M.	4	188	1907-1916
Williams		1	5	1878-1887
Williams		1	29	1878-1887
Williams		2	65	1887-1903
Williams		1	77	1878-1887
Williams	Albert	1	54	1878-1887
Williams	Albert	4	417	1907-1916
Williams	Amelia Margaret	1	30	1878-1887

CALHOUN COUNTY BIRTHS

Surname	Given Name	Book	Page	Year
Williams	Benjamin Hob.	2	5	1887-1903
Williams	Cecil	2	33	1887-1903
Williams	Clayton Martin	2	59	1887-1903
Williams	Della	2	50	1887-1903
Williams	Ellis Amiel	4	64	1907-1916
Williams	Geneva Igle	4	11	1907-1916
Williams	Giles Arthur	3	97	1903-1915
Williams	Laura E.	1	77	1878-1887
Williams	Mable Luretta	1	52	1878-1887
Williams	Mary	1	42	1878-1887
Williams	May	2	84	1887-1903
Williams	Nancy Jane	1	57	1878-1887
Williams	Nettie Leota	4	413	1907-1916
Williams	Norma Lee	2	43	1887-1903
Williams	Norman Leo	4	236	1907-1916
Williams	Paul Henry	2	66	1887-1903
Williams	Ruby Jane	1	65	1878-1887
Williams	Rush	2	1	1887-1903
Williams	Sadie Bell	2	18	1887-1903
Williams	Tresa Ann	1	6	1878-1887
Williams	Violet Marie	4	400	1907-1916
Williams	Zachariah	1	4	1878-1887
Williams	Zelpha Ann	1	50	1878-1887
Williams	David F.	2	116	1887-1903
Williamsmeyer	Mary	2	127	1887-1903
Willman		1	26	1878-1887
Willman	Alexander	1	41	1878-1887
Willman	James	2	45	1887-1903
Wilson		4	171	1907-1916
Wilson		1	76	1878-1887
Wilson		3	56	1903-1915
Wilson	(Still Born)	3	267	1903-1915
Wilson	Addie May	2	73	1887-1903
Wilson	Bertha Leona	2	109	1887-1903
Wilson	Birthie Clyde	1	44	1878-1887

CALHOUN COUNTY BIRTHS

Surname	Given Name	Book	Page	Year
Wilson	Byrle E.	4	500	1907-1916
Wilson	Charles E.	2	13	1887-1903
Wilson	Clara Frances	4	554	1907-1916
Wilson	Clora	1	47	1878-1887
Wilson	Dona	1	49	1878-1887
Wilson	Elba	4	461	1907-1916
Wilson	Geneva L.	4	327	1907-1916
Wilson	IrL	2	33	1887-1903
Wilson	James	2	128	1887-1903
Wilson	James Martin	1	15	1878-1887
Wilson	Jesse M.	2	69	1887-1903
Wilson	John H.	2	12	1887-1903
Wilson	John Timothy	1	28	1878-1887
Wilson	Lela Malie	3	223	1903-1915
Wilson	Levi Raymond	3	110	1903-1915
Wilson	Lillian	1	155	1903-1915
Wilson	Lyle Avery	2	52	1887-1903
Wilson	Martha E.	2	2	1887-1903
Wilson	Mary	2	103	1887-1903
Wilson	Mary Elizabeth	4	269	1907-1916
Wilson	Mary N.	2	48	1887-1903
Wilson	Nancy Elizabeth	1	4	1878-1887
Wilson	Nella E.	1	44	1878-1887
Wilson	Orville Russell	4	295	1907-1916
Wilson	Percy Willard	2	107	1887-1903
Wilson	Rachael J.	1	61	1878-1887
Wilson	Robert Clark	4	24	1907-1916
Wilson	Robert W.	2	14	1887-1903
Wilson	Rosa Belle	1	78	1878-1887
Wilson	Rose Ette	2	93	1887-1903
Wilson	Ruben Wesley	2	32	1887-1903
Wilson	Sarah Louise	4	89	1907-1916
Wilson	Silas Alfred	2	10	1887-1903
Wilson	Silas Jesse	2	75	1887-1903
Wilson	Stella Leona	1	64	1878-1887

CALHOUN COUNTY BIRTHS

Surname	Given Name	Book	Page	Year
Wilson	William Martin	1	77	1878-1887
Wilson	William Otto	2	82	1887-1903
Wimer		3	270	1903-1915
Winchen		2	13	1887-1903
Winchen		2	25	1887-1903
Windmiller	Ray Gilbert	4	293	1907-1916
Wineland	Annie Adelia	2	34	1887-1903
Wineland	Hollis Fredinano	4	21	1907-1916
Wineland	Holly Florence	4	21	1907-1916
Wineland	Lavina Faith	2	107	1887-1903
Wineland	Lillian	2	47	1887-1903
Wineland	Nellie Mabel	3	80	1903-1915
Wineland	Nola Irene	4	450	1907-1916
Wineland	Norman Lee	4	283	1907-1916
Wing	Hazel Rosa	2	52	1887-1903
Wing	William Orlo	2	42	1887-1903
Winkler		1	55	1878-1887
Winkler		4	296	1907-1916
Winkler		1	69	1878-1887
Winkler	Eva Matilda	3	257	1903-1915
Winkler	John	1	31	1878-1887
Winkler	Julia Virginia	4	566	1907-1916
Winkler	Lena Mary	4	172	1907-1916
Winkler	Paul W.	4	466	1907-1916
Winsell		4	330	1907-1916
Wintgen		4	11	1907-1916
Wintgen	Ina B.	4	9	1907-1916
Wintgen	Mary Lucille	4	579	1907-1916
Wintjen		2	2	1887-1903
Wintjen		4	550	1907-1916
Wintjen		4	143	1907-1916
Wintjen		2	80	1887-1903
Wintjen	Alvin Wesley	4	436	1907-1916
Wintjen	Anna Marcetis	4	388	1907-1916
Wintjen	Charles Richard	2	102	1887-1903

CALHOUN COUNTY BIRTHS

Surname	Given Name	Book	Page	Year
Wintjen	Dorothy E.	4	390	1907-1916
Wintjen	Everett	4	100	1907-1916
Wintjen	Genevieve Elanora	4	584	1907-1916
Wintjen	James Andrew	4	143	1907-1916
Wintjen	Laura	4	293	1907-1916
Wintjen	Letha Leona	3	250	1903-1915
Wintjen	Mourna	4	437	1907-1916
Wintjen	Oberton	3	112	1903-1915
Wintjen	Thalah	4	538	1907-1916
Wintjen	Winnie	2	124	1887-1903
Wintzin	Israel William	2	9	1887-1903
Wirth		1	65	1878-1887
Wirth	Gerome	4	383	1907-1916
Wirth	Joseph	4	382	1907-1916
Wistman	Beulah	4	514	1907-1916
Withaut		1	53	1878-1887
Wittmond	Carl H.	3	129	1903-1915
Wittmond	Clara Irene	4	311	1907-1916
Wittmond	Lena	2	30	1887-1903
Wittmond	Mary Bernadette	3	244	1903-1915
Woeful	John W.	1	60	1878-1887
Woehler	Anna Matilda	2	102	1887-1903
Woehler	Louisa (Still Born)	3	273	1903-1915
Woehler	Martin	3	70	1903-1915
Woelfel	Catherine Marie	4	62	1907-1916
Woelfel	George William	2	123	1887-1903
Woelfel	George Henry	2	36	1887-1903
Woelfel	Helena A.	2	21	1887-1903
Woelfel	Henry August	4	301	1907-1916
Woelfel	Marie Elizabeth	4	549	1907-1916
Woelfel	Mary Josephine	2	92	1887-1903
Woelfel	Rose Annie	2	6	1887-1903
Wood		2	10	1887-1903
Woodard	George Arthur	4	160	1907-1916
Woodard	Joseph R.	1	23	1878-1887

CALHOUN COUNTY BIRTHS

Surname	Given Name	Book	Page	Year
Woodeard		4	252	1907-1916
Woodeard	John Alonzo	4	535	1907-1916
Woodeard	Mary Alzina	4	331	1907-1916
Woodworth	Charles Henry	3	137	1903-1915
Woodworth	Clara M.	4	37	1907-1916
Workman		4	587	1907-1916
Workman	Anna Dorothy	3	123	1903-1915
Workman	Edith P. Jane	2	47	1887-1903
Workman	Mabel Lucile	2	66	1887-1903
Workman	William	2	92	1887-1903
Wright	Franklin P.	4	499	1907-1916
Wright	Oliver C.	4	357	1907-1916
Wurtz	Jennie E.	2	109	1887-1903
Younglove	Roy D.	2	50	1887-1903
Zahrli		1	74	1878-1887
Zahrli	Clarence Henry	4	193	1907-1916
Zahrli	Fred (Twin)	1	23	1878-1887
Zahrli	Louisa (Twin)	1	23	1878-1887
Zahrli	Nellie	2	37	1887-1903
Zigrand	Junita	4	116	1907-1916
Zigrang		3	142	1903-1915
Zigrang	Addelle Theresa Olive	3	249	1903-1915
Zigrang	Alfred Marion	2	117	1887-1903
Zigrang	Carl Otto	1	74	1878-1887
Zigrang	Carmen Izella	2	120	1887-1903
Zigrang	Cecilia Bernice	4	374	1907-1916
Zigrang	Helena May	4	343	1907-1916
Zigrang	Henry O.	1	60	1878-1887
Zigrang	Homer George	4	173	1907-1916
Zigrang	Lois	4	475	1907-1916
Zigrang	Ole Paul	4	126	1907-1916
Zigrang	Thelma L.	4	457	1907-1916
Zigrang	Theresa	1	16	1878-1887
Zigrang	Theresa Maria	4	187	1907-1916
Zigrang	Vencent D.	4	591	1907-1916

CALHOUN COUNTY BIRTHS

Surname	Given Name	Book	Page	Year
Zigrang	Vera Alice	4	178	1907-1916
Zigrang	Walter Dominic	2	79	1887-1903
Zimmerman		1	6	1878-1887
Zimmerman	Alice Mary	4	218	1907-1916
Zimmerman	Henry	4	526	1907-1916
Zimmerman	Katie	4	360	1907-1916
Zimmerman	Margaret Alma	4	199	1907-1916
Zipprich		2	40	1887-1903
Zipprich		4	96	1907-1916
Zipprich		4	253	1907-1916
Zipprich	Adan Frantz	1	66	1878-1887
Zipprich	Alfred Peter	4	499	1907-1916
Zipprich	Charles Joseph	1	59	1878-1887
Zipprich	Edward Frank	4	546	1907-1916
Zipprich	Frederick William	2	48	1887-1903
Zipprich	Helen Catherine	4	226	1907-1916
Zipprich	Henry Tony	4	6	1907-1916
Zipprich	John	2	30	1887-1903
Zipprich	John Frantz	2	4	1887-1903
Zipprich	Karl Joseph	1	41	1878-1887
Zipprich	Leonard (Twin)	1	30	1878-1887
Zipprich	Frank (Twin)	1	30	1878-1887
Zipprich	Margaret Mary	2	20	1887-1903
Zipprich	Martha Marie	4	360	1907-1916
Zipprich	Oswin Joseph	2	92	1887-1903
Zipprich	Peter Joseph	1	57	1878-1887
Zipprich	Petronilla W.	3	248	1903-1915
Zipprich	Rosa B.	4	117	1907-1916
Zumalt		4	134	1907-1916
Zumalt	Robbie Lee	4	551	1907-1916
Zumalwt	Lee	3	80	1903-1915
Zumalwt	Lethia	3	80	1903-1915
Zumwalt	Beula Cordelia	4	317	1907-1916
Zumwalt	Elmore Aluernice	2	74	1887-1903
Zumwalt	Irene Marie	4	289	1907-1916
Zumwalt	Pearl Belle	4	465	1907-1916

Calhoun County Deaths

1878 - 1915

CALHOUN COUNTY DEATHS

Surname	Given Name	Book	Page	Year
Abbott	Joseph WM.	1 & 2	11	1878-1903
Adams	Alonzo	3	86	1903-1910
Adams	Joseph	4	41	1910-1915
Adams	Sarah J.	1 & 2	45	1878-1903
Aderton	Amelia Jane	1 & 2	2	1878-1903
Aderton	George L.	3	82	1903-1910
Aderton	Henry K.	1 & 2	71	1878-1903
Ahrens	August	1 & 2	54	1878-1903
Alexander	Harriet L.	1 & 2	11	1878-1903
Alexander	Lilly A.	1 & 2	29	1878-1903
Algro	Margret	3	49	1903-1910
Aling	Elizabeth	4	94	1910-1915
Allen	Henry A.	1 & 2	65	1878-1903
Allen	Mary C.	1 & 2	28	1878-1903
Allen	Nathan Nelson	1 & 2	15	1878-1903
Almond	James	1 & 2	75	1878-1903
Altizer	A. Henry	3	12	1903-1910
Altizer		1 & 2	22	1878-1903
Altizer		4	79	1910-1915
Ambrose	Eliza	3	109	1903-1910
Ammott	William	3	186	1903-1910
Anderson	Fidella	1 & 2	7	1878-1903
Anderson	James C.	1 & 2	26	1878-1903
Anderson	John W.	3	73	1903-1910
Anderson	Martha	1 & 2	22	1878-1903
Anderson	Myrtle E.	3	74	1903-1910
Anderson	Wesley	3	97	1903-1910
Andrea	Edwin	3	16	1903-1910
Andrews	Catherine	1 & 2	2	1878-1903
Andrews	Grace	3	142	1903-1910
Andrews	Sue	1 & 2	13	1878-1903
Angel	Harvey	3	122	1903-1910
Angel	Margaret E.	1 & 2	30	1878-1903
Annott	Philip	1 & 2	9	1878-1903
Ansell	Albert Louis	4	58	1910-1915

CALHOUN COUNTY DEATHS

Surname	Given Name	Book	Page	Year
Ansell	Chas. A	1 & 2	34	1878-1903
Ansell	Ellen	1 & 2	9	1878-1903
Ansell	Francis	3	92	1903-1910
Ansell	J.J.	1 & 2	47	1878-1903
Ansell	John E.	3	148	1903-1910
Ansell	Louisa	1 & 2	76	1878-1903
Ansell	Malachia W.	1 & 2	19	1878-1903
Anthony	Amanda	1 & 2	13	1878-1903
Arende	Kattie	3	65	1903-1910
Argust	Arthur W.	1 & 2	37	1878-1903
Arling	Mary	1 & 2	35	1878-1903
Armentrout	Mary M.	1 & 2	14	1878-1903
Arnold	Lawrence	3	167	1903-1910
Arter	Roy L.	1 & 2	26	1878-1903
Aselage	William	3	142	1903-1910
Ashbrock	John	4	1	1910-1915
Athy	Thomas	1 & 2	29	1878-1903
Atwood	Elizabeth	3	37	1903-1910
Auer	Anna	1 & 2	50	1878-1903
Auer	Hannah	1 & 2	34	1878-1903
Bach	Louie	1 & 2	37	1878-1903
Bach		4	73	1910-1915
Bader	Albert	1 & 2	68	1878-1903
Bader	Alois A.	3	36	1903-1910
Bader	Tresa E.	3	179	1903-1910
Bailey	Annie F.	3	38	1903-1910
Bailey	Belinda	1 & 2	73	1878-1903
Bailey	E.W.	3	108	1903-1910
Bailey	Eliza	1 & 2	63	1878-1903
Bailey	Elizabeth	1 & 2	7	1878-1903
Bailey	Harrison	3	188	1903-1910
Bailey	John A.	1 & 2	38	1878-1903
Bailey	John A. L.	1 & 2	41	1878-1903
Bailey	Luella	1 & 2	10	1878-1903
Bailey	Vera Gladys	3	130	1903-1910

CALHOUN COUNTY DEATHS

Surname	Given Name	Book	Page	Year
Bain	James Gren	1 & 2	4	1878-1903
Bain	Norman C.	1 & 2	22	1878-1903
Bain	Rebecca	1 & 2	41	1878-1903
Bain	Rebecca	4	106	1910-1915
Baines	Snow	1 & 2	24	1878-1903
Baker	Annie M.	1 & 2	6	1878-1903
Baker	John	3	83	1903-1910
Baker	John	1 & 2	18	1878-1903
Baker	Margaret	3	104	1903-1910
Balckorby	Ella	4	78	1910-1915
Balke	Theresa	4	103	1910-1915
Ball	Frank A.	4	98	1910-1915
Ball	R.B.	3	60	1903-1910
Ball	Sarah A.	4	78	1910-1915
Ball	Willis	1 & 2	11	1878-1903
Baltesberger	Barbara	1 & 2	11	1878-1903
Baltesberger	John	1 & 2	1	1878-1903
Baltisberg	Mary Elmo	4	19	1910-1915
Banghart	William	1 & 2	14	1878-1903
Banker	Catherine	3	17	1903-1910
Barber	Bertram T.	1 & 2	65	1878-1903
Barber	Chas.	1 & 2	22	1878-1903
Barber	Nancy Margaret	1 & 2	4	1878-1903
Barber	Sarah M.	3	1	1903-1910
Barber	WM. E	1 & 2	10	1878-1903
Barber		1 & 2	75	1878-1903
Bare	Martha	1 & 2	35	1878-1903
Bare	Thomas G.	1 & 2	5	1878-1903
Barnard	Henry J.	1 & 2	57	1878-1903
Barnard	Rose	1 & 2	57	1878-1903
Barnard	Sarah L.	1 & 2	57	1878-1903
Barnard	WM. Riley	1 & 2	57	1878-1903
Barnes	Alta C.	4	81	1910-1915
Barnes	Daniel	1 & 2	36	1878-1903
Barnes	Elizabeth	3	162	1903-1910

CALHOUN COUNTY DEATHS

Surname	Given Name	Book	Page	Year
Barnes	John T.	1 & 2	33	1878-1903
Barnes	Millie	3	65	1903-1910
Barnes	Rosco S.	3	6	1903-1910
Barnes		1 & 2	51	1878-1903
Barnes		3	115	1903-1910
Barns	William	4	86	1910-1915
Barowman	Sarah E.	4	92	1910-1915
Barrowman	Olive George	1 & 2	10	1878-1903
Batchelder	Mary Louisa	1 & 2	57	1878-1903
Batchelder	W.W.	3	81	1903-1910
Batchelder		1 & 2	27	1878-1903
Baty	Mollie	1 & 2	2	1878-1903
Baumann	Grace	4	14	1910-1915
Baumann	Rachael	3	173	1903-1910
Beach	John Colvin	1 & 2	3	1878-1903
Beaty	R.C.	1 & 2	73	1878-1903
Beaty	Stephens R.	3	115	1903-1910
Beck	Caroline	1 & 2	53	1878-1903
Becker	Gregory	3	80	1903-1910
Becker	Henry	3	18	1903-1910
Becker	Henry G.	1 & 2	9	1878-1903
Becker	Julius E.	1 & 2	9	1878-1903
Becker	Roman	3	120	1903-1910
Becker	Theresa	1 & 2	120	1878-1903
Beech	Alice Ann	1 & 2	75	1878-1903
Beech		1 & 2	48	1878-1903
Beeman	Adoline	1 & 2	12	1878-1903
Beer	Chas.	3	54	1903-1910
Behrens	Berniden	3	182	1903-1910
Behrens	Clara	3	40	1903-1910
Behrens	Conrad	1 & 2	36	1878-1903
Behrens	Englebot	1 & 2	7	1878-1903
Behrens	Helen A.	4	77	1910-1915
Behrens	Sophia E.	1 & 2	4	1878-1903
Beisman	Laura Louise	1 & 2	15	1878-1903

CALHOUN COUNTY DEATHS

Surname	Given Name	Book	Page	Year
Belker	Frank P.	1 & 2	10	1878-1903
Bell	Chas. Taft	3	159	1903-1910
Bell	Harriet Eliza	4	21	1910-1915
Bell	Henry	1 & 2	1	1878-1903
Bell	Jas. R.	3	17	1903-1910
Bell	Jos.F.	3	39	1903-1910
Bell	Joseph	1 & 2	30	1878-1903
Bell	Joseph S.	1 & 2	69	1878-1903
Bell	Mrs. Harriet	1 & 2	16	1878-1903
Bell	Thomas A.	1 & 2	76	1878-1903
Bell	WM.	1 & 2	30	1878-1903
Bell	Zola O.	1 & 2	13	1878-1903
Bellm	Frank	1 & 2	28	1878-1903
Benken	Theo.	1 & 2	54	1878-1903
Benkin	Anna C.	4	92	1910-1915
Bennett	Chas.	1 & 2	51	1878-1903
Bennett	Mary J.	3	314	1903-1910
Bensinger	Martha Ann	3	171	1903-1910
Bentrup	Henry	4	115	1910-1915
Benz	Martin	3	136	1903-1910
Benz	Theresa	3	143	1903-1910
Benzinger	Eiza J.	1 & 2	2	1878-1903
Berendes	Annie M.	1 & 2	51	1878-1903
Berrey	Mary J.	1 & 2	64	1878-1903
Berrey	Ruth U.	1 & 2	37	1878-1903
Berrey	Stephens R.	1 & 2	42	1878-1903
Berry	Andrew W.	1 & 2	61	1878-1903
Berry	Emily J.	1 & 2	71	1878-1903
Berry	James	1 & 2	71	1878-1903
Berry	Mary R.	4	94	1910-1915
Besaw	Edna	1 & 2	20	1878-1903
Bess	E.L.	1 & 2	13	1878-1903
Bick	Henry	4	67	1910-1915
Bick	Robt.Theo	4	25	1910-1915
Bickhardt	Elizabeth	4	28	1910-1915

CALHOUN COUNTY DEATHS

Surname	Given Name	Book	Page	Year
Billings	Thomas	1 & 2	77	1878-1903
Birkhead	Helen Amos	4	19	1910-1915
Bizaillion	Francis I.	4	27	1910-1915
Bizaillion	Francis Z.	1 & 2	1	1878-1903
Bizaillion	G.D.	3	123	1903-1910
Bizaillion	Gideon	4	6	1910-1915
Black	Henry	3	86	1903-1910
Blackirby	Thomas	4	47	1910-1915
Blackorby	Henry	1 & 2	16	1878-1903
Blackorby	John	1 & 2	70	1878-1903
Blackorby	Pavy Belle	1 & 2	69	1878-1903
Blackorby	Richard	1 & 2	37	1878-1903
Blackorby	Richard Niles	4	61	1910-1915
Blackorby	WM. R.	1 & 2	42	1878-1903
Blackston	Jane	1 & 2	12	1878-1903
Blackston	Mrs. Lula May	4	99	1910-1915
Blackston	Otto	1 & 2	12	1878-1903
Blackston	Thomas Edward	4	102	1910-1915
Blackston	Thos. Leroy	1 & 2	14	1878-1903
Blackston	Thresia F.	1 & 2	71	1878-1903
Blackstun	Hannah	1 & 2	5	1878-1903
Blackstun	Ida I.	3	162	1903-1910
Blackstun	Maude	1 & 2	46	1878-1903
Blackstun	Norma L.	4	86	1910-1915
Blackstun	S. Lena	3	88	1903-1910
Blackwell	Elizabeth	3	106	1903-1910
Blackwell	Ida May	1 & 2	21	1878-1903
Blackwell	Isodor	1 & 2	23	1878-1903
Blackwell	Nona M.	4	117	1910-1915
Blackwell	Thos.	4	87	1910-1915
Blackwell	William Henry	1 & 2	10	1878-1903
Blain	John Henry	1 & 2	24	1878-1903
Blain	Julia	1 & 2	23	1878-1903
Bland	Sarah	1 & 2	18	1878-1903
Blooms	John Barney	1 & 2	66	1878-1903

CALHOUN COUNTY DEATHS

Surname	Given Name	Book	Page	Year
Bobin	Mary	1 & 2	6	1878-1903
Boch	Magdaline D.	1 & 2	2	1878-1903
Boede	Conrad	3	79	1903-1910
Boede	Nellie H.	1 & 2	69	1878-1903
Boedecker	G.W.	3	34	1903-1910
Boeing	Adaline	1 & 2	9	1878-1903
Bohl	Norbert	1 & 2	42	1878-1903
Bokamp	Elizabeth	1 & 2	42	1878-1903
Bonner	Frank G.	3	133	1903-1910
Bonner	Michael	1 & 2	5	1878-1903
Booth	John C.	1 & 2	52	1878-1903
Booth	Louisa N.	3	64	1903-1910
Booth	Margret E.	3	64	1903-1910
Booth	Turner	3	185	1903-1910
Booth	William Edward	4	39	1910-1910
Bopp	Joseph Henry	1 & 2	23	1878-1903
Bopp	Martin	1 & 2	46	1878-1903
Borchard	Lewis Loranda	1 & 2	11	1878-1903
Borrowman	Andrew	1 & 2	44	1878-1903
Borrowman	John	1 & 2	67	1878-1903
Bouyea	Willie F.	1 & 2	59	1878-1903
Bove	Caroline	3	55	1903-1910
Bovee	Evaline	1 & 2	24	1878-1903
Bovee	Luvena	1 & 2	14	1878-1903
Bovee	Mary S.	1 & 2	49	1878-1903
Bovee	Wesley	1 & 2	25	1878-1903
Bovee	Wesley	1 & 2	26	1878-1903
Bowvee	Vivian Jr.	4	115	1910-1915
Boyea	Chas.	1 & 2	78	1878-1903
Braden	Andrew J.	1 & 2	26	1878-1903
Bradley	Edward	1 & 2	42	1878-1903
Braksick	Edward	3	83	1903-1910
Braksick	Minnie	3	153	1903-1910
Brands	E. W.	3	112	1903-1910
Brands	john	1 & 2	26	1878-1903

CALHOUN COUNTY DEATHS

Surname	Given Name	Book	Page	Year
Brands	Maurice Leonard	3	20	1903-1910
Brangenberg	F.W.	3	96	1903-1910
Brangenberg	Jospeh	3	139	1903-1910
Brangenberg	Lula Mary	4	101	1910-1915
Brangenberg	Mary	1 & 2	11	1878-1903
Brannon	Eva Dora	1 & 2	16	1878-1903
Brant	William	1 & 2	10	1878-1903
Breaden	Andrew J.	1 & 2	6	1878-1903
Breden	Andrew Jackson	1 & 2	1	1878-1903
Breden	Edith	1 & 2	5	1878-1903
Breden	Frank	3	149	1903-1910
Breden	Irene L.	3	173	1903-1910
Breer	Mathias	4	38	1910-1915
Breer	Teckla	1 & 2	2	1878-1903
Breer	Teckla	4	98	1910-1915
Brenn	Annie	3	71	1903-1910
Brenn	Geo. Jacob	1 & 2	63	1878-1903
Brick	Elizabeth	1 & 2	18	1878-1903
Brinkman	Frederick A.	1 & 2	59	1878-1903
Brinkman	Zella Mrs.	1 & 2	8	1878-1903
Britton	Birdie Estella	1 & 2	21	1878-1903
Britton	Minnie	1 & 2	24	1878-1903
Broaden	Elizabeth	1 & 2	22	1878-1903
Brock	Henry	1 & 2	24	1878-1903
Brock	Frank	1 & 2	25	1878-1903
Brorkel	Warens	1 & 2	13	1878-1903
Brose	Barbara	1 & 2	32	1878-1903
Brose	Jacob	1 & 2	66	1878-1903
Brose	Katie E.	1 & 2	32	1878-1903
Brose	WM. B.	1 & 2	38	1878-1903
Broughton	Charles	1 & 2	17	1878-1903
Broughton	Jerry	3	67	1903-1910
Brown	L.B.	1 & 2	43	1878-1903
Browning	Jas. F.	1 & 2	17	1878-1903
Browning	Jos.	1 & 2	55	1878-1903

CALHOUN COUNTY DEATHS

Surname	Given Name	Book	Page	Year
Bruce	John	3	1	1903-1910
Brunz	Louis	3	36	1903-1910
Buchanan	Austin O.	3	9	1903-1910
Buchanan	Chas. E.	1 & 2	68	1878-1903
Buchanan	Samuel J.	4	33	1910-1915
Buchsuhl	Nevada	1 & 2	34	1878-1903
Buckingham	Irene A.	4	68	1910-1915
Buckner	Emma C.	1 & 2	12	1878-1903
Buckner	Jacob	1 & 2	51	1878-1903
Buckner	Katie C.	1 & 2	28	1878-1903
Buenger	August	3	183	1903-1910
Bugala	Henry	1 & 2	4	1878-1903
Bull	Ellen	1 & 2	64	1878-1903
Bull	Geo W.	1 & 2	24	1878-1903
Bull	Geo.	1 & 2	34	1878-1903
Bull	Hettie	1 & 2	29	1878-1903
Bull	Hettie J.	1 & 2	13	1879-1903
Bull	Mary	1 & 2	49	1878-1903
Bull	Nancy Ann	1 & 2	23	1878-1903
Bull	Nevada	1 & 2	64	1878-1903
Bull	Willis	1 & 2	6	1878-1903
Bull	WM. Warren	1 & 2	53	1878-1903
Bullier	Aloys	4	42	1910-1915
Bullion	Anna	1 & 2	73	1878-1903
Bunch	Isaac	3	85	1903-1910
Bunch	John Jr.	3	45	1903-1910
Bunch	Lena	1 & 2	78	1878-1903
Bunch	Margaret	3	90	1903-1910
Burge	Infant	4	47	1910-1915
Burge	Leota	3	117	1903-1910
Burns	Bobby Allen	1 & 2	2	1878-1903
Burns	E.H.	3	120	1903-1910
Burns	Fred	1 & 2	55	1878-1903
Burns	James B.	3	139	1903-1910
Burns	John	1 & 2	13	1878-1903

CALHOUN COUNTY DEATHS

Surname	Given Name	Book	Page	Year
Burns	Minnie	4	116	1910-1915
Burns	Minnie R	3	51	1903-1910
Burns	Nancy A.	3	89	1903-1910
Burns	Reuben H.	1 & 2	11	1878-1903
Burns		1 & 2	38	1878-1903
Burton	John	1 & 2	40	1878-1903
Burton	Mary C.	1 & 2	25	1878-1903
Bush	Mary	3	142	1903-1910
Buston	Catherine	1 & 2	31	1878-1903
Butler	Chas.	1 & 2	56	1878-1903
Butler	Joshua	3	8	1903-1910
Butler	Nancy	1 & 2	55	1878-1903
Byrd	Earl	3	52	1903-1910
Cahill	Mary	1 & 2	35	1878-1903
Calloway	Benj. H.	1 & 2	70	1878-1903
Calloway	Susan	1 & 2	57	1878-1903
Caloway	Hubert	1 & 2	2	1878-1903
Camera		3	9	1903-1910
Campbell	Alma Edith	1 & 2	64	1878-1903
Campbell	Eva M.	3	105	1903-1910
Campbell	Eva Maxine	3	105	1903-1910
Campbell	Gerald Victor	3	186	1903-1910
Campbell	Harrison Porter	4	12	1910-1915
Campbell	Jack	1 & 2	18	1878-1903
Campbell	Mary	1 & 2	14	1878-1903
Campbell	Sarah francis	1 & 2	13	1878-1903
Canan	Elizabeth M.	4	74	1910-1915
Canett	Frank	1 & 2	57	1878-1903
Cappel	Annie	3	26	1903-1910
Cappel	Ida	3	101	1903-1910
Capple	Casper	1 & 2	13	1878-1903
Caratlon		4	110	1910-1915
Carlton		4	34	1910-1915
Carmarko	Joe	4	59	1910-1915
Carner	Dolly	4	7	1910-1915

CALHOUN COUNTY DEATHS

Surname	Given Name	Book	Page	Year
Carnes	Alfred	1 & 2	21	1878-1903
Carnes	Cassie	1 & 2	20	1878-1903
Carren	Dennis Clarence	1 & 2	17	1878-1903
Carron	Sarah (Child)	1 & 2	1	1878-1903
Carter	Chas.	1 & 2	71	1878-1903
Caselton	Helen	4	96	1910-1915
Caselton	John Anton	3	159	1903-1910
Caselton	William	4	107	1910-1915
Cassaboon	Samuel H.	4	78	1910-1915
Causera	Mary Paulene	1 & 2	16	1878-1903
Cephes	Mary Ann	1 & 2	34	1878-1903
Cerlin	Theresa E.	1 & 2	19	1878-1903
Charlton		1 & 2	9	1878-1903
Child	Bertha	1 & 2	30	1878-1903
Child	Helen	3	4	1903-1910
Chism	Charley	1 & 2	43	1878-1903
Chittinden	C. E.	4	7	1910-1915
Christopher	Elda	1 & 2	26	1878-1903
Church	Dan	3	17	1903-1910
Churman	John H.	1 & 2	63	1878-1903
Cimmer	Annie	4	104	1910-1915
Claus	Catherine	4	84	1910-1915
Claus	Charles	4	5	1910-1915
Clemmons	Archibald W.	3	156	1903-1910
Clendenny	Asa	1 & 2	4	1878-1903
Clendenny	F.H.	3	99	1903-1910
Clendenny	Jacob	1 & 2	3	1878-1903
Clendenny	John	1 & 2	19	1878-1903
Clendenny	Lulu Miss	1 & 2	14	1878-1903
Clendenny	Mary E.	1 & 2	35	1878-1903
Cline	Ira Orville	4	99	1910-1915
Cloninger	Arthur	1 & 2	25	1878-1903
Cloninger	Bertha V.	1 & 2	22	1878-1903
Cloninger	John	1 & 2	56	1878-1903
Cloninger	Joseph H.	1 & 2	41	1878-1903

CALHOUN COUNTY DEATHS

Surname	Given Name	Book	Page	Year
Cloninger	Mabel	1 & 2	58	1878-1903
Cloninger	Mary E.	1 & 2	28	1878-1903
Cloninger	Philip	1 & 2	63	1878-1903
Cloninger		3	11	1903-1910
Clowers	Robt. Portor	1 & 2	67	1878-1903
Clugsten	Chas.	1 & 2	22	1878-1903
Clugsten	William P.	4	66	1910-1915
Clunk	Joseph	1 & 2	5	1878-1903
Coan	Michael	3	68	1903-1910
Cockrell	David Davis	4	115	1910-1915
Cockrell	Hattie J.	4	77	1910-1915
Cockrell	Olive E.	1 & 2	38	1878-1903
Cockrell	Sarah J.	1 & 2	62	1878-1903
Cockrell	Sarah Jane	1 & 2	65	1878-1903
Cockrell		3	50	1903-1910
Colbert	Anna M.	3	111	1903-1910
Collier	James	1 & 2	1	1878-1903
Collins	Joseph Frances	4	111	1910-1915
Collins	Stanley	4	6	1910-1915
Condon	Catherine	1 & 2	73	1878-1903
Condon	Emma	1 & 2	40	1878-1903
Cook	John	1 & 2	19	1878-1903
Corbett		4	63	1910-1915
Corbit	Mary	1 & 2	32	1878-1903
Cornant	Jos.B.	4	84	1910-1915
Cornelius	James Walton	4	32	1910-1915
Cornick	H.M.	3	71	1903-1910
Corwin	Goldie	3	7	1903-1910
Cosgrove	Joseph M.	4	35	1910-1915
Coughlin	Margaret	3	41	1903-1910
Courts	John	4	109	1910-1915
Cox	Emily E.	1 & 2	23	1878-1903
Cox	James W.	1 & 2	5	1878-1903
Cox	Jane	1 & 2	27	1878-1903
Cox	Mary	4	105	1910-1915

CALHOUN COUNTY DEATHS

Surname	Given Name	Book	Page	Year
Cox	Winterton	1 & 2	9	1878-1903
Crader	Abraham	1 & 2	54	1878-1903
Crader	America	1 & 2	32	1878-1903
Crader	Cassa	1 & 2	36	1878-1903
Crader	Deforrest	1 & 2	57	1878-1903
Crader	Irene	1 & 2	14	1878-1903
Crader	Isaac	3	149	1903-1910
Crader	Jacob Monroe	1 & 2	13	1878-1903
Crader	Kathryn L.	3	6	1903-1910
Crader	Lugene	1 & 2	46	1878-1903
Crader	Melare Ann	1 & 2	13	1878-1903
Crader	Minnie E.	3	19	1903-1910
Crader	Rebeca J.	1 & 2	54	1878-1910
Crader	Rosana	4	114	1910-1915
Crader	Rufus	1 & 2	29	1878-1903
Crader		4	2	1910-1915
Craigmiles	Doris	1	168	1903-1910
Craigmiles	Henry	1 & 2	12	1878-1903
Craigmiles	Lydiane	1 & 2	16	1878-1903
Crate	Abraham	1 & 2	1	1878-1903
Creech	Isaac Elmer	1 & 2	49	1878-1903
Cress	Clara Jane	1 & 2	18	1878-1903
Cress	Harry O.	1 & 2	72	1878-1903
Cress	James A.	1 & 2	34	1878-1903
Cress	Joseph M.	1 & 2	14	1878-1903
Cress	Stella Agnes	1 & 2	3	1878-1903
Cresswell	John	1 & 2	43	1878-1903
Cresswell	Jos.P.	3	24	1903-1910
Cresswell	Nora	3	30	1903-1910
Crist	Caroline	3	172	1903-1910
Crosby	Alma	1 & 2	29	1878-1903
Crosby	Elizabeth S.	1 & 2	10	1878-1903
Crosby	Evelane	1 & 2	21	1878-1903
Crosby	H. S.	1 & 2	34	1878-1903
Crosby	John D.	1 & 2	67	1878-1903

CALHOUN COUNTY DEATHS

Surname	Given Name	Book	Page	Year
Crosby	Margaret E.	1 & 2	67	1878-1903
Crosby		1 & 2	51	1878-1903
Crotty	Ellen	1 & 2	57	1878-1903
Crouch		1 & 2	21	1878-1903
Crull	Geo. W.	1 & 2	76	1878-1903
Crull	Margaret	4	42	1910-1915
Crull	Mrs. Mary A.	1 & 2	66	1878-1903
Cruose	Clarence	1 & 2	62	1878-1903
Culver	Mrs. Francis	1 & 2	11	1878-1903
Cunningham	Adaline	1 & 2	17	1878-1903
Cunningham	Eurzed	1 & 2	19	1878-1903
Cunningham	Henry	4	45	1910-1915
Curtis	Chas. C	1 & 2	21	1878-1903
Daack	Charotte	3	2	1903-1910
Daack	Henry	4	12	1910-1915
Daak	Christopher	4	80	1910-1915
Daak	Herman	1 & 2	25	1878-1903
Damnitz	HY. Chas. V.	1 & 2	4	1878-1903
Daniels	Alma	4	105	1910-1915
Darr	Henry	4	114	1910-1915
Darris	William	4	56	1910-1915
Daugherty	Elsadir	1 & 2	26	1878-1903
Davis	Albert W.	3	45	1903-1910
Davis	Hattie	1 & 2	72	1878-1903
Davis	Henry Z.	3	100	1903-1910
Davis	James E.	1 & 2	28	1878-1903
Davis	Katy	1 & 2	76	1878-1903
Davis	Levi M.	3	111	1903-1910
Davis	Nancy Jane	3	13	1903-1910
Davis	Otis Lindsey	1 & 2	16	1878-1903
Davis	Sarah	1 & 2	2	1878-1903
Davison	Goldie	1 & 2	14	1878-1903
Day	Bartholomew	3	4	1903-1910
Day	Jos. B.	1 & 2	19	1878-1903
Day	Perry	4	91	1910-1915

CALHOUN COUNTY DEATHS

Surname	Given Name	Book	Page	Year
Dean	Henry	1 & 2	60	1878-1903
Dean	Jacob	3	157	1903-1910
Dean	Rachael	4	22	1910-1915
Deen	Eliza J.	1 & 2	63	1878-1903
Degerlia	Claud	4	8	1910-1915
Degerlia	Harry	1 & 2	14	1878-1903
Degerlia	Nancy	1 & 2	12	1878-1903
Delaney	Emiline	3	5	1903-1910
Delaney	Gabriel	4	61	1910-1915
Delargy	Anna Agnes	4	102	1910-1915
Delargy	John	3	49	1903-1915
Delonay	Olive	4	20	1910-1915
Deloney	John H.	3	80	1903-1910
Deloney	Joseph	4	70	1910-1915
Deloney	Siversa E.	1 & 2	8	1878-1903
Deloney	WM. Samuel	1 & 2	21	1878-1903
DeLong	Guy	1 & 2	18	1878-1903
DeLong	Luther A.	3	58	1903-1910
DeLong	Nellie B.	3	25	1903-1910
Dennis	Gretta Loranie	1 & 2	15	1878-1903
Depper	Dolly	4	36	1910-1915
Depper	John	3	22	1903-1910
Depper	Peter	3	16	1903-1910
Depper	Theresa	3	116	1903-1915
Derking	Alma C.	1 & 2	8	1878-1903
DeScerns	Mrs. Matilda	1 & 2	12	1878-1903
DeSherley	Pearl	3	178	1903-1910
DeVault	John Lewis	1 & 2	11	1878-1903
DeVerger	Jos. H.	1 & 2	76	1878-1903
DeVine	Archy	1 & 2	69	1878-1903
DeVine	James Sr.	1 & 2	12	1878-1903
DeVine	Julia	1 & 2	46	1878-1903
Dewey	James M.	1 & 2	65	1878-1903
Dickman	August	1 & 2	8	1878-1903
Dierking	Garfield Arthur	3	103	1903-1910

CALHOUN COUNTY DEATHS

Surname	Given Name	Book	Page	Year
Dierking	John T.	3	117	1903-1910
Dierking	Joseph	4	25	1910-1915
Dillon	James M.	1 & 2	7	1878-1903
Dirksmeyer	Anton	3	162	1903-1910
Dirksmeyer	Henry L.	1 & 2	33	1878-1903
Dissernes	Chas.	3	14	1903-1910
Distle	Charles	1 & 2	2	1878-1903
Dixon	Fern	3	57	1903-1910
Dixon	Frank	3	178	1903-1910
Dixon	Jane	3	59	1903-1910
Dixon	John H.	1 & 2	70	1878-1903
Dixon	Marcy A.	1 & 2	26	1878-1903
Dixon	William Lewis	1 & 2	1	1878-1903
Doak	Ester	3	171	1903-1910
Doak	Hester	3	171	1903-1910
Doak	Loyd Henry	4	58	1910-1915
Doak	Mary	4	57	1910-1915
Docept	Jos.	1 & 2	24	1878-1903
Dohme	Sarah	1 & 2	8	1878-1903
Dorsey	Dorothy M.	4	94	1910-1915
Dorworth	Mandeville G.	1 & 2	7	1878-1903
Dorworth	Sam. W.	3	69	1903-1910
Doty	Rob't E.	1 & 2	41	1878-1903
Dougherty	WM.	1 & 2	72	1878-1903
Douglass	Ida Bracey	1 & 2	49	1878-1903
Douglass	Jas. R.	1 & 2	21	1878-1903
Droege	Anna Mary	3	11	1903-1910
Droege	Annie	1 & 2	54	1878-1903
Droege	Dan	1 & 2	52	1878-1903
Droege	Edward	3	47	1903-1910
Droege	Elizabeth	1 & 2	19	1878-1903
Droege	Elizabeth	1 & 2	70	1878-1903
Droege	Gabeulla	3	145	1903-1910
Droege	Henry	3	102	1903-1910
Duceo	Otto E.	3	89	1903-1910

CALHOUN COUNTY DEATHS

Surname	Given Name	Book	Page	Year
Ducep	Rose	4	46	1910-1915
Duetman	Mary Teckla	4	29	1910-1915
Dumsebach	Hellena	1 & 2	8	1878-1903
Dunneebach	Henry	1 & 2	11	1878-1903
Dunse	William	1 & 2	11	1878-1903
Dupey	Leona	4	11	1910-1915
Dutchy		1 & 2	45	1878-19036
Dwyer	Elizabeth	1 & 2	71	1878-1903
Earley	Nancy A.	3	76	1903-1910
East	John W.	1 & 2	11	1878-1903
Eastman	Hiram	1 & 2	5	1878-1903
Eaten	Nancy F.	1 & 2	71	1878-1903
Eberlin	Adeline	4	100	1910-1915
Eberlin	Antone	4	71	1910-1915
Eberlin	Blosse	1 & 2	36	1878-1903
Eberlin	Clement	4	61	1910-1915
Eckert	Harriet J.	3	56	1903-1910
Eckert	WM. R.	3	53	1903-1910
Edwards	George	1 & 2	17	1878-1903
Eilerman	Garret Herman	1 & 2	25	1878-1903
Eilerman	Henry	1 & 2	66	1878-1903
Eilerman	Louisa N.	1 & 2	57	1878-1903
Ellage	Estelle	1 & 2	59	1878-1903
Ellis	Caroline	1 & 2	21	1878-1903
Elmer	Julius	3	47	1903-1910
Elmer	Mrs. Bernard	3	183	1903-1910
Emerick	Andrew J.	3	133	1903-1910
Emerick	Geo. W.	1 & 2	50	1878-1903
Emerick	John	3	37	1903-1910
Emert	Chas.	3	126	1903-1910
Endris	William R.	4	28	1910-1915
Engle	Laural	1 & 2	10	1878-1903
Etter	Emma	1 & 2	74	1878-1903
Evering	Ida E.	4	76	1910-1915
Evering	Manervia J.	3	78	1903-1910

CALHOUN COUNTY DEATHS

Surname	Given Name	Book	Page	Year
Ewen	Elizabeth Jacobs	4	25	1910-1915
Ewen	Leonard	1 & 2	70	1878-1903
Ewing	Elizabeth Ann	1 & 2	36	1878-1903
Ewing	James	1 & 2	39	1878-1903
Fabrain	George	1 & 2	14	1878-1903
Fabrun	Lillian	3	58	1903-1910
Fanning	Samuel M.	1 & 2	16	1878-1903
Farnbach	Johanna	1 & 2	13	1878-1903
Farnbach	Johanna	1 & 2	12	1878-1903
Farnbach	Michael	1 & 2	58	1878-1903
Farrow	Charles	1 & 2	29	1878-1903
Feasel	Lawrence	1 & 2	14	1878-1903
Feidler	Clarence W.	1 & 2	15	1878-1903
Feidler	WM. Hobart	1 & 2	10	1878-1903
Ferguson	America	1 & 2	23	1878-1903
Ferguson	Benjamin	1 & 2	4	1878-1903
Ferguson	Chas.M.	1 & 2	38	1878-1903
Ferguson	Cordelia	1 & 2	42	1878-1903
Ferguson	David C.	1 & 2	8	1878-1903
Ferguson	Ellen	1 & 2	21	1878-1903
Ferguson	Grace E.	1 & 2	38	1878-1903
Ferguson	John	1 & 2	8	1878-1903
Ferguson	Luella	1 & 2	55	1878-1903
Ferguson	Peter Dyer	1 & 2	8	1878-1903
Festage	Herman	1 & 2	5	1878-1903
Fieg	Anna	1 & 2	4	1878-1903
Field	Willie	4	80	1910-1915
Fielder	Chris F. K.	3	85	1903-1910
Fielder	Etta.	1 & 2	66	1878-1903
Fielder	Henry	4	16	1910-1915
Fielder	Mary Etta	4	52	1910-1915
Fifer	Joshua	4	74	1910-1915
Fischer	Edward Jerome	3	163	1903-1910
Fischer	Ferdinand	1 & 2	23	1878-1903
Fisher	Henry	1 & 2	56	1878-1903

CALHOUN COUNTY DEATHS

Surname	Given Name	Book	Page	Year
Fisher	Henry	3	132	1903-1910
Fisher	Henry Cleo	1 & 2	17	1878-1903
Fisher	John G.	1 & 2	49	1878-1903
Fisher	Mary Emma	1 & 2	6	1878-1903
Fisher	Rose	1 & 2	40	1878-1903
Fisher	Sarah	3	104	1903-1910
Fisher	Sarah M.	1 & 2	38	1878-1903
Fitch	Samuel	1 & 2	31	1878-1903
Fitzgerald	James	1 & 2	19	1878-1903
Flagge	Henry	1 & 2	19	1878-1903
Flanigan	Aritus	1 & 2	74	1878-1903
Flanigan	Cora	1 & 2	76	1878-1903
Flanigan	Dora J.	1 & 2	75	1878-1903
Flanigan	Ida Z.	3	82	1903-1910
Fleming	Peter	4	21	1910-1915
Fluent	David	1 & 2	50	1878-1903
Fogal	Annie Mrs.	1 & 2	19	1878-1903
Foiles	Anna M.	1 & 2	35	1878-1903
Foiles	Chloe	1 & 2	74	1878-1903
Foiles	Dr. Lewis	4	57	1910-1915
Foiles	Edward	3	75	1903-1910
Foiles	Ernest	1 & 2	20	1878-1903
Foiles	Fredrie	1 & 2	54	1878-1903
Foiles	Hannah	1 & 2	28	1878-1903
Foiles	Henry V.	1 & 2	34	1878-1903
Foiles	Ira A.	1 & 2	75	1878-1903
Foiles	Isaiah	1 & 2	21	1878-1903
Foiles	James	1 & 2	66	1878-1903
Foiles	James B.	1 & 2	37	1878-1903
Foiles	James N.	1 & 2	59	1878-1903
Foiles	James S.	1 & 2	67	1878-1903
Foiles	John Jr.	1 & 2	36	1878-1903
Foiles	Luella	1 & 2	33	1878-1903
Foiles	Margaret	1 & 2	37	1878-1903
Foiles	Mary E.	1 & 2	33	1878-1903

CALHOUN COUNTY DEATHS

Surname	Given Name	Book	Page	Year
Foiles	Mary E.	1 & 2	34	1878-1903
Foiles	Mary E.	1 & 2	52	1878-1903
Foiles	Oren	1 & 2	16	1878-1903
Foiles	Parthena Ann	4	9	1910-1915
Foiles	Ruth A.	1 & 2	6	1878-1903
Foiles	Sidney Spencer	4	33	1910-1915
Foiles	Stacy	4	19	1910-1915
Fortschneider	Henry	4	1	1910-1915
Fortune	Mary	1 & 2	1	1878-1903
Foster	Otis	4	95	1910-1915
Foster	William	4	60	1910-1915
Fowler	Ida O.	3	31	1903-1910
Fowler	Oliver Roy	1 & 2	15	1878-1910
Fowler	WM. Peurrewale	1 & 2	24	1878-1903
Fox	Dutly Howland	1 & 2	24	1878-1903
Fox	Horatio	3	181	1903-1910
Frank	Anna	3	125	1903-1910
Frank	Cornelius	1 & 2	78	1878-1903
Frank	Harvey	1 & 2	22	1878-1903
Frank	John	1 & 2	43	1878-1903
Frank	John J.	3	106	1903-1910
Frank	Zophia K.	1 & 2	2	1878-1903
Franke	Clara F. E.	1 & 2	62	1878-1903
Franke	Fred K. H.	3	105	1903-1910
Franke	Martha	3	145	1903-1910
Franke	Nevada Augusta	3	185	1903-1910
Freeman	WM. H.	1 & 2	17	1878-1903
Freesmeyer	Elizabeth	3	184	1903-1910
Freesmeyer	Rotger	4	9	1910-1915
Freg	Anna	1 & 2	11	1878-1903
Freismeier	John P.	1 & 2	59	1878-1903
Fuhler	Margreta	1 & 2	2	1878-1903
Fulcher	Andrew J.	1 & 2	44	1878-1903
Fulkerson	Chas.	3	27	1903-1910
Fuller	Harriet J.	3	160	1903-1910

CALHOUN COUNTY DEATHS

Surname	Given Name	Book	Page	Year
Fulton	Mamie Pauline	4	55	1910-1915
Fulton	Mrs.	4	27	1910-1915
Fulton	Robert F.	4	3	1910-1915
Funk	Georgia	1 & 2	22	1878-1903
Funk	Mary H.	3	27	1903-1910
Funk	Nancy E.	4	112	1910-1915
Funk	William	1 & 2	3	1878-1903
Furgeson	David C.	3	34	1903-1910
Furgeson	Peter	1 & 2	21	1878-1903
Furie	Margaret	1 & 2	14	1878-1903
Futher	Margareth	1 & 2	3	1878-1903
Gardner	George Leonard	4	4	1910-1915
Gardner	George Leonard	3	187	1903-1910
Gardner	Noris	4	109	1910-1915
Garr	Louis	1 & 2	2	1878-1903
Gates	Anna	1 & 2	52	1878-1903
Gates	Enos W.	4	70	1910-1915
Gates	Jack	1 & 2	43	1878-1903
Gates	Nellie R.	3	48	1903-1915
Geers		3	76	1903-1915
Gerecke	WM.	1 & 2	52	1878-1903
Gerkin	Matilda	1 & 2	6	1878-1903
Gerkin	Sophia Marie	1 & 2	5	1878-1903
Gerrunt	Emily	1 & 2	8	1878-1903
Geymer	Maggie	1 & 2	20	1878-1903
Gheske	Lewis Abraham	4	107	1910-1915
Gilbert	Cecil	3	73	1903-1910
Gilbert	Eliza	3	132	1903-1910
Gilbert	Geo	1 & 2	24	1878-1903
Gilbert	Ray	4	51	1910-1915
Gill	Johanna	3	87	1903-1910
Glashen	Dennis	1 & 2	43	1878-1903
Glirken	Mrs. Rev	1 & 2	11	1878-1903
Glocke	Mary G.	1 & 2	6	1878-1903
Godar	Ellen	1 & 2	26	1878-1903

CALHOUN COUNTY DEATHS

Surname	Given Name	Book	Page	Year
Godar	Halena Mary	4	62	1910-1915
Godar		1 & 2	21	1878-1903
Godway	John	1 & 2	27	1878-1903
Gones	John W.	1 & 2	33	1878-1903
Goodwill	Mary	1 & 2	6	1878-1903
Goodyear	Mathias	1 & 2	4	1878-1903
Gorden	Mary Ann	1 & 2	45	1878-1903
Gorden	WM. F.	1 & 2	25	1878-1903
Gordon	Carry M.	3	39	1903-1910
Gordon	Edna	1 & 2	5	1878-1903
Gordon	Edward	3	175	1903-1910
Gordon	Elizabeth Ann	1 & 2	44	1878-1903
Gordon	John	1 & 2	64	1878-1903
Gordon	Laura L.	1 & 2	36	1878-1903
Gordon	Mary	3	161	1903-1910
Gose	George	3	101	1903-1910
Gotway	Joseph Peter	4	100	1910-1915
Gotway	Wealthy	1 & 2	19	1878-1903
Gotway	Zita	3	100	1903-1910
Graham	Mary Jane	1 & 2	74	1878-1903
Grall	Mary Jane	1 & 2	4	1878-1903
Grandsinger	Henry	1 & 2	11	1878-1903
Grandsinger	Henry	4	82	1910-1915
Grandsinger	Ida B.	3	107	1903-1910
Gras	Lorenz	1 & 2	58	1878-1903
Grasmann	WM. A.	1 & 2	56	1878-1903
Gray	Jacob	1 & 2	32	1878-1903
Gray	Marguerite Ellen	1 & 2	18	1878-1903
Gray	Nora	17	17	1878-1903
Gray	WM.	1 & 2	7	1878-1903
Greathouse	Charles Blaine	1 & 2	26	1878-1903
Green	Mrs. Pearl	4	39	1910-1915
Greer	Joseph P.	4	39	1910-1915
Grelle	Johanna	3	8	1903-1910
Gresham	Abner	1 & 2	39	1878-1903

CALHOUN COUNTY DEATHS

Surname	Given Name	Book	Page	Year
Gresham	Douglass	1 & 2	16	1878-1903
Gresham	Rachael	1 & 2	15	1878-1903
Gress	Henry	1 & 2	14	1878-1903
Gress	Louisia Mrs.	1 & 2	12	1878-1903
Gressam	Ernest Winfred	1 & 2	19	1878-1903
Grether	Louisa V.	1 & 2	43	1878-1903
Griffin	Bertha	1 & 2	25	1878-1903
Grosjean	John	1 & 2	42	1878-1903
Grover	Lucy H.	4	86	1910-1915
Grover	Sarah M.	4	101	1910-1915
Groves	Susan M.	3	54	1903-1910
Grueter	Lena	1 & 2	66	1878-1903
Grueter		3	60	1903-1910
Gueck	Elizabeth	1 & 2	78	1878-1903
Gueck	Fred	1 & 2	72	1878-1903
Gueck	John	3	90	1903-1910
Guesz	Andrew	1 & 2	3	1878-1903
Haar	Jermima	1 & 2	19	1878-1903
Habstad	John	4	81	1910-1915
Hadley	Clarence F.	3	14	1903-1910
Hadley	Hannah	1 & 2	12	1878-1903
Hagen	Christina	1 & 2	75	1878-1903
Hagen	Helen	3	90	1903-1910
Hagen	Henry	4	16	1910-1915
Hagen	Mary	1 & 2	67	1878-1903
Hagen	Theo J.	1 & 2	15	1878-1903
Hager	Margaret	1 & 2	15	1878-1903
Hagger	William	1 & 2	22	1878-1903
Halemeyer	Frances	1 & 2	77	1878-1903
Hall	Susan	1 & 2	16	1878-1903
Hall	William F.	3	41	1903-1910
Hallett	Harvey C.	4	76	1910-1915
Hallett	James V.	1 & 2	2	1878-1903
Hallett	William R.	3	140	1903-1910
Hamilton	Elias A.	1 & 2	37	1878-1903

CALHOUN COUNTY DEATHS

Surname	Given Name	Book	Page	Year
Hamilton	Issac	1 & 2	67	1878-1903
Hamilton	Mary L.	1 & 2	19	1878-1903
Hamilton	Rovezna	1 & 2	25	1878-1903
Hamilton	Ruby	1 & 2	17	1878-1903
Hammond	Benj	1 & 2	68	1878-1903
Hammond	Emma	1 & 2	76	1878-1903
Hammond	Reuben Allison	3	109	1903-1910
Hancock	Mary Ellen	1 & 2	19	1878-1903
Hanks	Walter	1 & 2	78	1878-1903
Hanks	Wilbur Herman	1 & 2	2	1878-1903
Hanneken	Elizabeth	1 & 2	61	1878-1903
Hanneken	Elizabeth Katherine	1 & 2	17	1878-1903
Hanneken	Garret	3	96	1903-1910
Hanneken	Helena	3	88	1903-1910
Hanneken	Helena	4	52	1910-1915
Hanneken	Hellena	1 & 2	9	1878-1903
Hanneken	Herman	1 & 2	16	1878-1903
Hanneken	Herman Joseph	1 & 2	18	1878-1903
Hanneken	John	3	139	1903-1910
Hanneken	Joseph	3	153	1903-1910
Hanneken	Mary	1 & 2	9	1878-1903
Hanneken		4	49	1910-1915
Hardesty	James S.	1 & 2	38	1878-1903
Harlow	Eddie Lee	1 & 2	40	1878-1903
Harlow	Ira	1 & 2	7	1878-1903
Harlow	Walter	1 & 2	54	1878-1903
Harmon	John B.	1 & 2	31	1878-1903
Harper	Mary Elizabeth	4	118	1910-1915
Harr	John	3	144	1903-1910
Harrell	Claude Forrest	3	99	1903-1910
Harrell	Emma	4	88	1910-1915
Harrell	Franics	1 & 2	43	1878-1903
Harrell	James H.	1 & 2	51	1878-1903
Harrell	James P.	1 & 2	20	1878-1903
Harrell	Ruby	3	145	1903-1910

CALHOUN COUNTY DEATHS

Surname	Given Name	Book	Page	Year
Harris	Matilda	1 & 2	18	1878-1903
Harrison	Edward R.	1 & 2	46	1878-1903
Harrison	George	1 & 2	9	1878-1903
Harrison	Joseph Charles	3	78	1903-1910
Harrison	William L.	1 & 2	46	1878-1903
Harrmond	Julia Ann	1 & 2	17	1878-1903
Hartford	Martin	4	2	1910-1915
Hartnagle	Geo. W.	1 & 2	77	1878-1903
Haselhorst	Anna	4	64	1910-1915
Haselhorst	Helena	3	101	1903-1910
Haselhorst	Martin	1 & 2	73	1878-1903
Haselhort	John	1 & 2	20	1878-1903
Hashchild	Daniel	1 & 2	10	1878-1903
Hasselmeyer	WM.	1 & 2	14	1878-1903
Hassetab	Barbara Anna	1 & 2	6	1878-1903
Hasson	W.E.	3	26	1903-1910
Hasty	Rebecca	3	132	1903-1910
Hauberg	Bernard	3	67	1903-1910
Haubs	Egbert	4	48	1910-1915
Haubs	Elizabeth T.	4	69	1910-1915
Haubs	J. Godfrey	3	50	1903-1910
Haug	William	4	18	1910-1915
Hausman	Augusta	3	113	1903-1910
Hausmann	Effie L.	3	60	1903-1910
Hausmann	Robert	4	40	1910-1915
Hausmann	WM.	3	24	1903-1910
Hayden	L.D.	1 & 2	36	1878-1903
Hayn	Simon	1 & 2	16	1878-1903
Hazelwonder	Clara Lucinda	4	13	1910-1915
Heart	John	1 & 2	6	1878-1903
Heaton	Edward	3	39	1903-1910
Heavner	Jesse Olive	4	103	1910-1915
Heavner	Sarah	3	184	1903-1910
Heavner	Weltha Geneva	3	155	1903-1910
Heavner		3	121	1903-1910

CALHOUN COUNTY DEATHS

Surname	Given Name	Book	Page	Year
Heffer	Gesina	3	64	1903-1910
Heffington	Emma S.	3	91	1903-1910
Heffington	Hubert Carol	3	159	1903-1910
Heffington	Jospeh M.	3	127	1903-1910
Heffington	Mary	4	73	1910-1915
Heffington	Roland	4	7	1910-1915
Heffner	Joseph	1 & 2	9	1878-1903
Hegger	Herman	3	147	1903-1910
Heidenrich	Peter J.	1 & 2	5	1878-1903
Heimer	Anna I.	4	82	1910-1915
Heiser	Joseph	3	146	1903-1910
Held	Anna	4	35	1910-1915
Held	Edward	3	141	1903-1910
Helfrich	Katherine	4	110	1910-1915
Heller	Johnannah	1 & 2	28	1878-1903
Hemphill	David V.	1 & 2	23	1878-1903
Hennel	Augusta	1 & 2	46	1878-1903
Hergott		3	28	1903-1910
Herkert	Alexander	1 & 2	46	1878-1903
Herkert	August	1 & 2	29	1878-1903
Herkert	Gertrude	1 & 2	61	1878-1903
Herkert	Lena	3	72	1903-1910
Herman	Gottlieb A.	3	25	1903-1910
Herman	John	1 & 2	15	1878-1903
Herman	Paul	3	73	1903-1910
Herron	Albert	1 & 2	53	1878-1903
Herron	Fulton	1 & 2	6	1878-1903
Herron	Scott	3	164	1903-1910
Hess	Orbie Roy	4	27	1910-1915
Hesse	Edward	4	21	1910-1915
Hessen	WM.	1 & 2	34	1878-1903
Hetzer	Chas.	3	18	1903-1910
Hetzer	Fred	4	53	1910-1915
Hetzer		3	110	1903-1910
Hicks	Mrs.	1 & 2	21	1878-1903

CALHOUN COUNTY DEATHS

Surname	Given Name	Book	Page	Year
Higgerson	Alta	1 & 2	9	1878-1903
Higgerson	Joseph	1 & 2	12	1878-1903
Higgerson	Leroy	1 & 2	40	1878-1903
Higgerson	Margaret	3	65	1903-1910
Higman	Chas.	1 & 2	60	1878-1903
Higman	John	1 & 2	23	1878-1903
Higman	Lindley J.	1 & 2	18	1878-1903
Higman	Mary F.	1 & 2	27	1878-1903
HIgman	Nathan	1 & 2	46	1878-1903
Higman	Nathan A.	1 & 2	60	1878-1903
Hill	Bessie	4	112	1910-1915
Hill	George	3	165	1903-1915
Hill	Henry TZ.	1 & 2	6	1878-1903
Hill	John Edward	4	85	1910-1915
Hill	Minnie Edith	4	101	1910-1915
Hill	Rebecca Jane	4	53	1910-1915
Hill	Thomas M.	1 & 2	8	1878-1903
Hill	Westley	1 & 2	2	1878-1903
Hillan	Anna	1 & 2	3	1878-1903
Hillen	Mary	3	131	1903-1915
Hillen	William	1 & 2	21	1878-1903
Hiller	William	4	107	1910-1915
Hirst	William	3	51	1903-1910
Hix	John W.	1 & 2	21	1878-1903
Hoag	Sarah E.	1 & 2	45	1878-1903
Hock		1 & 2	72	1878-1903
Holly	Albert	4	50	1910-1915
Holmes	William	3	11	1903-1910
Holterfield	James	1 & 2	26	1878-1903
Holterfield	Lucinda	3	46	1903-1910
Holzwarth	Conrad	3	164	1903-1910
Holzwarth	Lena R.	3	95	1903-1910
Holzwarth	WM. E.	3	89	1903-1910
Holzwarth	Zelphia	3	181	1903-1910
Homady	Nathan	1 & 2	43	1878-1903

CALHOUN COUNTY DEATHS

Surname	Given Name	Book	Page	Year
Hosey	Henry	3	53	1903-1910
Houseman	Katie L.	1 & 2	63	1878-1903
Housemann	Chas.	3	172	1903-1910
Housmann	Leanore	3	155	1903-1910
Howard	Ordela	1 & 2	16	1878-1903
Howardton	WM. A.	1 & 2	41	1878-1903
Howland	Annie	1 & 2	60	1878-1903
Howland	Chas. S.	1 & 2	16	1878-1903
Howland	Mary E.	1 & 2	70	1878-1903
Howland	Mary E.	1 & 2	52	1878-1903
Howland	Princella	1 & 2	37	1878-1903
Howland	Roy Lee	1 & 2	65	1878-1903
Howland	William	3	43	1903-1910
Howland	WM. C.	1 & 2	29	1878-1903
Hubbard	Fredie M.	1 & 2	71	1878-1903
Hubbard	John	1 & 2	56	1878-1903
Hubbard	Jos. C.	1 & 2	74	1878-1903
Huff	Luella	1 & 2	71	1878-1903
Huffstutler	John W.	1 & 2	26	1878-1903
Huffstutler	Julia	1 & 2	56	1878-1903
Huffstutler	Martha E.	1 & 2	17	1878-1903
Hughes	Ada	1 & 2	15	1878-1903
Hughes	Chas. B	1 & 2	1	1878-1903
Hughes	John	1 & 2	61	1878-1903
Hughes	Louis Thos.	1 & 2	33	1878-1903
Hughes	Louis Thos.	1 & 2	32	1878-1903
Hughes	Margaret	3	96	1903-1910
Hughes	Thos.	4	71	1910-1915
Hughey	Cyrus W.	3	187	1903-1910
Hunnicutt	William	1 & 2	12	1878-1903
Hunt	Cora Lee	1 & 2	24	1878-1903
Hunt	Jefferson T.	3	122	1903-1910
Hunter	Martha	1 & 2	40	1878-1903
Hurst	Arthur A.	1 & 2	27	1878-1903
Husamann	Katherine K.	1 & 2	11	1878-1903

CALHOUN COUNTY DEATHS

Surname	Given Name	Book	Page	Year
Husman	Veronica	4	4	1910-1915
Imming	Evangeline	1 & 2	48	1878-1903
Imming	Herbert	3	40	1903-1910
Ingersoll	Cora Edna	1 & 2	36	1878-1903
Ingersoll	Frances Opal	3	188	1903-1910
Ingersoll	Samuel Sconce	4	95	1910-1915
Ingle	William T.	1 & 2	75	1878-1903
Inman	Charles Henry	3	177	1903-1910
Inna	John	1 & 2	4	1878-1903
Irene	Della	1 & 2	4	1878-1903
Jackson	Anderson	1 & 2	25	1878-1903
Jackson	John	1 & 2	14	1878-1903
Jackson	John K.	4	91	1910-1915
Jacobs	Henry W.	3	116	1903-1910
Jacobs	Homer Ean	1 & 2	19	1878-1903
Jacobs	John	1 & 2	76	1878-1903
Jacobs	Jos. C.	1 & 2	15	1878-1903
Jacobs	Joseph A.	4	81	1910-1915
Jacobsmeyer	Joseph	1 & 2	6	1878-1903
Jacobsmeyer	Martin O.	1 & 2	5	1878-1903
Jansen	Herman	1 & 2	52	1878-1903
Jennings	Christine	1 & 2	60	1878-1903
Jennings	Margaret W.	1 & 2	23	1878-1903
Jennings	Thos. S.	1 & 2	7	1878-1903
Jewett	Christina E.	1 & 2	1	1878-1903
Jewsbury	Velma Martha	3	182	1903-1910
Johnes	Anna Louisa	3	3	1903-1910
Johnes	Frederika	3	144	1903-1910
Johnes	Henry	3	72	1903-1910
Johnes	M. Leota	3	66	1903-1910
Johns	Allen	1 & 2	63	1878-1903
Johns	Frederick	1 & 2	61	1878-1903
Johns	Henry H.	4	72	1910-1915
Johns	Mary	1 & 2	61	1878-1903
Johns	William	4	24	1910-1915

CALHOUN COUNTY DEATHS

Surname	Given Name	Book	Page	Year
Johnson	Barbara Alice	3	160	1903-1910
Johnson	Cassie	3	35	1903-1910
Johnson	E. W.	1 & 2	13	1878-1903
Johnson	Elizabeth Ann	4	18	1910-1915
Johnson	James	1 & 2	53	1878-1903
Johnson	James	1 & 2	6	1878-1903
Johnson	Louisa	1 & 2	53	1878-1903
Johnson	Patsy Ann	3	151	1903-1910
Johnson	Richard M.	4	20	1910-1915
Johnson	Viola	4	31	1910-1915
Johnston	Author	1 & 2	62	1878-1903
Johnston	Bertha	1 & 2	56	1878-1903
Johnston	Clay	1 & 2	64	1878-1903
Johnston	Elba	1 & 2	62	1878-1903
Jones	Ada	1 & 2	12	1878-1903
Jones	Christian	3	62	1903-1910
Jones	Emaline A.	1 & 2	20	1878-1903
Jones	John	1 & 2	22	1878-1903
Jones	John W.	1 & 2	26	1878-1903
Jones	Johny	1 & 2	32	1878-1903
Jones	Mariah J.	1 & 2	45	1878-1903
Jones	Mrs. Charles	4	17	1910-1915
Jones	Rosa A.	1 & 2	39	1878-1903
Jones	Volney	3	84	1903-1910
Jones		3	128	1903-1910
Joy	Paul	1 & 2	74	1878-1903
Joy	Robert	1 & 2	21	1878-1903
Joy	Robert	1 & 2	13	1878-1903
Judd	Mary Kimble	1 & 2	24	1878-1903
Kaible	Grace Viola	1 & 2	21	1878-1903
Kamp	Alvin	1 & 2	25	1878-1903
Kamp	John	3	145	1903-1910
Kamp	Josie	3	138	1903-1910
Kamp	Mary C.	3	137	1903-1910
Kamp	Mrs. John	3	150	1903-1910

CALHOUN COUNTY DEATHS

Surname	Given Name	Book	Page	Year
Kanellekan	Anton Edward	4	17	1910-1915
Kapple	Gerdrate	1 & 2	6	1878-1903
Keating	William	1 & 2	50	1878-1903
Keehner	Frederick	1 & 2	18	1878-1903
Keeting	Lora Irena	1 & 2	20	1878-1903
Keeton	Lizzie J.	3	31	1903-1910
Keeton	Viola M.	3	64	1903-1910
Kehri	Theresa	1 & 2	17	1878-1903
Keil	Catherine	1 & 2	12	1878-1903
Keintey	Genevieve	1 & 2	2	1878-1903
Kelby	Elizabeth	1 & 2	22	1878-1903
Keller	Rebecca	1 & 2	65	1878-1903
Kelly		3	156	1903-1910
Kendrick	Rolla S.	1 & 2	52	1878-1903
Kenedy	Samel H.	1 & 2	1	1878-1903
Kennedy	Miss.	3	167	1903-1910
Kerch	Jennie	1 & 2	11	1878-1903
Kerton	Andrew S.	1 & 2	29	1878-1903
Ketchum	Catherine	1 & 2	33	1878-1903
Ketchum	Victoria	4	102	1910-1915
Kiehl	Henry B.	3	42	1903-1910
Kiel	Catherine	3	102	1903-1910
Kiel	Henry Sr.	3	66	1903-1910
Kiel	Mary S.	3	85	1903-1910
Killian	Maria Ann	1 & 2	16	1878-1903
Kimberly	Alice Alma	1 & 2	41	1878-1903
Kimberly	Mary Alice	1 & 2	40	1878-1903
Kimberly	Nona Alta	1 & 2	28	1878-1903
Kinder	Caroline	1 & 2	77	1878-1903
Kinder	Elvin Kermit	3	134	1903-1910
Kinder	Harry	4	32	1910-1915
Kinder	Henry Martin	4	34	1910-1915
King	Henrietta	1 & 2	63	1878-1903
Kinkade	P.G.	3	130	1903-1910
Kinman	Margo E.	1 & 2	23	1878-1903

CALHOUN COUNTY DEATHS

Surname	Given Name	Book	Page	Year
Kinman	Mollie	1 & 2	25	1878-1903
Kinscherff	Bernard	1 & 2	10	1878-1903
Kinsie	William Jacob	1 & 2	24	1878-1903
Kinter	Frederick	1 & 2	35	1878-1903
Kirkhoff	Henry	1 & 2	4	1878-1903
Kirn	Milton Robert	4	69	1910-1915
Kitson	Hulda E.	1 & 2	5	1878-1903
Kitson	Nettie A.	1 & 2	54	1878-1903
Kitson	Saller	1 & 2	24	1878-1903
Kitson	William R.	3	12	1903-1910
Kitson	Wilmar A.	3	33	1903-1910
Kitson		3	46	1903-1910
Kizer	Mathias	1 & 2	5	1878-1903
Klaas	Angela	1 & 2	75	1878-1903
Klaas	Anna M.	3	19	1903-1910
Klaas	Barney	3	127	1903-1910
Klaas	Chas.	3	141	1903-1910
Klaas	Jospeh	4	54	1910-1915
Klaas	Liborius	3	151	1903-1910
Klaas	Martin	4	11	1910-1915
Klaas	Mary	1 & 2	59	1878-1903
Klaas	Mary	1 & 2	51	1878-1903
Klaas	Tillie	1 & 2	72	1878-1903
Klaas	Tukla	1 & 2	72	1878-1903
Klammer	Ernest Winfred	1 & 2	23	1878-1903
Klemme	Lucy	4	15	1910-1915
Klemme	Mathias	1 & 2	8	1878-1903
Klerin	Elizabeth	1 & 2	9	1878-1903
Klocke	Frances	3	98	1903-1910
Klockenkemper	Bernard Urben	3	105	1903-1910
Klockenkemper	Raphael	3	160	1903-1910
Klocker	Catherine	1 & 2	19	1878-1903
Klunk	Adam	1 & 2	73	1878-1903
Klunk	Michael	1 & 2	66	1878-1903
Klunk	Michael	4	89	1910-1915

CALHOUN COUNTY DEATHS

Surname	Given Name	Book	Page	Year
Klunk	Peter	1 & 2	69	1878-1903
Knese	Mary	1 & 2	66	1878-1903
Knight	Edward	3	179	1903-1910
Knight	Ella	1 & 2	36	1878-1903
Knight	Sarah	3	56	1903-1910
Knight	William	1 & 2	67	1878-1903
Knowlton	Edw. M.	1 & 2	14	1878-1903
Koch	Frank	1 & 2	12	1878-1903
Kohn	Tekla	3	31	1903-1910
Kohne	Katy	1 & 2	70	1878-1903
Kooke	Christian	1 & 2	64	1878-1903
Korte	Marcia C.	1 & 2	27	1878-1903
Kost	Ambros	1 & 2	13	1878-1903
Koulp	Henry	1 & 2	18	1878-1903
Kramer	John G.	3	76	1903-1910
Krating	Blanche	1 & 2	38	1878-1903
Krause	August Frederick Martin	1 & 2	26	1878-1903
Krause	August H.	3	55	1903-1910
Krause	Augusta	3	98	1903-1910
Krause	Lilly	3	83	1903-1910
Kraut	John	3	21	1903-1910
Kraut	Roscoe	3	13	1903-1910
Kremer	Cordelia	3	163	1903-1910
Krempel	Mary	3	176	1903-1910
Krites	Clara	1 & 2	37	1878-1903
Krites	Laura	1 & 2	36	1878-1903
Kroeschel	Mary	4	11	1910-1915
Kronable	Barney	1 & 2	68	1878-1903
Kronable	Caroline	4	66	1910-1915
Kronable	John WM.	1 & 2	68	1878-1903
Krooms	Malinda	4	55	1910-1915
Kuck	Anna	4	23	1910-1915
Kuckinmeister	Frank	1 & 2	50	1878-1903
Kuckmistor	William	1 & 2	45	1878-1903
Kuhne	Gerhard Henick	1 & 2	1	1878-1903

CALHOUN COUNTY DEATHS

Surname	Given Name	Book	Page	Year
Kulp	Henrietta	4	31	1910-1915
Kulp	Henry August Deedtrich	1 & 2	16	1878-1903
Kulp	Lillie	3	51	1903-1910
Kuntz	Frank	1 & 2	44	1878-1903
Kurtz	Ruth	1 & 2	70	1878-1903
Labbee	Alfred	1 & 2	8	1878-1903
Labert	Chas. F.	1 & 2	4	1878-1903
Laird	Isaac	1 & 2	1	1878-1903
Laird	Jennie	3	70	1903-1910
Laird	Lucinda E.	1 & 2	7	1878-1903
Laird	Mary C.	1 & 2	26	1878-1903
Laird	Mary E.	1 & 2	15	1878-1903
Laird	Rody	1 & 2	63	1878-1903
Laird	Sarah J.	1 & 2	44	1878-1903
Lamar	Sarah	4	95	1910-1915
Lamar	Zeprian	3	174	1903-1910
Lamaster	Logan	1 & 2	43	1878-1903
Lammy	Ethel	1 & 2	29	1878-1903
Lammy	John C.	3	122	1903-1910
Land	Rosa	1 & 2	15	1878-1903
Lane	John Stock	1 & 2	67	1878-1903
Lane	Mary Ann	1 & 2	32	1878-1903
Lane	WM. Henry	1 & 2	16	1878-1903
Lara	Levina	1 & 2	23	1878-1903
Lawson	Arthur W.	3	152	1903-1910
Lawson	Elizabeth	4	51	1910-1915
Lawson	Ira	1 & 2	8	1878-1903
Lawson	Mary Jane	4	68	1910-1915
Lawson	Walter	1 & 2	48	1878-1903
Lebbets	Lucas	1 & 2	15	1878-1903
Lee	James	4	30	1910-1915
Lee	Virginia S.	3	33	1903-1910
Leicheier	Henry	1 & 2	17	1878-1910
Leiser	Barbar	1 & 2	40	1878-1903
Leistrick	Chas	1 & 2	31	1878-1903

CALHOUN COUNTY DEATHS

Surname	Given Name	Book	Page	Year
Leistritz	Chas. A.	3	120	1903-1910
Leistritz	Edward	3	5	1903-1910
Leistritz	Harold L.	3	97	1903-1910
Lesseg	Clara	4	54	1910-1915
Lestrich	Augusta	1 & 2	8	1878-1903
Levis	Christopher C.	1 & 2	42	1878-1903
Levis	Farmer	1 & 2	51	1878-1903
Levis	Lucy Jane	1 & 2	8	1878-1903
Lewis	James Henry	3	44	1903-1910
Likes	David	3	178	1903-1910
Likes	Dora V.	3	112	1903-1910
Likes	Edward	1 & 2	22	1878-1903
Likes	Jane	3	38	1903-1910
Lind	Godfrey	3	124	1903-1910
Linder	Magdelina	1 & 2	74	1878-1903
Lippincott	David E.	1 & 2	22	1878-1903
Lirkogle	Cappie	1 & 2	11	1878-1903
Lloyd	N. Edna	3	103	1903-1910
Lloyd	Naomi Adna	3	103	1903-1910
Lock	Alice	1 & 2	24	1878-1903
Lockart	Ellery A.	4	6	1910-1915
Long	Chas	1 & 2	23	1878-1903
Long	Christina	4	58	1910-1915
Long	Floyd U.	1 & 2	76	1878-1903
Long	Homer	3	167	1903-1910
Long	Jesse	1 & 2	11	1878-1903
Long	Jospeh Barnett	4	106	1910-1915
Long	Leah	4	41	1910-1915
Longevin	Madaline	1 & 2	50	1878-1903
Love	Edward P.	1 & 2	13	1878-1903
Love	John D.	1 & 2	1	1878-1903
Love	William	3	12	1903-1910
Lowe	Caroline	1 & 2	15	1878-1903
Lowe	John	1 & 2	15	1878-1903
Lowe	Mary M.	3	133	1903-1910

CALHOUN COUNTY DEATHS

Surname	Given Name	Book	Page	Year
Luippold	Gottlieb	1 & 2	13	1878-1903
Lumby	Elza R.	1 & 2	58	1878-1903
Lumby	Kitty E.	1 & 2	60	1878-1903
Lumby	Marion T.	1 & 2	58	1878-1903
Lumby	Nancy	1 & 2	60	1878-1903
Lumby	Thos	1 & 2	58	1878-1903
Lynch	William	1 & 2	69	1878-1903
Lynn	Chester A.	1 & 2	35	1878-1903
Lynn	Mary	1 & 2	2	1878-1903
Lynn	Mary Jane	1 & 2	44	1878-1903
Mace	Lonzo C.	1 & 2	49	1878-1903
Machetton	Juanita	1 & 2	25	1878-1903
Madison	Elizabeth	4	83	1910-1915
Mager	Allie T.	1 & 2	10	1878-1903
Mager	Bernice Katherine	4	113	1910-1915
Mager	Howard Curtis	1 & 2	15	1878-1903
Mager		4	62	1910-1915
Mager		4	63	1910-1915
Maines	August	3	74	1903-1910
Malone	Cloe	1 & 2	10	1878-1903
Malone	Loraine	1 & 2	21	1878-1903
Malone	Mary	4	22	1910-1915
Manker	Marion S.	3	153	1903-1910
Manning	William	3	47	1903-1910
Mappen	John J.	4	9	1910-1915
Marion	Beulah	1 & 2	75	1878-1903
Marion	Franics	1 & 2	17	1878-1903
Marion	Frank	3	22	1903-1910
Marion	Sarah A.	1 & 2	17	1878-1903
Marks	Mary J.	1 & 2	26	1878-1903
Marsching	John	1 & 2	65	1878-1903
Martin	Charles Paul	4	111	1910-1915
Martin	John Martin	4	54	1910-1915
Martin	Laura	1 & 2	24	1878-1903
Martin	Mabel Florence	4	30	1910-1915

CALHOUN COUNTY DEATHS

Surname	Given Name	Book	Page	Year
Martin	Virgil L.	3	74	1903-1910
Mason	Marion E.	1 & 2	23	1878-1903
Mason	Mary	1 & 2	59	1878-1903
Massey	Rosa	3	125	1903-1910
Matthew	Denize	4	12	1910-1915
May	Mattie	1 & 2	20	1878-1903
Mcauley	Leander	4	47	1910-1915
McBride	John	3	20	1903-1910
McCallister	WM.	1 & 2	23	1878-1903
McClimens	Daniel Grisby	1 & 2	1	1878-1903
McClimens	Lulu	1 & 2	78	1878-1903
McClimens	Nancy E.	1 & 2	78	1878-1903
McClimens	Robert	1 & 2	49	1878-1903
McConnell	Jesse	1 & 2	3	1878-1903
McConnell	John S.	1 & 2	53	1878-1903
McConnell	Olive A.	1 & 2	20	1878-1903
McConnell	Robt	1 & 2	67	1878-1903
McConnell	Vera	1 & 2	67	1878-1903
McCoy	James N.	3	93	1903-1910
McCoy	William M.	4	14	1910-1915
McDonald	Lucy J.	3	63	1903-1910
McDonald	Mary	3	30	1903-1910
McFarland	Thos	1 & 2	68	1878-1903
McGee	Eliza A.	3	61	1903-1910
McGee	Isaac Paul	3	77	1903-1910
McGee		3	98	1903-1910
McGinnis	John	1 & 2	52	1878-1903
McGregor	Jesse Lee	1 & 2	66	1878-1903
McGuire	Milis	1 & 2	65	1878-1903
McGuire	Sophia	4	96	1910-1915
McGuire	Sophia L.	3	134	1903-1910
McGuire	William T.	3	75	1903-1910
McGunnis	Bridget	1 & 2	20	1878-1903
McGunnis	Thomas	1 & 2	22	1878-1903
McIntire	Alonzo	1 & 2	68	1878-1903

CALHOUN COUNTY DEATHS

Surname	Given Name	Book	Page	Year
McIntire	Charlotte	1 & 2	28	1878-1903
McIntire	Geo G.	1 & 2	6	1878-1903
McIntire		1 & 2	76	1878-1903
McLaughlin	Amanda M.	1 & 2	21	1878-1903
McLaughlin	Myrtle I.	1 & 2	26	1878-1903
McLaughlin	Robert	1 & 2	9	1878-1903
McLaughlin	Thorld C.	1 & 2	24	1878-1903
McLester	Biddy Belle	1 & 2	64	1878-1903
McLester	Liberty B.	1 & 2	70	1878-1903
McNabb	Frances	1 & 2	50	1878-1903
McNabb	Hugh	1 & 2	49	1878-1903
McNabb	John	3	50	1903-1910
McVeigh	Daniel	1 & 2	23	1878-1903
Mefford	A.J.	1 & 2	13	1878-1903
Mefford	Fred M.	3	15	1903-1910
Meilke	Caroline	1 & 2	28	1878-1903
Meilke	William	1 & 2	28	1878-1903
Meisenheimer	Carrie	1 & 2	4	1878-1903
Menke	Anna M.	3	110	1903-1910
Merida	Juanita	3	54	1903-1910
Merida	Laura E.	3	62	1903-1910
Merida	Margaret	1 & 2	7	1878-1903
Merida	Sam	1 & 2	62	1878-1903
Meseke	Wilhelmina	3	154	1903-1910
Mest	Henry	3	19	1903-1910
Meyer	Anton	1 & 2	26	1878-1903
Meyer	August	3	136	1903-1910
Meyer	Chas	1 & 2	34	1878-1903
Meyer	Clarence J.	3	116	1903-1910
Meyer	Frances	3	136	1903-1910
Meyer	Leo Garret	3	81	1903-1910
Meyer	Louis	4	22	1910-1915
Meyer	Mary	3	11	1903-1910
Meyer	Russell Drake	1 & 2	12	1878-1903
Meyer	Walter	1 & 2	26	1878-1903

CALHOUN COUNTY DEATHS

Surname	Given Name	Book	Page	Year
Mielke	August	3	140	1903-1910
Milke	William	1 & 2	28	1878-1903
Miller	Arimenta	4	18	1910-1915
Miller	Benjamin	1 & 2	18	1878-1903
Miller	Isabella	4	26	1910-1915
Miller	Jane Adelaide	4	90	1910-1915
Miller	Mary	1 & 2	69	1878-1903
Miller	Mary	1 & 2	76	1878-1903
Miller	Milley	1 & 2	6	1878-1903
Miller	William	1 & 2	3	1878-1903
Miller	Zip	1 & 2	69	1878-1903
Miner	Mrs. Eunice A. Lane	4	45	1910-1915
Miner	William W.	3	143	1903-1910
Minesinger	James H.	1 & 2	20	1878-1903
Mitchell	George Hubert	3	2	1903-1910
Modlin	Charles Paul Ray	4	50	1910-1915
Modlin	Pauline Fay	4	52	1910-1915
Moffett	George W.	3	138	1903-1910
Moffett	Lee	4	43	1910-1915
Moffett	Valeria	4	43	1910-1915
Monroe	William	1 & 2	52	1878-1903
Moore	Amanda E.	3	168	1903-1910
Moore	Clara	1 & 2	12	1878-1903
Moore	Elizah R.	1 & 2	14	1878-1903
Morgan	Anderson	3	135	1903-1910
Mortland	Mary A.	1 & 2	1	1878-1903
Mortland	Mary I.	3	35	1903-1910
Mortland	Mattie M.	1 & 2	29	1878-1903
Mortland	William	4	5	1910-1915
Mortland		1 & 2	52	1878-1903
Morton	Elizabeth	3	188	1903-1910
Morton	Fay Howe	3	172	1903-1910
Morton	Mahalia T.	3	131	1903-1910
Moses	Frank	1 & 2	17	1878-1903
Moses	Orinda B.	1 & 2	8	1878-1903

CALHOUN COUNTY DEATHS

Surname	Given Name	Book	Page	Year
Mossmann	Anna M.	3	70	1903-1910
Motaz	A. Mary	1 & 2	31	1878-1903
Motaz	Adolph	1 & 2	38	1878-1903
Motaz	Sarah E.	1 & 2	30	1878-1903
Motaz	Sophia	4	51	1910-1915
Motaz		1 & 2	62	1878-1903
Mottaz	Louise	3	184	1903-1910
Moultry	Robert Carroll	4	23	1910-1915
Mueller	Henry	1 & 2	60	1878-1903
Mueller	Hilda V.	4	66	1910-1915
Mulkey	Loyd A.	1 & 2	60	1878-1903
Mulkey	Thomas	1 & 2	32	1878-1903
Muller	Peter	3	95	1903-1910
Nairn	Christopher C.	4	8	1910-1915
Nairn	Elizabeth Jane	4	104	1910-1915
Nairn	James	4	63	1910-1915
Nairn	John	1 & 2	5	1878-1903
Nairn	Luna P.	4	49	1910-1915
Narup	Kathryne	3	166	1903-1910
Nash	Harriett	1 & 2	19	1878-1903
Neal	William Mckinly	1 & 2	21	1878-1903
Neil	Maria Ann	1 & 2	21	1878-1903
Neimier	Hary	4	113	1910-1915
Nelson	Albert	4	87	1910-1915
Nelson	Douglass	1 & 2	56	1878-1903
Nevius	Jane	1 & 2	7	1878-1903
Nevius	Otis H.	1 & 2	63	1878-1903
Newman	John Henry	3	176	1903-1910
Nicholas	Chris	3	71	1903-1910
Nicholas	Leroy	1 & 2	60	1878-1903
Nicholas	Lulu	1 & 2	39	1878-1903
Nicholas	W.P.	1 & 2	25	1878-1903
Nickolas	Mary Alice	1 & 2	14	1878-1903
Niel	John P.	4	88	1910-1915
Nimerick	Bridget	3	165	1903-1910

CALHOUN COUNTY DEATHS

Surname	Given Name	Book	Page	Year
Nimerick	Rosana	1 & 2	22	1878-1903
No Name		3	23	1903-1910
No Name		3	63	1903-1910
Nodston	John	1 & 2	18	1878-1903
Nold	Malchor	3	84	1903-1910
Nolte	August	3	21	1903-1910
Nolte	Elmer H.	4	72	1910-1915
Nolte	Joseph	1 & 2	30	1878-1903
Nolte	Mary	4	10	1910-1915
Nolte	Sarah	3	123	1903-1910
Norberta	Agnes	1 & 2	18	1878-1903
Norris	Jos. C.	1 & 2	21	1878-1903
Northcutt	Eliza	1 & 2	64	1878-1903
Northman	Johanna	4	15	1910-1915
Nutz	John B.	1 & 2	1	1878-1903
Oberjohann	William F.	4	97	1910-1915
Oberjohn	Earl Ervin	1 & 2	20	1878-1903
Oberry	Gustave W.	1 & 2	26	1878-1903
Oden	Melvin	3	131	1903-1910
Oettle	Albrecht	4	33	1910-1915
Oettle	Andria	1 & 2	19	1878-1903
Oettle	Angelia	4	97	1910-1915
Oettle	Anna Katherine	4	117	1910-1915
Oettle	Christopher	4	41	1910-1915
Oettle	Fred	3	109	1903-1910
Oettle	Jesse	4	26	1910-1915
Oettle	John	1 & 2	15	1878-1903
Oettle	Marie Garnet	3	170	1903-1910
Oettli	Gotlieb	1 & 2	23	1878-1903
Oezenn	Oscar	1 & 2	42	1878-1903
Ogden	Ernest Sherry	3	166	1903-1910
Ortleb	Frank H.	1 & 2	74	1878-1903
Ortleb	Margreth K.	1 & 2	9	1878-1903
Osborne	Murton Auer	4	3	1910-1910
Osgood	Samuel N.	1 & 2	14	1878-1903

CALHOUN COUNTY DEATHS

Surname	Given Name	Book	Page	Year
Osterman	Charlotte	4	111	1910-1915
Osterman	Elizabeth Mary	1 & 2	24	1878-1903
Osterman	John	1 & 2	1	1878-1903
Osterman	Mary E.	3	53	1903-1910
Osterman	William	1 & 2	74	1878-1903
Otle	Carl	1 & 2	13	1878-1903
Otten	Herman	1 & 2	39	1878-1903
Ottle	Mary	3	32	1903-1910
Otwell	William J.	3	183	1903-1910
Otwell		3	59	1903-1910
Owens	Drann	1 & 2	70	1878-1903
Owens	Ruth	1 & 2	50	1878-1903
Owens	Sarah	1 & 2	6	1878-1903
Owens	Sarah J.	3	41	1903-1910
Pach	Mary	1 & 2	15	1878-1903
Pankey	Jospeh	1 & 2	10	1878-1903
Parker	Gideon	1 & 2	44	1878-1903
Parker	John	1 & 2	31	1878-1903
Parker	Leona	4	2	1910-1915
Parker	Malinda	1 & 2	63	1878-1903
Patrick	Mary	1 & 2	5	1878-1903
Patterson	Martha	1 & 2	19	1878-1903
Peacock	Edith	1 & 2	10	1878-1903
Peacock	Jermina	1 & 2	39	1878-1903
Pearson	Bessie	4	113	1910-1915
Peeler	Bernard	1 & 2	75	1878-1903
Peeler	Forest I.	3	165	1903-1910
Pehm	Anna	1 & 2	35	1878-1903
Pehm	Anna	1 & 2	10	1878-1903
Pehm	Anna A.	1 & 2	41	1878-1903
Pehm	Anna C.	3	154	1903-1910
Pehm	Herman	4	82	1910-1915
Pehm	Regina	1 & 2	35	1878-1903
Pehm	Regina	3	28	1903-1910
Pehm	Rudotph	4	108	1910-1915

CALHOUN COUNTY DEATHS

Surname	Given Name	Book	Page	Year
Peller	Eustash	1 & 2	40	1878-1903
Pellican	Abraham	1 & 2	31	1878-1903
Pellicann	Bartholomew	1 & 2	46	1878-1903
Pepper	John M.	1 & 2	15	1878-1903
Pepper	Joseph	1 & 2	8	1878-1903
Peppers	William	3	49	1903-1910
Perard	August	1 & 2	42	1878-1903
Percentina	Antone	1 & 2	33	1878-1903
Percentina	Antone	1 & 2	32	1878-1903
Percentina	Eliza	1 & 2	55	1878-1903
Percentina	Joseph	1 & 2	6	1878-1903
Percentina	Lenora J.	1 & 2	62	1878-1903
Perkins	Clarence	3	88	1903-1910
Perry	Jacob W.	4	90	1910-1915
Perry	John W.	1 & 2	30	1878-1903
Peters	Sarah	1 & 2	6	1878-1903
Petersen	Andrew P.	3	57	1903-1910
Petre	Peter	3	57	1903-1910
Peuterbaugh		3	140	1903-1910
Philipps	Lobry	1 & 2	37	1878-1903
Philips	Kise K.	1 & 2	39	1878-1903
Philips	Mary	1 & 2	26	1878-1903
Phillips	James Edward	3	175	1903-1910
Phillips	Ruth	4	99	1910-1915
Phillips	WM. M.	1 & 2	45	1878-1903
Picket	Moses	1 & 2	25	1878-1903
Pickett	Juranda K.	1 & 2	52	1878-1903
Pieper	Henry L.	3	180	1903-1910
Pieper	Mary	3	154	1903-1910
Pipen	Olive C.	1 & 2	41	1878-1903
Piper		1 & 2	55	1878-1903
Pluester	Barney	1 & 2	64	1878-1903
Pluester	Mary	1 & 2	64	1878-1903
Plummer	Carry Allen	1 & 2	17	1878-1903
Plummer	Ethel	4	15	1910-1915

CALHOUN COUNTY DEATHS

Surname	Given Name	Book	Page	Year
Plummer	Hettie May	3	156	1903-1910
Plummer	Lizzie	1 & 2	70	1878-1903
Plummer	Orlena	1 & 2	46	1878-1903
Plummer	Ray	1 & 2	65	1878-1903
Plummer	Rose E.	3	126	1903-1910
Plummer	William Henry	4	35	1910-1915
Plummer		3	126	1903-1910
Poettler	Peter	3	146	1903-1910
Pohlman	Ann	1 & 2	18	1878-1903
Pohlman	Anna	1 & 2	66	1878-1903
Pohlman	Anna Margaret	1 & 2	23	1878-1903
Pohlman	Jos. C.	1 & 2	77	1878-1903
Pohlman	Mary	4	97	1910-1915
Pohlman		3	123	1903-1910
Pointsalot	Anna E.	3	148	1903-1910
Pointsalot	Ray V.	3	68	1903-1910
Polman	Katie	1 & 2	19	1878-1903
Pontero	Mary Anna	4	24	1910-1915
Pontero	Nicholas	4	59	1910-1915
Pontius	Walter	4	110	1910-1915
Poor	Abner V.	4	104	1910-1915
Poor	Allen	4	97	1910-1915
Poor	Andrew J.	1 & 2	5	1878-1903
Poor	E. Olive	3	79	1903-1910
Poor	Gevert L.	1 & 2	35	1878-1903
Poor	James	1 & 2	44	1878-1903
Poor	Margaret	1 & 2	25	1878-1903
Poor	Margaret Elizabeth	4	112	1910-1915
Poor	Mary Amanda	1 & 2	2	1878-1903
Poor	Melissa F.	1 & 2	30	1878-1903
Poor	Milo Mirl	3	163	1903-1910
Poor	Nancy E.	3	92	1903-1910
Poor	Samuel	3	43	1903-1910
Poor	William	1 & 2	72	1878-1903
Poor	William	1 & 2	61	1878-1903

CALHOUN COUNTY DEATHS

Surname	Given Name	Book	Page	Year
Poor		1 & 2	3	1878-1903
Poor		3	174	1903-1910
Pope	Geo M.	1 & 2	77	1878-1903
Post	Oliver	3	170	1903-1910
Potney	E.	1 & 2	9	1878-1903
Powell	David	1 & 2	52	1878-1903
Powell	Jacob	3	27	1903-1910
Powell	Johanna	1 & 2	76	1878-1903
Powell	Nora Lura	1 & 2	20	1878-1903
Praul	Mary E.	1 & 2	27	1878-1903
Praul	Rudolph	1 & 2	22	1878-1903
Presley	George William	4	100	1910-1915
Presley	Sarah C.	3	52	1903-1910
Pressey	David	3	147	1903-1910
Pressey	Henry	1 & 2	22	1878-1903
Pressey	John Baptiste	4	108	1910-1915
Pressey	Margreth C.	1 & 2	31	1878-1903
Pressley	Frances Hazel	4	116	1910-1915
Pressley	Julia L. A.	4	85	1910-1915
Pressley	Perry	4	96	1910-1915
Preston	James	1 & 2	49	1878-1903
Preston	William	3	67	1903-1910
Pruit		1 & 2	74	1878-1903
Puls	WM. Clifford	1 & 2	18	1878-1903
Qualls	John	1 & 2	16	1878-1903
Quiller	Delli	1 & 2	43	1878-1903
Raker	Henry	3	129	1903-1910
Rall	Benjamin	1 & 2	11	1878-1903
Ramsey	Chancey R.	1 & 2	41	1878-1903
Ramsey	James	1 & 2	13	1878-1903
Ramsey	Larkin	1 & 2	21	1878-1903
Ramsey	Mary Maynard	3	180	1903-1910
Randall	Mary	4	65	1910-1915
Randel	James M.	4	65	1910-1915
Rayborn	Chas. H.	3	10	1903-1910

CALHOUN COUNTY DEATHS

Surname	Given Name	Book	Page	Year
Read	Joseph	1 & 2	5	1878-1903
Recker	Joseph	1 & 2	19	1878-1903
Reed	Albert	3	164	1903-1910
Reed	Carrie A.	1 & 2	60	1878-1903
Reed	Charles	1 & 2	17	1878-1903
Reed	Huldy Ann	1 & 2	9	1878-1903
Reed	Joel	1 & 2	49	1878-1903
Reed	Jospeh	1 & 2	25	1878-1903
Reed	Martha	1 & 2	25	1878-1903
Reed	Opal	3	109	1903-1910
Reed	Pearl	4	46	1910-1915
Reed	Wesley	1 & 2	14	1878-1903
Reeves	Elizabeth	1 & 2	47	1878-1903
Reeves	Travis	1 & 2	12	1878-1903
Reeves		1 & 2	17	1878-1903
Reigenhart	Marietta	1 & 2	19	1878-1903
Reimenschneider	Anna Mary	1 & 2	45	1878-1903
Reimenschneider	John	1 & 2	54	1878-1903
Reimenschneider	Lena	1 & 2	68	1878-1903
Reimenschneider	Mary	1 & 2	65	1878-1903
Reineke	Adam	3	84	1903-1910
Reineke	Dina	4	57	1910-1915
Reis	Louis	1 & 2	8	1878-1903
Rengenhardt	Louis	1 & 2	41	1878-1903
Renode	George F.	4	65	1910-1915
Rentz	Hellena	1 & 2	22	1878-1903
Rentz		1 & 2	34	1878-1903
Retzer	Frank H.	4	60	1910-1915
Retzer	Theresa	1 & 2	55	1878-1903
Retzer	Tracy	1 & 2	3	1878-1903
Rexrod	Fred	1 & 2	20	1878-1903
Rhinsocker	Mary Elizabeth	1 & 2	9	1878-1903
Richard	Cecil Forest	4	23	1910-1915
Richardson		1 & 2	9	1878-1910
Richey	Lora	1 & 2	51	1878-1903

CALHOUN COUNTY DEATHS

Surname	Given Name	Book	Page	Year
Richter	Annie	3	29	1903-1910
Richter	Christian	3	48	1903-1910
Richter	Elizabeth	3	138	1903-1910
Richter	Garret	1 & 2	48	1878-1903
Richter	WM.	1 & 2	48	1878-1903
Ringhausen	Adaline Beckie	1 & 2	9	1878-1903
Ringhausen	Delighia	4	13	1910-1915
Ringhausen	Ester	1 & 2	78	1878-1903
Ringhausen	Levis	1 & 2	31	1878-1903
Ritter	Evalina H.	4	89	1910-1915
Roach	Laura	4	67	1910-1915
Roberts	Levis	1 & 2	20	1878-1903
Robinson	Ella	1 & 2	31	1878-1903
Rodgers	Abner U.	1 & 2	21	1878-1903
Rodgers	Columbus	3	99	1903-1910
Rodgers	Mollie	1 & 2	73	1878-1903
Roehl	John	1 & 2	59	1878-1903
Roentz	William	3	158	1903-1910
Roman	Bopp	1 & 2	34	1878-1903
Rosa	Caroline	1 & 2	37	1878-1903
Rosa	Elvira	3	108	1903-1910
Rosa	Hellia Melonia	1 & 2	4	1878-1903
Rosa	James	3	28	1903-1910
Rosa	Marie Celia	1 & 2	2	1878-1903
Rosa	Roy E.	1 & 2	67	1878-1903
Rosa	William T.	4	83	1910-1915
Rose	America	4	13	1910-1915
Rose	Anton Jr.	3	52	1903-1910
Rose	Charles B.	4	42	1910-1915
Rose	Etta	1 & 2	59	1878-1903
Rose	Eva M.	1 & 2	60	1878-1903
Rose	Harry A.	1 & 2	49	1878-1903
Rose	Paul J.	4	55	1910-1915
Rose	Plenny W.	1 & 2	67	1878-1903
Rose	Thomas B.	4	28	1910-1915

CALHOUN COUNTY DEATHS

Surname	Given Name	Book	Page	Year
Rose	John	3	173	1903-1910
Ross	Frank H.	4	73	1910-1915
Roth	Anna	4	70	1910-1915
Roth	August	3	158	1903-1910
Roth	Bridget	3	86	1903-1910
Roth	Catherine	1 & 2	36	1878-1903
Roth	Emma	3	63	1903-1910
Roth	John	1 & 2	22	1878-1903
Roth	Julia E.	3	120	1903-1910
Roth	Mary	3	29	1903-1910
Roth	Michael A.	1 & 2	58	1878-1903
Roth	Peter	3	121	1903-1910
Roth	Peter M.	3	77	1903-1910
Roth	Rosina	1 & 2	55	1878-1903
Roundcount	Edwan	1 & 2	16	1878-1903
Ruffs	Hubert	1 & 2	53	1878-1903
Rulon	Alice	1 & 2	35	1878-1903
Rulon	Walter A.	1 & 2	30	1878-1903
Rulon		3	69	1903-1910
Russel	Riley Estella	1 & 2	3	1878-1903
Russel	Tolba	1 & 2	10	1878-1903
Russell	Johan	1 & 2	29	1878-1903
Russell		1 & 2	9	1878-1903
Rustemeyer	Oscar	1 & 2	70	1878-1903
Ruyle	John Robt.	1 & 2	1	1878-1903
Ruyle	Joseph	1 & 2	62	1878-1903
Ruyle	Levis A.	1 & 2	39	1878-1903
Ruyle	Mary M.	3	42	1903-1910
Ruyle	Nancy Elizabeth	1 & 2	20	1878-1903
Ruyle	Nona M.	3	143	1903-1910
Ruyle	Zomia	3	124	1903-1910
Sager	Dorothy B.	3	152	1903-1910
Sagress	James D.	3	94	1903-1910
Salbert	Chas. Frederick	1 & 2	4	1878-1903
Sampier	Felix	1 & 2	45	1878-1903

CALHOUN COUNTY DEATHS

Surname	Given Name	Book	Page	Year
Sampier	Mary	1 & 2	68	1878-1903
Sampson	Charley	1 & 2	69	1878-1903
Sanders	Richard H.	1 & 2	48	1878-1903
Sands	Benj. Franklin	1 & 2	65	1878-1903
Santon	Herman	1 & 2	5	1878-1903
Saunders	Elizabeth	1 & 2	4	1878-1903
Saunders	Ellen	3	180	1903-1910
Saunders	Henry	1 & 2	22	1878-1903
Saunders	Major	3	37	1903-1910
Sawyer	Robt.	1 & 2	18	1878-1903
Schaper	Ernst	3	137	1903-1910
Schemider	Charles	4	4	1910-1915
Scheppard	HY	1 & 2	75	1878-1903
Scherah	Louis	1 & 2	11	1878-1903
Schiekler	Mary B.	4	44	1910-1915
Schilling	Barbara	1 & 2	17	1878-1903
Schlee	Barbara	3	5	1903-1910
Schleeper	Frank	1 & 2	15	1878-1903
Schleeper	Fred	3	45	1903-1910
Schleeper	John	4	91	1910-1915
Schleeper	Leonard J.	3	151	1903-1910
Schleeper	Mary	1 & 2	7	1878-1903
Schleeper	Mary Anna Minnie	3	169	1903-1910
Schleeper	Mathias	4	26	1910-1915
Schleeper	Ralhennie	1 & 2	69	1878-1903
Schleeper	Virgil	3	175	1903-1910
Schlieper	Charles Sr.	3	108	1903-1910
Schlieper	Henry	4	89	1910-1915
Schlieper	Paul	3	161	1903-1910
Schlippe	Daniel	1 & 2	10	1878-1903
Schmidt	Mary	4	36	1910-1915
Schmitz	John	3	40	1903-1910
Schneider	Catherine	1 & 2	62	1878-1903
Schneider	Gertrude	3	75	1903-1910
Schneider	Mathias B.	1 & 2	9	1878-1903

CALHOUN COUNTY DEATHS

Surname	Given Name	Book	Page	Year
Schuler	Elizabeth Jane	4	76	1910-1915
Schulte	Anna Maria	3	157	1903-1910
Schulte	Herman	1 & 2	5	1878-1903
Schulte	Mary	3	80	1903-1910
Schulze	Herman	3	46	1903-1910
Schuman	Caroline	4	118	1910-1915
Schuman	Christian	1 & 2	69	1878-1903
Schuman	Louisa	1 & 2	35	1878-1903
Schumann	John M.	1 & 2	64	1878-1903
Schumann	Leonard	3	117	1903-1910
Schuyler	Francis Marion	1 & 2	16	1878-1903
Schuyler	Laura E.	3	26	1903-1910
Sconce	Lucinda	3	36	1903-1910
Sconce	Sarah	1 & 2	12	1878-1903
Scott	John	4	87	1910-1915
Scott	Kattie	1 & 2	5	1878-1903
Scott	Rebecca (Heaton)	1 & 2	1	1878-1903
Scott	Rebeccah Heston	1 & 2	1	1878-1903
Scott	William	4	30	1910-1915
Scranton	Vera Lucile	4	46	1910-1915
Sebbus	August	1 & 2	72	1878-1903
Seibanmann	Clarence Chas.	1 & 2	25	1878-1903
Seidler	Mary	4	85	1910-1915
Seidler		3	94	1903-1910
Seidler		3	95	1903-1910
Seiferman	Nicholas	3	4	1903-1910
Seimore	Mrs. Meinard	1 & 2	10	1878-1903
Seiver	Henry	1 & 2	22	1878-1903
Selby	Amanda	3	130	1903-1910
Selzer	Luise	1 & 2	14	1878-1903
Senatz	Volentine	1 & 2	56	1878-1903
Sevier	Arthur	1 & 2	17	1878-1903
Sevier	Martha Alice	1 & 2	73	1878-1903
Sevier		3	2	1903-1910
Sharing	Sarah	1 & 2	32	1878-1903

CALHOUN COUNTY DEATHS

Surname	Given Name	Book	Page	Year
Shaw	Bertha	3	44	1903-1910
Sheff	Joseph	1 & 2	5	1878-1903
Sheidan	Elmer P.	3	93	1903-1910
Shephard	Franklin	1 & 2	50	1878-1903
Sherard	Christina	1 & 2	13	1878-1903
Shoeful	Geo	1 & 2	43	1878-1903
Shores	Geneva Estell	4	1	1910-1915
Sibley	Catherine M.	3	114	1903-1910
Sibley	John	1 & 2	41	1878-1903
Sidwell	Abraham Lincoln	4	10	1910-1915
Sidwell	Catherine	4	108	1910-1915
Sidwell	Charles A.	3	10	1903-1910
Sidwell	Elish	1 & 2	71	1878-1903
Sidwell	John WM.	1 & 2	43	1878-1903
Sidwell	Louisiana	1 & 2	8	1878-1903
Sieberman	Caroline L.	3	22	1903-1910
Sieberman	Edward	1 & 2	24	1878-1903
Sieberman	Mary	3	114	1903-1910
Siebus	Louisa	3	112	1903-1910
Siebus	Simon	1 & 2	77	1878-1903
Siebus	Stephen	4	93	1910-1915
Siemer	Franklin	1 & 2	72	1878-1903
Siemer	Garrett	1 & 2	13	1878-1903
Siemer	Geo	1 & 2	72	1878-1903
Siemer	John	3	29	1903-1910
Sievers	Mary Annie	1 & 2	24	1878-1903
Simon	John	4	64	1910-1915
Simon	John H.	3	72	1903-1910
Simon	Mark	1 & 2	3	1878-1903
Simons	Teresa	4	34	1910-1915
Simons		1 & 2	30	1878-1903
Simpson	Alonzo	1 & 2	18	1878-1903
Simpson	Chas.	1 & 2	16	1878-1903
Sitton	Chas. A.	1 & 2	15	1878-1903
Sitton	Dr. Joshua W.	1 & 2	15	1878-1903

CALHOUN COUNTY DEATHS

Surname	Given Name	Book	Page	Year
Sitton	Martha E.	1 & 2	7	1878-1903
Sitton	Robert	1 & 2	20	1878-1903
Skirvin	Susan A.	3	70	1903-1910
Slyter	Addly	1 & 2	56	1878-1903
Slyter	Richard	1 & 2	53	1878-1903
Smidt	Frank	1 & 2	2	1878-1903
Smith	Alta	1 & 2	39	1878-1903
Smith	August Woodrow	4	106	1910-1915
Smith	Augustus	1 & 2	54	1878-1903
Smith	Birdie Lee	1 & 2	66	1878-1903
Smith	Catherine	1 & 2	3	1878-1903
Smith	Chas. H.	1 & 2	24	1878-1903
Smith	Edith	1 & 2	48	1878-1903
Smith	Edward	3	177	1903-1910
Smith	George Andrew	4	29	1910-1915
Smith	James Frank	4	62	1910-1915
Smith	James G.	1 & 2	45	1878-1903
Smith	John D.	3	23	1903-1910
Smith	Lena	1 & 2	18	1878-1903
Smith	Mary	1 & 2	3	1878-1903
Smith	Mary	1 & 2	8	1878-1903
Smith	Mary	1 & 2	18	1878-1903
Smith	Rachel	1 & 2	24	1878-1903
Smith	Samatha	3	186	1903-1910
Smith	Sarah	1 & 2	44	1878-1903
Smith	Walter Willard	4	53	1910-1915
Smith	William H.	3	82	1903-1910
Smith		1 & 2	27	1878-1903
Smith		1 & 2	8	1878-1903
Smyth	Anna T.	1 & 2	58	1878-1903
Smyth	Clara Jane	1 & 2	59	1878-1903
Snider	Betsy E.	1 & 2	40	1878-1903
Snider	Nancy Eva	4	32	1910-1915
Snider	Rebecca	4	84	1910-1915
Snow	Maxine Letha	4	103	1910-1915

CALHOUN COUNTY DEATHS

Surname	Given Name	Book	Page	Year
Snyder	Abraham	1 & 2	30	1878-1903
Snyder	Arthur Leroy	1 & 2	30	1878-1903
Snyder	Bertha May	1 & 2	12	1878-1903
Snyder	John	1 & 2	11	1878-1903
Snyder	Pauline Teresa	1 & 2	15	1878-1903
Snyders	Elizabeth	1 & 2	59	1878-1903
Snyders	Helen C.	1 & 2	27	1878-1903
Snyders	John	3	91	1903-1910
Snyders	Lillian	3	91	1903-1910
Snyders	Mary Rosina	3	189	1903-1910
Snyders	Peter	1 & 2	31	1878-1903
Snyders	Regina Ann	1 & 2	77	1878-1903
Sourbeck	John	1 & 2	66	1878-1903
Sowards	Sara	4	59	1910-1915
Spang	Frank	1 & 2	64	1878-1903
Spang	raymond	4	93	1910-1915
Spears	Frank	1 & 2	59	1878-1903
Spencer	rebecca	1 & 2	56	1878-1903
Spers	Catherine	1 & 2	4	1878-1903
Springstun	Ladonia A.	3	7	1903-1910
Springstun	Lemuel A.	1 & 2	15	1878-1903
Springstun	Ruby	3	62	1903-1910
Squier	Carl	1 & 2	10	1878-1903
Squier		1 & 2	27	1878-1903
Squier		3	25	1903-1910
Starks	Chirstopher H.	1 & 2	33	1878-1903
Starnes	Norah	1 & 2	71	1878-1903
Starr	Caroline	3	87	1903-1910
Starr	Dena	4	75	1910-1910
Starr	Geo F.	1 & 2	77	1878-1903
Starr	Henry	1 & 2	26	1878-1903
Stearns	Lubinda Adeline	3	181	1903-1910
Stearns	Paul	4	71	1910-1915
Stein	John	3	3	1903-1910
Stein	John	3	141	1903-1910

CALHOUN COUNTY DEATHS

Surname	Given Name	Book	Page	Year
Stelbrink	Elizabeth	1 & 2	68	1878-1903
Stelbrink	John	1 & 2	34	1878-1903
Stelbrink	Mary	3	130	1903-1910
Sternes	Joseph	1 & 2	28	1878-1903
Stiles	Cecil	4	75	1910-1915
Stiles	Josephine	1 & 2	8	1878-1903
Stinebaugh	John	1 & 2	36	1878-1903
Stinnett	Virgil	3	124	1903-1910
Stoffel	Elizabeth S.	3	20	1903-1910
Stoffel	Lizzie	1 & 2	21	1878-1903
Stoffel	William	3	21	1903-1910
Stone	Jennetta	1 & 2	32	1878-1903
Stone	John M.	1 & 2	54	1878-1903
Stone	Shollis	1 & 2	22	1878-1903
Stratmeyer	Catherine	1 & 2	19	1878-1903
Stratwyer	Augusta	1 & 2	11	1878-1903
Stumbeaugh	Luther	1 & 2	41	1878-1903
Styers	Rulph	1 & 2	20	1878-1903
Styros	Andy	1 & 2	19	1878-1903
Sudbrack	F.W.	1 & 2	63	1878-1903
Sudbrack	Fredericke	4	90	1910-1915
Sullivan	WM. H.	1 & 2	11	1878-1903
Surbeck	Maria D.	1 & 2	27	1878-1903
Surgeon	James	3	43	1903-1910
Surgeon	James H.	3	32	1903-1910
Sutter	John B.	3	61	1903-1910
Sutter	Magdalina	4	43	1910-1915
Sutton	Nathan R.	4	72	1910-1915
Swan	Hubert L.	3	94	1903-1910
Swan	James W.	4	83	1910-1915
Swan	John	4	117	1910-1915
Swandgen		1 & 2	26	1878-1903
Swanson	Andrew	4	31	1910-1915
Swarnes	Jersey	1 & 2	73	1878-1903
Swarnes	Maholn	1 & 2	10	1878-1903

CALHOUN COUNTY DEATHS

Surname	Given Name	Book	Page	Year
Swarnes	William	3	16	1903-1910
Sweeney	Andrew J.	1 & 2	5	1878-1903
Sweeney	WM A.	1 & 2	26	1878-1903
Sweet	Brokaw	3	177	1903-1910
Sweet	George G.	3	81	1903-1910
Sweetman	Alfred	1 & 2	9	1878-1903
Sweetman	Florence I.	3	6	1903-1910
Sweney	Elizabeth	4	93	1910-1915
Sword	George Washington	1 & 2	1	1878-1903
Synders	P. Bernice	3	97	1903-1910
Tadlock	Abigail	1 & 2	20	1878-1903
Talbert	Richard Alvin	4	50	1910-1915
Tarpey	Michael	1 & 2	77	1878-1903
Tavenier	Ferdinard	1 & 2	10	1878-1903
Tavernier	Ernestine Augusta	4	38	1910-1915
Tavernier	Louis Francis	1 & 2	17	1878-1903
Tayon	Johanna	1 & 2	42	1878-1903
Tellkamp	Mary	1 & 2	39	1878-1903
Temple	Arthur C.	3	155	1903-1910
Temple	Elizabeth	3	44	1903-1910
Temple	James	3	168	1903-1910
Temple	Julia Ann	1 & 2	15	1878-1903
Temple	Parsia	1 & 2	25	1878-1903
Tepen	William	4	68	1910-1915
Teppen	Lucas	1 & 2	48	1878-1903
Terneus	Myrtle	4	44	1910-1915
Tharp	Naney A.	1 & 2	37	1878-1903
Thomas	Levi	1 & 2	17	1878-1903
Thomas	Mary Ann	1 & 2	18	1878-1903
Thompson	Chas.	3	169	1903-1910
Thompson	Samuel	1 & 2	61	1878-1903
Thorp	Anna	4	60	1910-1915
Thorp	James Collins	4	67	1910-1915
Tilbitt	Chas. M.	1 & 2	39	1878-1903
Tilly	Eliza	1 & 2	35	1878-1903

CALHOUN COUNTY DEATHS

Surname	Given Name	Book	Page	Year
Tilly	Henry Earl	1 & 2	51	1878-1903
Titus	Catherine	3	150	1903-1910
Tobin	Margaret	1 & 2	23	1878-1903
Todd	Erbe	3	152	1903-1910
Todd	Homer	3	14	1903-1910
Todd	Mary Bell	1 & 2	14	1878-1903
Tolbert	Frances O.	3	148	1903-1910
Tolbert	Geo W.	1 & 2	39	1878-1903
Tolbert	Jesse	1 & 2	78	1878-1903
Tolbert	Lous	3	161	1903-1910
Toll	Gatia	1 & 2	62	1878-1903
Tops	Anna	1 & 2	34	1878-1903
Towbridge	John H.	3	48	1903-1910
Trankley	Ida	1 & 2	73	1878-1903
Traufler	Mary	4	37	1910-1915
Tribble	Edith Alice	1 & 2	64	1878-1903
Trobridge	David	1 & 2	8	1878-1903
Trossen	Herman	3	87	1903-1910
Trussen	Tabata	3	157	1903-1910
Tucker	Geo G.	1 & 2	40	1878-1903
Turnbaugh	Alma	3	3	1903-1910
Turnbaugh	Ariana C.	1 & 2	44	1878-1903
Turnbaugh	Mary	1 & 2	12	1878-1903
Turnbaugh	Silas E.	1 & 2	24	1878-1903
Turnbull	James M.	1 & 2	6	1878-1903
Turnbull	Mildred Elizabeth	4	16	1910-1915
Turner	Albert	1 & 2	7	1878-1903
Turner	Sarah Elizabeth	4	45	1910-1915
Tuttle	Mark P.	1 & 2	4	1878-1903
Twichell	Chesby W.	1 & 2	15	1878-1903
Twichell	Emma J.	1 & 2	56	1878-1903
Twichell	Johnie C.	1 & 2	71	1878-1903
Twichell	Leonard	3	78	1903-1910
Twichell	Oberia	4	79	1910-1915
Twichell	Serella	1 & 2	12	1878-1903

CALHOUN COUNTY DEATHS

Surname	Given Name	Book	Page	Year
Ulery	David	3	135	1903-1910
Ulery	Elizabeth	1 & 2	33	1878-1903
Ulery	Janie	4	88	1910-1915
Ulery	Shelton	3	13	1903-1910
Vaambik	Susanna	1 & 2	12	1878-1903
Vancill	Cora	1 & 2	20	1878-1903
Vanul	Napoleon	1 & 2	13	1878-1903
Varner	Israel	1 & 2	7	1878-1903
Vaughan	Robert Lee	4	38	1910-1915
Veetman	Henry	1 & 2	51	1878-1903
Vetter	Gracie	4	56	1910-1915
Vetter	Louis	1 & 2	39	1878-1903
Vetter	Mary	1 & 2	46	1878-1903
Vetter	William	1 & 2	48	1878-1903
Vetter		3	15	1903-1910
Vetter		3	77	1903-1910
Voss	John Henry	1 & 2	5	1878-1903
Waddle	Susan	1 & 2	56	1878-1903
Waddle	Susan	1 & 2	51	1878-1903
Waddle	WM. Jesse	1 & 2	18	1878-1903
Wagoner	Eckard	1 & 2	18	1878-1903
Wagoner	Joseph Eckert	4	105	1910-1915
Wagoner	Katie L.	3	92	1903-1910
Wahl	Catherine Jane	4	92	1910-1915
Wahl	John	3	9	1903-1910
Waldhauser	John G.	1 & 2	58	1878-1903
Waldhauser	Valentine	1 & 2	52	1878-1903
Waldow	Elizabeth Ann	3	176	1903-1910
Waldow	Mary L.	3	24	1903-1910
Walhauser	Agatha	1 & 2	50	1878-1903
Wallace	John J.	3	147	1903-1910
Wallendorff	Doris	4	29	1910-1915
Wallendorff	Eliz J.	1 & 2	74	1878-1903
Wallendorff	Joseph	1 & 2	27	1878-1903
Wallendorff	Mary Ann	1 & 2	22	1878-1903

CALHOUN COUNTY DEATHS

Surname	Given Name	Book	Page	Year
Wallendorff	Osca	1 & 2	4	1878-1903
Wallmann	Helena	4	14	1910-1915
Ward	Lessie	1 & 2	77	1878-1903
Waschkowsky	Fred	4	17	1910-1915
Watson	Amanda	1 & 2	69	1878-1903
Watson	C.A.	3	113	1903-1910
Watson	Earl F.	1 & 2	46	1878-1903
Watson	James	1 & 2	62	1878-1903
Watson	Leslie	1 & 2	75	1878-1903
Watson	Milly	3	128	1903-1910
Watson	Vermia	1 & 2	5	1878-1903
Watts	Alta S.	1 & 2	51	1878-1903
Watts	Emilie	3	66	1903-1910
Watts	Hallie May	3	155	1903-1910
Watts	Maud Elizabeth	3	170	1903-1910
Watts	Sarah E.	3	110	1903-1910
Watts	Uriah	1 & 2	20	1878-1903
Watts	William	3	68	1903-1910
Watts		3	108	1903-1910
Weaver	Joseph Daley	4	48	1910-1915
Webb	Mary A.	4	109	1910-1915
Webb	William	3	129	1903-1910
Webben	Henry	1 & 2	21	1878-1903
Webster	Amrey	1 & 2	17	1878-1903
Webster	Geo.	1 & 2	19	1878-1903
Webster	Herman	3	36	1903-1910
Weigel	Lucile	4	36	1910-1915
Weir	J.	1 & 2	74	1878-1903
Weir	Mamie B.	1 & 2	73	1878-1903
Weisenhamer	Marion	1 & 2	7	1878-1903
Weishaupt	Frank A.	4	74	1910-1915
Weishaupt	Roseus Teresa	1 & 2	23	1878-1903
Weishaupt	Thresa	4	77	1910-1915
Welch	Walter	1 & 2	24	1878-1903
Wheeler	Jno B.	3	59	1903-1910

CALHOUN COUNTY DEATHS

Surname	Given Name	Book	Page	Year
Whisman	Ann	1 & 2	38	1878-1903
Whisman	Isaac	1 & 2	38	1878-1903
Whisman	John M.	1 & 2	61	1878-1903
Whisman	Mildred M.	3	30	1903-1910
Whisman	Wilhelmina	1 & 2	45	1878-1903
Whisman		3	146	1903-1910
White	Frank	1 & 2	11	1878-1903
White	Garnette Sylva	4	44	1910-1915
White	Jane Sarah	1 & 2	8	1878-1903
White	John	1 & 2	54	1878-1903
White	John	1 & 2	54	1878-1903
White	Johnny	1 & 2	51	1878-1903
White	Julia	1 & 2	71	1878-1903
White	Minnie	1 & 2	8	1878-1903
White	Ralph	3	1	1903-1910
White	Samuel Allen	3	102	1903-1910
White	William F.	3	8	1903-1910
Wick	Geo.	1 & 2	25	1878-1903
Wick	Mary	3	150	1903-1910
Wickert	Mary	3	114	1903-1910
Wiedman	Roscoe E.	3	129	1903-1910
Wiegard	Matilda Mary	1 & 2	10	1878-1903
Wieneke	Annie E.	3	38	1903-1910
Wieneke	Melvin	3	137	1903-1910
Wigand	Rollin	1 & 2	48	1878-1903
Wiggands	WM.	1 & 2	44	1878-1903
Wihl	Charles	1 & 2	1	1878-1903
Wildhagen	Charlotte	3	125	1903-1910
Wilhelm	Maria Ann	1 & 2	16	1878-1903
Wilkinson	Alfred	1 & 2	1	1878-1903
Wilkinson	Amanda	3	113	1903-1910
Wilkinson	Benjamin F.	3	165	1903-1910
Wilkinson	Elizah	1 & 2	5	1878-1903
Wilkinson	Ella	1 & 2	17	1878-1903
Wilkinson	George W.	3	106	1903-1910

CALHOUN COUNTY DEATHS

Surname	Given Name	Book	Page	Year
Wilkinson	Harry L.	3	166	1903-1910
Wilkinson	James	3	7	1903-1910
Wilkinson	Jane	4	56	1910-1915
Wilkinson	Mrs. Etta	1 & 2	42	1878-1903
Wilkinson	William Montfm	1 & 2	16	1878-1903
Wilkinson	WM.	1 & 2	29	1878-1903
Willard	Ben	3	15	1903-1910
Williams	George A.	3	93	1903-1910
Williams	Hallie	3	42	1903-1910
Williams	Irene	1 & 2	24	1878-1903
Williams	Isabel J.	3	18	1903-1910
Williams	John H.	1 & 2	23	1878-1903
Williams	Lutitia	1 & 2	12	1878-1903
Williams	Mary	1 & 2	6	1878-1903
Williams	Myra	3	107	1903-1910
Williams	Nathaniel	3	169	1903-1910
Williams	Nellie	1 & 2	30	1878-1903
Williams	Olive	1 & 2	40	1878-1903
Williamsmeyer	Martin	1 & 2	26	1878-1903
Williby	O.F.	4	10	1910-1915
Willson	Nora	1 & 2	36	1878-1903
Wilson	Nancy	3	134	1903-1910
Wilson	Andrew Cook	4	49	1910-1915
Wilson	Austin	1 & 2	6	1878-1903
Wilson	Hulda J.	1 & 2	9	1878-1903
Wilson	John	1 & 2	31	1878-1903
Wilson	Laura	1 & 2	25	1878-1903
Wilson	Mary E.	3	69	1903-1910
Wilson	Mary E.	1 & 2	65	1878-1903
Wilson	Olive L.	1 & 2	13	1878-1903
Wilson	Rachael	1 & 2	250	1878-1903
Wilson	Robert	1 & 2	48	1878-1903
Wilson	Samuel	3	179	1903-1910
Wilson	Silos	1 & 2	18	1878-1903
Wilson	Sophromia B.	1 & 2	23	1878-1903

CALHOUN COUNTY DEATHS

Surname	Given Name	Book	Page	Year
Winecka	S.	1 & 2	20	1878-1903
Wineland	Clara	1 & 2	15	1878-1903
Wineland	Holly F.	3	115	1903-1910
Winkler	John	1 & 2	20	1878-1903
Winkler	Theo	1 & 2	76	1878-1903
Winsell		4	48	1910-1915
Winterhalter	Jos.	1 & 2	74	1878-1903
Wintjen	Andreas	4	20	1910-1915
Wintjen	Lizzie	4	75	1910-1915
Wintjen	Lorence	3	55	1903-1910
Wintjen	Verna	4	37	1910-1915
Wintzen	Matilda	1 & 2	14	1878-1903
Wirth	Michael	3	103	1903-1910
Wirth	Michael	3	103	1903-1910
Wismann	Samuel	1 & 2	31	1878-1903
Witt	Arthur O.	4	40	1910-1915
Wittmond	Francis	1 & 2	21	1878-1903
Wittmond	Petter	1 & 2	1	1878-1903
Woelfel	Carlyle Gertrude	4	116	1910-1915
Woelfel	Henry	3	182	1903-1910
Woeller	Engle	1 & 2	69	1878-1903
Woltman	Catherine M.	4	80	1910-1915
Wood	Alma	1 & 2	24	1878-1903
Wood	Mrs. Mary	1 & 2	22	1878-1903
Woodard	Mr.	4	24	1910-1915
Woodard	Sylvina L.	3	35	1903-1910
Woodeard	Jessie Josephine	4	40	1910-1915
Workman	J.H.	3	100	1903-1910
Workman	Mary Jane	4	6	1910-1915
Wright	Cecil	3	32	1903-1910
Wright	Flora Allie	1 & 2	62	1878-1903
Wright		1 & 2	72	1878-1903
Young	Henry	1 & 2	60	1878-1903
Zahrli	Amnot	1 & 2	58	1878-1903
Zahrli	Elizabeth	1 & 2	44	1878-1903

CALHOUN COUNTY DEATHS

Surname	Given Name	Book	Page	Year
Zahrli	Fred	3	10	1903-1910
Zahrli	John	1 & 2	4	1878-1903
Zahrli	Sophia	3	79	1903-1910
Zigrang	Dominick	3	127	1903-1910
Zimmerman	Mary	1 & 2	2	1878-1903
Zipprich	Barbara Rose	4	8	1910-1910
Zipprich	Michael	4	64	1910-1915
Zumalt	Minnie Clora	4	69	1910-1915
Zumwalt	Emma	3	174	1903-1910
Zumwalt	Lee	3	33	1903-1910

About Personal Touch Genealogy

J. L. Dickson and Personal Touch Genealogy offer research services to obtain public record documents from any of the following Kentucky counties or locations:

- Boyle
- Frankfort (State Archives)
- Garrard
- Jessamine (Documents Only)
- Lincoln
- Madison
- Rockcastle (Documents Only)
- Genealogy research in other counties available by request.

My professional services focus on customer service and satisfaction, and are based on years of quality training and experience.

Don't skimp on qualifications when you are looking for accuracy.

My credentials include:

- Genealogy Instructor and Family Archivist

- Taught by a genealogist with 45 years of professional experience for 3 years

- Positions held at genealogical and historical societies include Vice President, Board of Directors, Webmaster, Staff Genealogist, Archivist and Newsletter Editor

- Over a decade of experience working on my own personal research

- Listed as a Kentucky County Research Specialist by the Kentucky State Archives

- My main focus is documentation ... let the documents tell the story!

Visit my website at **www.PersonalTouchGenealogy.com** to
learn more, or to contact me.

ORDER FORM

Name _____

Address _____

City _____

State _____ ZIP _____

Area Code/Phone _____

Email _____

Calhoun County, Illinois — Births & Deaths
1878-1916

Quantity: _____ @ $40 each (shipping included)   _____

Kentucky residents add 6% for state sales tax   _____

                                          TOTAL: _____

Bulk purchasing, shipping and handling quotes
available upon request.

Mail this form with your check or money order to:
J. L. Dickson
P. O. Box 333
Stanford, KY 40484

You may also order on our website
www.PersonalTouchGenealogy.com or
email us at personaltouch.genealogy@yahoo.com